THOMAS JEFFERSON

Also by Merrill D. Peterson

The Jefferson Image in the American Mind

Democracy, Liberty, and Property: The State Constitutional
  Convention Debates of the 1820's

Major Crises in American History (General Editor
  with Leonard Levy)

Thomas Jefferson
A PROFILE

EDITED BY

MERRILL D. PETERSON

AMERICAN PROFILES

General Editor: Aïda DiPace Donald

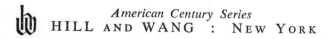
American Century Series
HILL AND WANG : NEW YORK

First edition May 1967
Second printing (first American Century Series edition) April 1968
Third printing September 1968
Fourth printing August 1969

Manufactured in the United States of America

Contents

Introduction

Thomas Jefferson holds a secure place in the American pantheon. This was not always true. Hated, vilified, and despised while he lived, these feelings pursued him far beyond the grave, even as the principles and practices associated with his name became the orthodoxy of American democracy. Only in the last quarter century has Jefferson been installed in the front rank of the nation's heroes, a spiritual event of the utmost significance symbolized by the consecration in 1943, the bicentennial of Jefferson's birth, of the magnificent memorial in the national capital triangulated to the monuments honoring Washington and Lincoln and dedicated to the man who, in President Franklin D. Roosevelt's words, "led the steps of America into the paths of the permanent integrity of the Republic."

The jarring passions and opinions that for so long agitated the American mind on the subject of Thomas Jefferson left their imprint on nearly everything written about him. Biography and history perpetuated the rage of partisanship that had engulfed his life. The twin hysterias of exaltation and denunciation tended to obliterate the authentic Jefferson, raising in its place fantastic images arrayed in partisan colors. Moreover, the man's works and teachings seemed to have a peculiar relevance to posterity, with the result that he was repeatedly mustered into the service of one cause or another and, in this way, kept alive in the public consciousness of successive generations. Taking possession of Jefferson for their own purposes, Americans were unable to render justice to the historical Jefferson, the elusive man himself. It should not be inferred from these circumstances that all of the older literature is without value or, for that matter, that everything of recent date is free of the tincture of partisanship or other vitiating error. Jefferson is one of those figures, like Cromwell or Napoleon, who will perhaps never be seen with a coldly neutral and objective eye. Nevertheless, the writing of more recent vintage makes a stronger claim to truth. When the man became a monument, when the chaos of emotion succeeded to a uniform climate of veneration and praise, historians won the freedom to restore the integrity of the historical personage.

But posterity's affair with Jefferson is only the first of the problems that confront serious students of his life and work. Sufficiently complex in itself was his own affair with history. Born in 1743, he came upon the stage at the opening of the "age of the democratic revolution," and he did not withdraw (he died in 1826) until its force was spent. Indeed he helped make the age, as well as the American nation, which was its best achievement. He was a prodigy of talents, wrote voluminously, and worked incessantly at countless tasks. Yet he never revealed the inner recesses of his heart and mind. Of the great subjects of American biography, Jefferson is probably the largest and most difficult.

His life exhibited bewildering conflicts and contradictions. By birth, taste, and training he was an aristocrat, yet his principles crossed the threshold of modern democracy and by their espousal he earned both the curses and the plaudits of his contemporaries. He loved his native land, dedicated his life to it, and gave such compelling expression to the nation's genius that, in the opinion of a modern biographer, he should forever be remembered as "The Apostle of Americanism." On the other hand, he was a man of elevated tastes and sensibilities, more at home in Parisian salons than in the impoverished American world, more cosmopolitan than national in thought and feeling. "Jefferson," wrote Henry Adams, "aspired beyond the ambition of a nationality, and embraced in his view the whole future of man." He was both philosopher and politician. Despite his mastery in the latter role, politics were a perpetual torment to him, and it was the great disappointment of his life that he had been yoked to the labors of government instead of the infinitely more serviceable tasks of science and philosophy and art to which he believed he had been born. Aristocrat and democrat, cosmopolitan and American, philosopher and politician: the life of Jefferson reveals a congeries of conflicts and tensions of this order. They cannot be ignored or explained away. Yet the dangerously abstract and superficial polarity of the terms may lead to overwrought interpretations, cleverly couched in the language of irony, paradox, and contradiction, which deprive Jefferson's life of the underlying unity and coherence it actually had. It is easy enough to split that life into pieces and make of him a figure of contradiction; far more difficult, and surely more valid, is the task of resolving the ambivalent elements of his life and character in a common pattern of experience.

The same problem in another aspect is that of theory and practice, two dimensions of experience which can never be continuous but which in Jefferson's case often seem radically fractured. Speculative, idealistic, doctrinaire ("visionary" was the epithet of his enemies), his tendency was to reduce everything that came before his senses to some scheme of theoretical rationality. He believed in the power of ideas, seldom changed his principles, and derived more satisfaction from unfolding future possibilities than from the command of immediate problems. "His political thinking," Gilbert Chinard writes, "was governed by several articles of faith which withstood modification by reasoned argument or practical demonstration." But this is a half-truth. He traveled outside his principles when, in his opinion, the national interest demanded it. The Louisiana Purchase is the classic case, for it upset most of his constitutional principles and he knew it. He generally subscribed to a theory of political economy that gave paramount importance to agriculture; but he did not adhere to it in the actual conduct of American affairs. He kept his political principles on a loose tether, always ensuring, however, that the stake—the ultimate end of freedom—was firmly planted in the ground. In scientific investigation he was exceedingly hardheaded, skeptical of every theory until proven in practice. Even in architecture, where he followed the classical models, he showed impressive freedom and invention in adapting a design to the situation at hand. Chinard, one of the pioneers of modern Jefferson scholarship, has noted his happy faculty for holding ideals intact on a plane apart from operative realities. "Far from being a single-track mind, his was decidedly a double-track intellect with two lines of thought running parallel without any apparent contradiction, for theory never interfered with his practice." Chinard saw in this trait the beginnings of a highly creative American outlook, "practical idealism." However this may be, his observation states the problem without solving it, for there is obviously something wrong with a conception of Jefferson as a kind of intellectual switchyard where all the trains marked "theory" and all the trains marked "practice" move hither and thither without ever coming together.

Another kind of problem for the biographer—less for the historian—arises from the wall of silence Jefferson threw around his emotional life. What is called his private, or domestic, life is abundantly documented. There are account books, farm books, garden books, family letters, reminiscences, and so on, to say nothing of Monticello, the most vivid presentment of his heart and mind. Yet in all this it is quite impossible to sound the depths of the man. The biographer catches him only at the surface—a vast unruffled surface. The Epicurean motto, "Hide thy life," might have been Jefferson's own, as Albert J. Nock observed. "He was the most approachable and the most impenetrable of men, easy and delightful of acquaintance, impossible of knowledge." His affections ran deep, but through what channels it is hazardous to say. Almost nothing is known of his wife; her early death in 1782 devastated him, but so far as the record shows he buried his feelings with her. Anger was an emotion he never vented in the open air. Even the imperturbable Washington could explode and hurl epithets under the strain of political controversy, but not Jefferson. He is often denied a sense of humor, which is unjust, though it cannot be considered a strong point of his personality. Never doubting the uprightness of his intentions, he rarely admitted a mistake, stared into the shadows of motive, or indulged in self-reflection. He wrote an autobiography, but it is a mere chronicle of events, cut short in 1789, and virtually useless to the biographer who would like to know what Thomas Jefferson thought of Thomas Jefferson. The personality is elusive—as remote as the Olympian heights where he built his house. He had many momentous decisions to make during his public career, and he made them, astonishingly without ever disclosing the pain and the agony they must have cost. Everything seemed to come effortlessly to him: words, ideas, actions. The sense of inner struggle is missing, and with it the dramatic intensity and moral significance that give a peculiar interest to some great lives.

It is Jefferson's intellectuality that holds the strongest interest for thinking men in the middle of the twentieth century. Of course, his enduring greatness must always be essentially political, for he fixed the course of American democracy, and so long as men the world around cherish liberty and repeat the words of the Declaration of Independence, Jefferson will be remembered. But the political Jefferson is taken for granted. He is a monument. His ideals are ours; and we are no longer enthralled by his now outmoded methods of pursuing them. Turning to the intellectual Jefferson, scholars have formed from the many facets of his mind new images of the cultural hero and the civilized man. He was so much more than a republican statesman—philosopher, scientist, architect, educator, linguist, inventor, geographer, musician, and so on—that when his political doctrines became axiomatic or, as in the case of some of them, fell into disuse before the march of history, he challenged understanding in the terms of intellect, imagination, and the civilizing arts. This understanding has not been easy. The tributaries of his mind meander in all directions before feeding into the main stream. No single scholar can trace their courses and map the immense intellectual terrain. The areas of knowledge he embraced are now divided and subdivided into so many pieces that no man can grasp the whole. The body of assumptions that gave a certain unity to his thought are from another world, "a lost world" as Daniel Boorstin has demonstrated, which can be recovered, if recovered at all, only after the most painstaking investigations. Jefferson never reduced the totality of his thought to a system. If a system existed, historians must re-create it from the assorted parts. So far as the search has gone, it seems apparent that all the parts do not cohere. The architect in the Roman mode indulged a fondness for the rococo in landscape. The philosopher who believed in the natural unity of mankind, hence in equality of rights, was unable to embrace the Negro race in his theory. The visionary of enlightenment and progress subscribed to theories of society and government, faintly archaic in his own time, which tended to narrow the field and check the powers of change. Historians have searched out the dominant spirit of Jefferson's thought. Some, like Karl Lehmann, have found in it the humanism derived from the ancient world and the Renaissance, while others, like Boorstin, have accented the naturalism of an early scientific age. Both were important. And the biographer who takes the whole man as his subject must endeavor to establish their connections and interactions within a unifying pattern.

Public events crowded Jefferson's life remorselessly. He constantly bewailed his fate, and the biographer cannot help but sympathize with him. His public services are his principal claim to fame, of course, yet they were less expressive of his true nature than the retired life of science and philosophy he craved but never found until the end. To bring the figure into relief from the thick texture of public events, every one a story in itself, is not the least of the biographer's tasks. His life of Jefferson becomes perforce a life of the times, scarcely distinguishable from narrative history. Of Jefferson, he must sometimes feel, recalling the Emersonian aphorism, there is properly no biography, only history.

Although the writings assembled for this profile reveal the problems of Jefferson biography, they have been selected for a better reason: their contribution to our understanding of the historical figure. Each of the eleven pieces is self-contained. Two are chapters from books, one is a lecture in a recent series, and the others are journal articles. All are scholarly, though some are more scholarly than others. The earliest date of first publication of any of the essays is 1941; four of them appeared in 1943, the bicentennial year, also a banner year in Jefferson studies; and others appeared as late as 1965. The interpretations remain fresh.

Taken together, they do not offer a consistent and complete profile of Jefferson. That is not the intent, and indeed it would be impossible to encompass the subject in a modest anthology such as this one. Regrettably, on some of the most important phases of Jefferson's life almost nothing new and significant has been said in recent years. This is conspicuously true of the Presidency, where Henry Adams' magnificent *History of the United States During the Administrations of Jefferson and Madison* still holds sway seventy-five years after its publication. None of the essays centers on Jefferson the President. Nor is Jefferson the scientist or Jefferson the educator adequately represented in this volume. Yet even these subjects, unfortunately neglected, are illuminated by interpretations in adjacent areas.

The opening essay, "Thomas Jefferson, The Gentle Radical," by Dixon Wecter, portrays the man and the career in the light of the images he projected to his contemporaries and to posterity. Wecter really has two subjects: the historical figure and the heroic symbol. The risk of mixing them has already been noted, yet each has something to say of the other, and Wecter's deftly composed counterpoint justifies the risk. If he is somewhat less than successful in explaining how Jefferson became a hero seemingly against the decrees of nature, he is keenly sensitive to the nuances of Jefferson's character and to the subtle process by which he became, more than is usually supposed, what people wanted or feared him to be. The hero, so far from being self-made, was made by the political fortunes of his time, indeed even more by the distant fortunes of American democracy with which the name of this "diffident aristocrat" was inextricably connected.

Carl Becker's "What Is Still Living in the Political Philosophy of Thomas Jefferson?" is a fine restatement of the theme first developed in his famous book, *The Declaration of Independence,* in 1922. And yet the tone and the conclusion are quite different. In the book he was openly patronizing toward the philosophy of natural law and natural rights condensed in the second paragraph of the Declaration. While a "humane and engaging faith," it had been undermined by the modern intelligence and the realities of the modern world; and to ask whether it was true or false was "a meaningless question." Returning to the subject in 1943, however, in the depths of the Second World War, he called this philosophy "a living force," as modern as when it was written into the nation's birthright. What was *not* still living in Jefferson's political philosophy were his essentially negative political means—states' rights, strict construction, *laissez faire,* and so on—which no longer served the ends of freedom. This is the modern liberal view. (Wecter rightly associates it with the revision of the democratic tradition that occurred during the administration of Franklin D. Roosevelt.) Becker's analysis of Jefferson's political thought, admirable in most respects, is unjust in attributing to him a wholly negative and static conception of the functions of government; for *laissez faire* was not a fixed principle with him, and he believed that government should advance "hand in hand with the progress of the human mind." Becker is most arresting in his reading of Jefferson's mind and character through the felicities of his literary style. "Jefferson," he concludes, "was a democrat by intellectual conviction, but by temperament and training a Virginia aristocrat." The opinion is shared by most present-day scholars.

John Dos Passos is deservedly better known as a novelist than as a historian or biographer, but his "A Portico Facing the Wilderness" is one of the most wonderfully evocative chapters in the Jefferson literature. With the aid of the Chevalier de Chastellux's recollections, he depicts Jefferson in retirement at Monticello in the spring of 1782, the agonies and defeats of his wartime Governorship just behind him, the abyss of his wife's death only a few months before him, and from this point looks back over the Virginian's life. This was the turning point, Dos Passos says, when Jefferson had to decide whether to retreat deeper into obscurity or return to the path of greatness he had already traveled not a little way. In the end, it was probably Martha's passing that determined his fate, for the loss shattered his idyllic dream of Monticello. If Dos Passos occasionally indulges his poet's license with fact, as in furnishing Monticello with park, garden, and other amenities it did not possess in 1782, this is a small price to pay for the grace and the charm of his portrait. And his conception of Monticello, "portico facing the wilderness," somehow captures the spirit of the man who brought the nobility of the ancients to the untamed, untutored American world.

Robert R. Palmer's article, "The Dubious Democrat: Thomas Jefferson in Bourbon France," is an original variation on an old theme, Jefferson's response to the French Revolution. Beginning in 1792 his political enemies charged that he became a convert to revolutionary democracy while in France and, upon his return, set out to introduce "Jacobinism" into the United States. These opinions pervaded American historiography until finally dispelled by Gilbert Chinard in 1929. Chinard argued that Jefferson's political thought was fixed before he went to France and that his experience there had no effect other than to strengthen his convictions and to awaken him to the unique potentialities of American life. Palmer, without denying the valuable truth in this position, nevertheless believes that the French Revolution profoundly altered Jefferson's political outlook. His first reactions were conservative; gradually, hesitantly, as Palmer demonstrates, he came to accept the revolutionary reality and its democratic promise. The article is interesting not only for what it has to say on the specific subject but also for its disclosure of an essentially pragmatic, perhaps even expediential, political temper.

The next two selections treat economic aspects of Jeffersonian thought and politics. My own article gives great weight to considerations of foreign commerce in Jefferson's conception of national policy from 1783 to his retirement as Secretary of State a decade later. In this interpretation the agrarian motivations of his politics, still so much emphasized, are submerged in a larger design encompassing American wealth and power in the Atlantic world. William D. Grampp, an economic historian, defines three varying systems of economic doctrine held by Jefferson at successive times. The first featured agrarian self-sufficiency, the second *laissez faire,* the third economic nationalism. As a political economist, Jefferson repeatedly shifted ground in order to meet the changing demands of republicanism and the national interest. Grampp's perceptive article dispels confusion on this point and also says a good deal about the reciprocity between theory and practice in Jefferson's politics.

Dumas Malone and Julian P. Boyd are the foremost Jefferson scholars of our time. They are best known through their major works: Malone's multivolume *Jefferson and His Times* and Boyd's incomparable edition of *The Papers of Thomas Jefferson*. They are represented in this volume, not by snippets from these monumental works still in progress, but by broadly interpretive essays in a lighter vein. Returning to the old theme of Jefferson and Hamilton, Malone examines the clash between these two giants with reference particularly to the Constitution. He sees a "forbidding rigidity," quite uncharacteristic of Jefferson's mind, in the strict constructionism developed in opposition to Hamilton's measures, and he attributes it to Jefferson's deep political distrust of the Federalist leader. In the final analysis, Malone believes that Jefferson is to be forgiven more than Hamilton because he valued freedom more than power; yet both were essential in their time, as in ours, and the historian who gives entire allegiance to one or the other of these great rivals runs serious risks. Boyd, while aware of the problem, passionately affirms as the Jeffersonian ideal the identification of power with freedom. Beginning with the premier statement of this ideal, the First Inaugural Address, Boyd demotes Jefferson's niggardly constitutional doctrines to a merely instrumental role, transient and incidental, and instead sees his commitment to human rights as—much more than airy rhetoric—the ultimate force and unifier of a great and disparate nation. "The salient fact that we have too long overlooked is that the cardinal principle of Jefferson's life was his uncompromising devotion to the Union because of its identity with human rights." From this striking observation, Boyd goes on to examine Jefferson's conception of an "empire of liberty" and its influence on the growth of the American West.

The articles by Louis B. Wright and Horace M. Kallen offer contrasting views of Jefferson's intellectual style and cultural ideal. The former's survey of Jefferson's lifelong intercourse with the ancients emphasizes the persistent influence of classical norms of conduct, art, and manners. No pedant, his classicism breathed the fullness of life, Wright says. The point is well made; nevertheless, the question arises how a man thus saturated in the classical tradition could so proudly inhale the air of his native land and give voice to the still silent American mind. Kallen addresses himself to this question in "The Arts and Thomas Jefferson." "Fundamentally," he writes, "Jefferson's aesthetic involved a dissolution of classical attitudes in spontaneously pioneer sentiments and practices." Despite his education in the gentle traditions of art and learning, he was more concerned with technique than with beauty itself, with manipulation than with contemplation, with function than with form; and in all this he expressed the matter-of-fact pragmatism of American life. Even his classicism was new: not that of Renaissance humanism but that of the Newtonian world machine with its scientific passion for order, precision, and balance.

Except for politics, the subject of religion has invited more writing on Jefferson than any other. The subject has many aspects, the most important being Church and State relations, religion in education, and Jefferson's own religious (or irreligious) profession. While he lived, and for decades after his death, he was extravagantly abused as an atheist, corruptor of youth, destroyer of Christianity, and no respectable sect put in a claim to his spiritual remains. But this hysteria, too, has passed away. It is now generally recognized that, however limited or mistaken his religious ideas may have been, they were the product of a mind deeply committed to the search for truth and open to the channels of religious experience. The article by George Harmon Knoles is a straightforward and judicious report on these ideas. The subject is elusive, for the reasons Knoles cites, yet much too important to be ignored. The article concludes, and it is hoped rounds out, this historical profile of the man.

MERRILL D. PETERSON

Thomas Jefferson, 1743-1826

Thomas Jefferson was born at Shadwell, Albemarle County, Virginia, on April 13, 1743. He attended William and Mary College, studied law and was admitted to the bar, and practiced his profession for several years. He married Martha Wayles Skelton in 1772. She died a decade later, after bearing six children, two of whom lived to adulthood. Entering the Virginia House of Burgesses in 1769, he served for six years, and was then elected to the Continental Congress. He drafted the Declaration of Independence in 1776. Returning to Virginia, he went into the legislature and attempted to reform the laws and institutions of the commonwealth. His Statute for Religious Freedom, submitted in 1779, was finally adopted in 1786. He served as Governor of the war-torn state from 1779 to 1781. In 1783, he returned to Congress. His plans for a monetary system on the decimal unit and for the government of the territories laid important groundwork. Sent to France in 1784 as a commissioner to negotiate commercial treaties, he succeeded Benjamin Franklin as Minister to France the next year. While in France he published *Notes on the State of Virginia,* his only book. He witnessed the coming of the French Revolution before returning to the United States, and in 1790 became Secretary of State in President Washington's administration. The friction that developed between him and the Secretary of the Treasury, Alexander Hamilton, principally on fiscal and foreign policies, contributed to the conflict that resulted in the organization of political parties. He resigned his post at the end of 1793. While in retirement he commenced the rebuilding of Monticello, originally begun in 1769, but now redesigned on a more elaborate scale. Elected Vice-President in 1796, he rapidly assumed the leadership of the Republican party. In this role he secretly drafted the Kentucky Resolutions of 1798 protesting the unconstitutionality of the Alien and Sedition Acts and proposing "nullification" as the ultimate recourse. He became President in 1801 after a bitterly contested election not only in the country but in the House of Representatives, which made the final choice. The measures of his first administration, climaxed by the Louisiana Purchase, were exceedingly popular. Re-elected by the votes of all but two states in 1804, he encountered frustration and defeat in his second term. He failed to obtain the Floridas from Spain and met with no greater success, despite the rigors of the Embargo (1807–1809), in enforcing America's neutral rights on the belligerent powers of Europe. Retiring to Monticello in 1809, he labored in vain to restore his debt-ridden estate. His last years were devoted to the establishment of the University of Virginia (1819), which he conceived, planned, and supervised in every detail. He died at Monticello on the fiftieth anniversary of American independence, July 4, 1826.

M.D.P.

THOMAS JEFFERSON

✪

Thomas Jefferson, The Gentle Radical

> This is an ignorant year
> Within a cruel time.
> If he were here
> We might rebuild
> The firm wall raised by him,
> The column felled.
> —LAWRENCE LEE, "The Tomb of Thomas Jefferson"
> (1940)

I

Nature did not intend Thomas Jefferson for a hero. Temperament, physique, and background were all against it. If destiny had not plucked him from the ivory tower he built at Monticello, and hurled him into the thick of public turmoil, Jefferson would have lived and died a bookish, fastidious Virginia squire. He might have become, more easily than a hero, a writer of belles-lettres, a college don, or an amateur philosopher sunning himself on the leeward side of John Locke. He is like no other American leader, although there are faint resemblances in Woodrow Wilson and Franklin D. Roosevelt of which their friends have made the most.

Certainly Jefferson the idol was not hewn from the same stone as Washington, Israel Putnam, Francis Marion. He had a seden-

---

tary man's shrinking from military discipline. The drums and trumpets passed him by. His only sight of advancing redcoats was through a telescope, from a knoll near Monticello called Carter's Mountain, in June, 1781, and in later years his enemies were quick to assert that his headlong flight after that vision spoke for itself. He was a man of exquisite perceptions, an artist with nerves attuned to the age of sensibility. At the death of his wife he fell into a swoon so deep that his life was feared for; those who disliked Jefferson did not hesitate to call him "womanish" and "feline."

Loose-jointed in appearance and in talk—lacking Franklin's homely vigor without achieving the majesty of Washington— "Long Tom" Jefferson wore his elegance of mind and raiment with an insouciance that some misjudged for sloppiness. As President he received a British Minister in slippers and dressing gown (a democratic style that Huey Long once tried to copy, in receiving a German dignitary). Even at his inauguration Jefferson had quietly walked from Conrad's boardinghouse to take the oath in the Senate chamber of the unfinished Capitol; though legend persistently repeats that he arrived on horseback, dismounted casually, and hitched his horse to the "palisades" of the Capitol fence. He owned ten thousand acres and two hundred slaves, and recoiled from courting the masses or playing the political bully-boy. Yet he became "the People's friend," a highhanded imperialist, and a saber-rattler before the Barbary pirates. For all his agrarian background, he was far less the full-blooded country gentleman than were Washington and Jackson. He raised tobacco but never used it, never kept a playing card in his house, bred fine horses but never loved the race track. Dueling did not tempt him. He drank no spirits, but was fond of French wines and cookery—one of those gentlemen, as Patrick Henry said, who "abjured their native victuals." He was virtually a vegetarian, as he told Dr. Ulley— and, like most vegetarians, proved to be a terrifying idealist, tinged with fanaticism. His mores were not those of the carnivorous mammal. And his mind was a brilliant, delicate, complex mechanism. In fact, as Henry Adams remarked, all our early Presidents save Jefferson can be drawn with "a few broad strokes of the brush"—but the master of Monticello, with his shifting lights and shades, nuances and translucencies, defies even the finest pencil. Did the People ever have a more extraordinary friend?

Let us see how Jefferson came to be a hero. Born in 1743 among the red clay hills of Albemarle County, Virginia, he sprang from good stock. His mother, Jane Randolph Jefferson, made him cousin to numerous purse-proud Tuckahoes. Jefferson affected to pass lightly over the old pedigree of the Randolphs, "to which let every one ascribe the faith and merit he chooses," and to stress the homespun simplicity of his father, Peter, whose "education had been quite neglected."[1] With this help, legend has made Peter Jefferson into a clodhopper, stressing the democratic rather than the patrician heritage of his son. Late research, however, has shown that Peter Jefferson owned a great acreage of rich land, had five overseers, served as vestryman and justice of the peace and sheriff, and displayed a skill in map-making that bears witness to his cultivation of hand and brain.[2] He was no Thomas Lincoln.

At William and Mary College young Thomas Jefferson was something of a bookworm, who as his classmate John Page recalled "could tear himself away from his dearest friends and fly to his studies." A century later, drawing heavily upon imagination, John Esten Cooke wrote a novel called *The Youth of Jefferson, or a Chronicle of College Scrapes.* Tom, or "Sir Asinus," here figures as a tall, freckled, sandy-haired lad with a prankish temper. Thinking he is pursued by the proctor, he flies down the corridor in a faded dressing gown, and barricades himself gun in hand, crying out: "Beware! I am armed to the teeth, and rather than be captured I will die in defence of my rights—namely, liberty, property, and the pursuit of happiness under difficulties!" (The mature Jefferson did not include "property" among the inalienables; that belonged to Hamilton's point of view.)

"Under temptations and difficulties," young Jefferson wrote, "I

[1] Jefferson's Autobiography, Paul L. Ford, ed., *The Writings of Thomas Jefferson* (New York, 1892–1899), I, 2.

[2] Information from Miss Maude H. Woodfin, University of Richmond, and from Professor T. P. Abernethy, University of Virginia. A scholarly study of Peter Jefferson, by D. Edgar Hickisch of Portsmouth, Virginia, is yet unpublished.

would ask myself what would Doctor Small, Mr. Wythe, Peyton Randolph, do in this situation?" His three youthful heroes were a Scotch mathematician, a jurist and college tutor, and a tidewater gentleman of Jefferson's own blue blood. To the end of his life, indeed, Jefferson's ideal was blended of two types, the scholar and the intellectual aristocrat, which have rarely been popular with the masses of Americans. It was the dash of liberalism which Jefferson himself added to the *beau ideal* that made him an unforgettable favorite. Meanwhile, Jefferson gained notice at the Virginia bar and in 1769 was chosen by his native county for the House of Burgesses. He fell under the spell of Patrick Henry, who "appeared to me to speak as Homer wrote." Sympathetic with Henry's hostility to the Crown, Jefferson was still cool enough to perceive the orator's defects in logic and learning. Jefferson came early to distrust the spell of rhetoric. In part it may have been a rationalization: a weak throat and unconquerable diffidence in large groups kept Jefferson from ever becoming himself a spellbinder. His pen was mightier than his voice. Three silent men—Franklin, Washington, Jefferson—were the first great idols of the republic: the age of silver tongue and spread eagle, of Webster and Hayne, Grady and Bryan, was yet unborn.

Quickly gaining note as a pamphleteer for independence, Jefferson was sent as a Virginia delegate to the Continental Congress. New Englanders liked him as a penman, even as they admired Washington as a soldier. "Though a silent member of Congress, he was so prompt, frank, explicit and decisive upon committees and in conversation," wrote John Adams, ". . . that he soon seized upon my heart." This popularity was very important to Jefferson's budding career. In June, 1776, as a tribute to his fine literary gift, legal training, and eagerness to work, he was named first of a committee of five to draft the Declaration of Independence.

Jefferson was not then aware of the world-shaking import of his document. Later he took it retrospectively in his stride, as it were. In the face of contrary facts he stated so vehemently that the Declaration had been signed by Congress on the Fourth of July— even to the extent of imagining a "paper" draft signed on that date, when confronted with the parchment undoubtedly engrossed on August 2[3]—that indulgent posterity, in the main, has let Jefferson have his way. With due respect to his fellow-committeemen, Jefferson was truly the author of the Declaration—the proud boast of his tombstone, and his supreme claim among the Founding Fathers. If he is something less than the divinely inspired creator of this noble document—whose theories, spirit, and even phrases are the products of a long evolution—he is surely the amanuensis of Americanism. To Lee in 1825 he wrote that the Declaration "was intended to be an expression of the American mind." Its clarity, vigor, beauty, and fighting affirmation of the democratic faith endear Jefferson forever to his countrymen. No one else could have seen so well or expressed so finely the ultimate, as well as the immediate, aims of the new American spirit. It was addressed to the people. Hence it omitted a few underlying subtleties. Chief of these was the vital distinction Jefferson saw between *natural* rights (those which man can exercise "without the aid of exterior assistance," such as freedom of thought and speech) and *civil* rights (like gaining and holding property, in which men agree to abdicate a measure of individualism, and to act only "under the guarantee of society"). This was the reason why property was not one of the "inherent and inalienable rights," since it lay under the hand of social control. Jefferson's individualism was one of rights plus duties; Hamilton's tended to stress property rights above other matters, and paved the way for that ideal later called "rugged individualism"—a term, said Herbert Hoover in 1934, which "I should be proud to have invented," but which to others meant an industrial philosophy active in the creation of slums and economic misery, while it destroyed the green countryside and the domestic handicrafts that Jefferson loved. But Jefferson did not put his distinction into writing until after he had quit Philadelphia and gone back home, "being alone and wanting amusement," and it

[3] See Jefferson's Autobiography, *Writings of Thomas Jefferson* (Ford ed.), I, 29, 38; Carl Becker, *The Declaration of Independence* (1922), p. 184; and John C. Fitzpatrick, *The Spirit of the Revolution* (1924), pp. 8, 16.

remained unpublished for more than a century after his death.[4] This was typical of the casualness of Jefferson.

After firing the salvo of the Declaration, Jefferson returned to Virginia, convinced that his next duty was to sow the liberal seed at home—by abolishing entails, revising the criminal code, setting up free schools, and cleaving Church from State. Jefferson had no stomach for soldiering; his aptitude lay in "mental fight." Certain keen partisans of Washington, Hamilton, and the Federalists have never forgiven Jefferson for failing to expose himself to hunger, frostbite, and bloodshed in the cause to which he had rallied his countrymen. The late Senator Beveridge, biographer of John Marshall, by playing up a phrase in one of Washington's letters, imagines the shivering soldiers in their smoky huts at Valley Forge thinking of the penman of their faith, asking each other with chattering teeth, "Where is Jefferson?"[5] Yet there is no real evidence that Jefferson was looked upon at this time as a quitter. He was craven only in the subtler sense of T. E. Hulme's saying, that "a non-muscular man is inevitably physically a coward."

In 1779 Jefferson succeeded Patrick Henry as Governor of Virginia. He did not make a good wartime Governor, as even loyal Virginians admit. He was too timorous about overstepping his strict legal rights, even in an emergency, and in practical matters his judgment was undeveloped. And Jefferson had the sudden violence of the sedentary man. With his four thousand British prisoners he was alternately too soft and too hard—at first arranging musicales and philosophical causeries for them and opening his library to the officers, and then, upon hearing of Americans abused on board British prison ships, loading his captives with irons and preparing to treat them as common criminals until Washington intervened. In later years he showed the same bursts of violence: demanding that Aaron Burr be hanged out of hand, and in the War of 1812 proposing that if the British touched our coasts "we must

---

[4] It was published from the Jefferson Papers in the Library of Congress by Gilbert Chinard in 1929, in his *Thomas Jefferson, The Apostle of Americanism*, pp. 80–82. The distinction, of course, was implicit throughout Jefferson's thought.

[5] Albert J. Beveridge, *Life of John Marshall* (1916), I, 126–128.

burn the city of London, not by expensive fleets or congreve rockets, but by employing an hundred or two Jack-the-painters, whom nakedness, famine, desperation and hardened vice, will abundantly furnish among themselves." This is a strain in Jefferson's nature, supposedly mild and calm, which has never colored his legend and even been ignored by most of his biographers.[6] Hero-worship and symbol-making call for simplification, in dealing with a man so complex as Jefferson.

In the late spring of 1781, with Virginia's treasury bankrupt and the British overrunning the Old Dominion, Jefferson desperately prepared to resign in favor of a military governor. At that juncture, the redcoats swooped down on Monticello and would have caught him but for the warning of Jack Jouett, "the Southern Revere." The head of a government should avoid capture by the enemy if he can, as many European sovereigns and premiers have lately decided. A statesman who runs away may govern some other day. No discredit should arise if he has first done his best—as Tom Paine pointed out in 1805, in defense of Jefferson. It is true that after the invasion was over Jefferson had to face a charge of insufficient preparedness; on December 19, 1781, he appeared before the legislature, was acquitted and voted thanks. But his prestige in Virginia was clouded by the disasters of his Governorship, and by his having given up the helm in a storm. Thin-skinned to criticism, Jefferson looked forward to "the all-healing grave." It was his first and last public failure. In Virginia its memory lasted until—during his absence as Minister to France—the progressives under Madison came into local power, and loyally rehabilitated Jefferson as their master. Many years later, in Jefferson's first term as President, when a rash of newspaper libels broke out against him, the facts were deliberately twisted to make it seem that Jefferson had been rebuked by the Virginia legislature for his cowardice, in running away from the British! The charge was absurd, but strangely passed into common belief, especially in the North. Federalists dwelt upon the spectacle of this long-legged statesman leaving Monticello with more haste than grace. Even a

[6] As Chinard notes, p. 113. The quotation is from Jefferson to Duane, October 1, 1812.

generation ago, the great historian Edward Channing used to lecture vividly to his Harvard classes about the affrighted agrarian, "coattails flying in the wind." Chronologically, this is the first libel against Thomas Jefferson.

II

In France, Jefferson was overshadowed by the remembrance of Franklin. He lacked Franklin's easy bonhomie, and quaintly enough was more of a Puritan than the great *Bostonian* had been. Jefferson too was a widower, but no lovely ladies found him apt at flirtation and banter, nor did any crown him with laurel at *fêtes champêtres*. At forty-three he was older than Franklin at seventy-five. "A dozen years ago this scene would have amused me," Jefferson wrote to Mrs. Trist, "but I am past the age for changing habits!"

Abroad, Jefferson grew more aggressively American, seeing England as an aristocracy besotted with liquor and horse-racing, and France as a land where marital fidelity is "an ungentlemanly practice." He also loved to magnify the virtues of his native land, solemnly assuring Crevecœur that New Jersey farmers probably learned how to make "the circumference of a wheel of one single piece" from Greek epic poetry, "because ours are the only farmers who can read Homer." Jefferson fondly imagined himself the typical American farmer.

France also confirmed Jefferson's aversion to "priestcraft" and hereditary aristocracy. At the news of Shays's Rebellion at home, he rejoiced—believing in a little bloodletting at intervals for the health of the body politic. After his return to America the full fury of the French Revolution broke. At first Jefferson hailed it with almost fanatic tranquillity: "Was ever such a prize won with so little innocent blood? . . . rather than it should have failed I would have seen half the earth desolated."[7] Even today, conservatives who hold to "sound Jeffersonian principles" try to forget his reckless remark about watering the tree of liberty periodically with

[7] Jefferson to Short, January 3, 1793, *The Writings of Thomas Jefferson,* Memorial edition (1903), IX, 9.

blood. Jefferson maintained that only the sickly timid tory fears the People, whereas the strong leader loves and trusts them. In later years Jefferson disliked the radial plan upon which L'Enfant had laid out the city of Washington—knowing it was designed to keep mobs from throwing up impassable barricades, while soldiers massed in its "circles" could command the approaches to the Capitol with artillery.[8] Let the People come, he said.

Yet in practice, Jefferson was the gentlest of Girondists. Upon the eve of the Revolution the French Foreign Minister had smiled upon meetings of the disaffected in Jefferson's house, "being sure," as Jefferson wrote, "that I should be useful in moderating the warmer spirits." After Jefferson's orderly election to the Presidency (which he loved to style "the revolution of 1800"), he reassured bankers and industrialists that he abhorred the spirit of unrest bred by the "blood and slaughter" in France, and was so temperate that radicals could hardly believe their ears. Out of office he was an idealist and revolutionary; within, a conservative and opportunist. Moreover, Jefferson the agrarian, urging that we "let our work-shops remain in Europe," had as deep a fear as did Hamilton of the mobs of Old World cities. Jefferson compared such mobs to "sores" on the face of a nation. Convinced that those who labor in the earth are God's chosen people, and that tillers of the soil have an instinct for order and justice, Jefferson was ready at any time to sign up with embattled farmers. A revolution with pitchforks he understood, but pikestaves unnerved him.

Returning from France to serve as Secretary of State, Jefferson came into collision with Hamilton, and soon retired to Monticello. Shy by nature, disliking to fight hand-to-hand, he tried to convince himself that he wanted nothing so much as to plant his corn and beans in peace. "I have no passion to govern men; no passion which would lead me to delight to ride in a storm," he wrote his friend Rutledge on December 27, 1796. But events helped to draft him. Leadership was needed in the fight for "republicanism," what a later age would call democracy. An immersed scholar like John Taylor of Caroline was no vote-getter, while an eager man like Patrick Henry (already hardening into reaction) had fallen into

[8] See Albert Jay Nock, *Jefferson* (1926), pp. 288–289.

the mud too often while scrambling for prizes and profits. The younger generation in Virginia, Madison and Monroe, frankly looked to Jefferson as their master. And the Federalists, by training their guns upon Jefferson even out of office, roused his slow-kindling anger and also drew more public notice to him. He thus became the focus for discontent. At fifty-four—still protesting he preferred "the prattle of my grandchildren and senile rest"— Jefferson began to fight. He entered upon the Vice-Presidency, under John Adams. The threat of Aaron Burr's election in 1800 could be blocked only by a man like Jefferson. His duty was clear, and success followed. And so, like many other political leaders in a land where undue anxiety for office is bad form, Jefferson was carried forward upon the shoulders of his friends. Hero-worship was quick to respond.

The first *Jefferson Almanac* appeared in 1800, for the year 1801; its publisher, George Keating, guaranteed "to give the Purchaser an Almanac for 1802 in case Thomas Jefferson is not elected President of the United States." Campaign pamphlets and thumbnail biographies of Jefferson now poured from the press by dozens. Typical is J. J. Beckley's *Epitome of the Life & Character of Jefferson* (Philadelphia, July, 1800), lauding the "ardent mind of Jefferson, eagerly pursuing the principles of the revolution" (trusting apparently that readers would assume he meant the American rather than the French one); calling him "a man of pure, ardent, and unaffected piety . . . the adorer of one God . . . the friend and benefactor of the whole human race . . . the MAN OF THE PEOPLE . . . the brightest luminary of the western world." Robert Treat Paine's lyric "For Jefferson and Liberty" was sung at innumerable Jefferson rallies and "festivals," along with Rembrandt Peale's song "The People's Friend":

> Devoted to his country's cause,
>   The Rights of Men and equal Laws,
>   His hallow'd pen was given:
> And now those Rights and Laws to save
> From sinking to an early grave,
>   He comes employ'd by Heaven.

Among the Berkshire hills of Massachusetts, Elder John Leland of Cheshire, who had preached electioneering sermons for Jefferson, conceived a magnificent victory tribute. To his Baptist flock he proposed that they should make the biggest cheese in the world in honor of Thomas Jefferson. An eyewitness reported:

Every man and woman who owned a cow was to give for this cheese all the milk yielded on a certain day—only no *Federal cow* must contribute a drop. A huge cider-press was fitted up to make it in, and on the appointed day the whole country turned out with pails and tubs of curd, the girls and women in their best gowns and ribbons, and the men in their Sunday coats and clean shirt-collars. The cheese was put to press with prayer and hymn singing and great solemnity. When it was well dried it weighed 1600 pounds. It was placed on a sleigh, and Elder Leland drove with it all the way to Washington. It was a journey of three weeks. All the country had heard of the big cheese, and came out to look at it as the Elder drove along.[9]

Upon his arrival in Washington, "Leland the cheese-monger," as scoffing Federalists called him, preached on Sunday before the joint Houses of Congress, from the text, "And behold, a greater than Solomon is here"—praising the President with such zeal as one might expect from a godly man who had driven for three weeks with the largest cheese in the world. A segment of this cheese was still uneaten in 1805; it was served at a Presidential reception with cake and a huge urn of hot punch. This tribute was rivaled belatedly in 1837, when a New York admirer of outgoing President Jackson conveyed to the White House, "with banners and bands of music," a cheese weighing fourteen hundred pounds.

Although James Fenimore Cooper knew a Federalist parson who refused, at the font, to christen an infant "Thomas Jefferson," namesakes quickly began to appear. Among many namesake letters found in Jefferson's private papers, now in the Library of Congress, is one written with the painful care of a hand unaccustomed to the pen. The writer, Thomas Harris, says that he is "a free black man" of Sterling, Connecticut, and that his wife has

---

[9] Harriet Taylor Upton, *Our Early Presidents* (1890), pp. 165–166.

presented me with a pair of *twin boys*. A pair of *black twin boys* are, Sir, I believe no common sight. Such a pair however claim protection and support from me, which I fear I shall not be able to afford them. But Sir, as a testimony of my gratitude, for those principles of Justice and humanity by you so boldly advanced and ably advocated, and of the very great respect in which I hold the Father of his Country, the friend of freedom and equal rights, the benefactor of mankind, and of people of colour in particular, I have named one of my twins *Thomas,* and the other *Jefferson.*[10]

In regard to Jefferson as the Negro's friend, one of the most popular stories circulated about him was that he had returned the bow of an old darky, in order that a Negro "might not outdo him in politeness." Popular in school readers a generation ago, the anecdote usually went hand in hand with one about an old wayfaring man, wishing to ford a stream, who picked out Jefferson from a company of gentlemen on horseback as "the kindest-looking person." Jefferson's benevolence toward the poor and the slave was a legitimate part of his legend, though his attitude toward slavery— as the owner of two hundred blacks himself—was never quite clear to the public. For Jefferson himself (while favoring some gradual emancipation) was loath openly to endorse abolition when asked to do so by the French Society for the Abolition of the Slave Trade. It was another issue upon which the theoretical and the practical Jefferson never quite got together.

Jefferson's fan mail, as a later day would call it, is luckily preserved in the Library of Congress but of course unpublished. It reveals some interesting things. The President's known scientific bent, for example, attracted a host of letter writers unknown to fame or to Jefferson. They send a sample of cotton wadding made by a new process, a bit of old Peruvian earthenware, "a plan of aerial navigation" which needs federal support, a new type of loom, an apple-paring machine, "an invention for traveling under water." American ingenuity felt that a kindred spirit was in the White House. Sometimes Jefferson's humble admirers caution him to take better care of himself, hinting that he runs the risk of

[10] Thomas Harris to Jefferson, March 26, 1804, Jefferson Papers, Library of Congress.

assassination. Sometimes he is told that a Jefferson debating club has been formed in his honor, or a play or epic poem dedicated to him, often with the proposal that he produce or print it. That Jefferson was, in a sense unknown to Washington and John Adams, "the People's President," here stands revealed. A mechanic writes in to say that he and his wife have had "the fever," and need a loan of five hundred dollars which they are sure the President will supply. Another laborer writes that he is averse to hard work, and so needs money to get an education and become a literary man; all credit will then belong to Jefferson. A Kentuckian reports that a dislocated shoulder prevents his doing heavy labor, and therefore he wishes two thousand dollars to finance him while he studies law; apparently getting no answer, he repeats his request six weeks later with growing irritation. The pastor of a flock of Baptist Republicans in Lebanon, Ohio, tells Jefferson that his church has lost money in a legal dispute and needs a loan; other letters, incidentally, testify to cordial relations between Jefferson and a number of Baptist preachers and congregations. Many petitions come from needy veterans of the Revolution, debtors, and petty offenders in jail. Perhaps the most singular demand is a letter to Jefferson from one William Esenbeck, January 11, 1806; as a citizen of the national capital, he wants the President to detail six Indians to help him hunt wild beasts around the city.

Although one finds the curious complaint, in a letter of January 25, 1801, that "you will carry on the Government in a most parsimonious manner," it is plain that Jefferson in his first term won vast popular favor by abolishing the excise (the cause of the Whisky Rebellion, in Washington's day), the land tax, stamp tax, and other direct levies which had been made during the war scare of 1798. This pruning won Jefferson an abiding place in the heart of the American farmer. But the most widely applauded act of Jefferson's regime was the Louisiana Purchase. It was a shrewd and simple bargain which everybody could understand, although Jefferson himself took little subsequent pride in the Purchase and did not number it among the great "works" listed by his epitaph— probably because he knew how unconstitutional his methods had been. But the average American, in an age of land-hunger and expansionism, felt no such misgivings, and was quick to approve Jefferson the empire-builder. A typical letter, from an unknown admirer, James Garner of Pendleton, South Carolina, June 7, 1807, relates that he has just been "taking a small view of the western Country, Natchez & Lower Louisiana":

I Returnd Home, & having a higher (if possible) Regard & Esteem for your Personal Qualifications, in that great Acquisition of the western world & Numberless Measures mild and Advantageous to the American People in General, Excites me to Write, to inform you that I never Expect to See you, & in order to Get as nigh as possible have Taken the freedom of Calling my Second and Last Son Th. Jefferson.

After Jefferson's sweeping re-election, carrying all states save Connecticut and Delaware, his reputation seems to have reached its peak. His Second Inaugural shows that Jefferson, like other great leaders in world history, had become the mouthpiece of his age. Here occurs his famous counsel of "commerce and honest friendship with all nations—entangling alliances with none." Unlike Washington, Jefferson was an adept literary artist, and it is significant that posterity has mistakenly put into the mouth of Washington one of Jefferson's most captivating phrases.

About 1806—when Jefferson the expansionist was laying claim, incidentally, to the Gulf Stream as an American preserve, "in which hostilities and cruising are to be frowned on"—his popularity was almost overwhelming. The Embargo had not yet reared its head. As early as November of that year, and increasingly through the next twelve-month, letters poured in begging him to consider a third term. From Bergen County, New Jersey, he was told that "It is the duty of every man to submit his individual wishes to the general will"; "at a crisis when the flames of war are raging in Europe with unabated violence," added the Chenango County Republicans of New York. In Delaware the Kent County Republicans wrote: "Your services is [sic] necessary . . . men are ridiculing the Declaration of Independence." A few admirers dissented, one reminding him that "if JEFFERSON retiring with éclat enforces the principle of Rotation . . . what man would in future have the temerity to avow a contrary doctrine? He would be immediately and deservedly denounced, as an enemy to the sovereign People. . . . None ever can be more universally beloved."[11] But, whether tempted or not, Jefferson followed Washington's precedent.

Sensitive to censure, Jefferson also had the shy man's dislike of being lionized. Although a great democrat, he wanted to keep popularity at arm's length. This had been evident in earlier days— when in the late winter of 1797, approaching Philadelphia to take his seat as Vice-President, he had tried to enter the city by stealth. As usual, American enterprise frustrated the scheme: "A body of troops were on the lookout for him and signalled his approach by a discharge of artillery, and, marching before him into the city, bore a banner aloft on which were inscribed the words: 'Jefferson, the Friend of the People.' "[12] As President he made it a rule to send back even small tokens offered by admirers, lest he be suspected of taking perquisites and bribes; near the end of his second term he meticulously returned an ivory cane to Samuel Hawkins, saying he desired no reward save the "consciousness of a disinterested administration." When Boston citizens sought to make his birthday a patriotic anniversary, he disapproved "transferring the honors and veneration for the great birthday of the Republic to any individual, or of dividing them with individuals." The Fourth of July was enough glory for Jefferson. At the zenith of his popularity Jefferson looked icily upon Sullivan's proposal that he take a swing around the circle, to let the provincials have a look at their beloved chief; the President declared himself "not reconciled to the idea of a chief magistrate parading himself through the several States as an object of public gaze and in quest of an applause which, to be valuable, should be purely voluntary."[13] For all his mastery of some political arts and his secret thirst for approval, Jefferson never overcame a feeling, like that of Shakespeare's Coriolanus,

[11] "A Citizen of Washington County, Maryland," to Jefferson, February 23, 1807.
[12] Sarah N. Randolph, *The Domestic Life of Thomas Jefferson* (1871), p. 242.
[13] Nock, 260–261.

about cheapening himself to court the mob, "the mutable, rank-scented many." Jefferson's self-knowledge—that kept him from any illusions about his power of oratory or his personal magnetism —may have added to this feeling. Yet it is safe to say that no man today, Democratic or Republican, could become a major political hero who showed one half of Jefferson's aristocratic diffidence.

Still, he took a very human interest in what people thought about him. Jefferson kept a personal scrapbook, now in the University of Virginia Library. The first fifty pages are filled with political songs and verses, panegyrics and lampoons, accounts of dinners and Republican picnics, bearing chiefly upon himself. One tells of a monster celebration on the banks of the Ohio near Cincinnati, on the Fourth of July, 1806, at which Jefferson was toasted as "the supporter of the rights of man . . . whose integrity and virtue will live in the remembrance of a free and enlightened people, when calumniators are buried in oblivion," and cheered in the playing of "Jefferson's March" with a two-gun salute (George Washington received only one gun). Lyrics in praise of Jefferson are set to the tune of "Hail, Columbia" and "Anacreon in Heaven" (subsequently that of "The Star-Spangled Banner"). In this album one finds "Original Thoughts on the Election of Thomas Jefferson—composed by an obscure Alien," in faltering meter but full of rhapsody. There is a satire sung at a Federalist rally on Independence Day in New Hampshire, which begins:

> Great Washington's hobby, from first dawning youth,
> Was virtue, and valor, and wisdom, and truth.
> While Jefferson's hobby, on Chesterfield's plan,
> Was to *rise* in the Statesman, but *sink* in the Man.

Beside this aspersion is the retort of a loyal Jeffersonian; he leaves the first two lines intact, but emends—

> And Jefferson's hobby (on Washington's plan)
> To unite in the Statesman, the PATRIOT and MAN—

for good measure adding that "John Adams's hobby is dullness profound."

Jefferson's album includes the verses of one brave poet who exclaims

Huzza for the prudent Embargo!

Yet, as is well known, the Embargo Act of 1807 was the one keenly unpopular deed of Jefferson's eight years. Highhanded, it infringed upon American trade, "making many smugglers and traitors, but not a single hero," as Henry Adams remarked. If this be thought New England prejudice, one may hear Mr. Albert Jay Nock, that warm Jeffersonian of our own day, call it "the most arbitrary, inquisitorial, and confiscatory measure formulated in American legislation up to the period of the Civil War."[14] Forbidding the sailing of American ships upon the high seas lest they fall into the clutches of warring Europeans, the Embargo was humiliating to patriots and disastrous to traders. Except for theorists who shared Jefferson's hope that "economic sanctions" might come to be a moral equivalent for the War of 1812, nobody loved the Embargo. Yet, as an experiment, much could have been said for it. At the end of his very successful administration Jefferson was left temporarily discredited. Many families in the South, as well as in the Middle States and New England, were ruined by Jefferson's prudential isolation; they never forgave him, and handed to the next generation their hatred along with their insolvency. Fredrika Bremer in 1850 on a railway journey through Georgia met a man "in person not unlike a meal-sack, whose father had lost $50,000 by the Embargo; he said 'I regard Tom Jefferson as the compound of everything which is rascally, mean, wicked, dishonorable.' "[15]

III

Indeed, in speaking of Jefferson the hero it is necessary to take account of that obbligato of hatred heard throughout his Presidency. Some of the First Families of Virginia had detested him

[14] *Ibid.*, p. 266; cf. Henry Adams, *History of the United States During the Administrations of Jefferson and Madison* (1891–1893), Vol. IV, Chap. XII, "The Cost of Embargo."
[15] F. Bremer, *America of the Fifties* (1924), pp. 124–125.

since the Revolution, because he fought to end aristocratic privileges like entail, and the Episcopal clergy because he divorced Church and State. In fact, parsons and "economic royalists" were Jefferson's born enemies. In Jefferson's day the charge of irreligion was a much more effective weapon of attack, before the eyes of the common man, than the charge of economic heresy. John Adams, although as much the skeptic as Jefferson, held economic views approved by the traders of New England, and hence was never set in the public pillory among the godless. A good many politicians who did not themselves give a rap for the divinity of Christ or inspiration of the Scriptures seized upon the theological brush with which to tar Jefferson. Jefferson avoided public utterance of his gravest doubts, but at heart seems to have been a deist. He disliked all sects, but came closest to being a Unitarian. He held vague hopes of immortality, but believed above all else in the religion of progress, of human betterment, "passing over us like a cloud of light." "It does me no injury for my neighbor to say there are twenty gods, or no god. It neither picks my pocket nor breaks my leg," he wrote in the *Notes on Virginia,* in tolerant words which irritated many. Although his views had been fixed long before he went abroad, Jefferson upon returning from France found he was suspected of being "Frenchified" or "contaminated" by alien nonsense. From Virginia the prejudice spread elsewhere as soon as Jefferson began to fill federal office.

Dr. Timothy Dwight, president of Yale, "Pope" of Connecticut, and akin by blood or marriage to those Hillhouses and Wolcotts and Wadsworths who held the purse-strings of southern New England, led the assault. In a typical *Discourse preached on the Fourth of July* he predicted in 1800 that under Jefferson all Bibles would be burnt, children "wheedled or terrified" into singing *Ça ira,* and "we may see our wives and daughters the victims of legal prostitution." The nationalization of women, as Dr. Dwight well knew, is always a clarion call. In his later book *The Character of Thomas Jefferson* Dr. Dwight charged that this heretic was also vain, insincere, double-faced, and "would descend to the low means and artifices of a practiced intriguer and demagogue to gain favor with the lowest classes of the community." To have become the People's President was, in fact, an act of perfidy! Stephen Cullen Carpenter announced that Jefferson had denied "the right of property, marriage, natural affection, chastity, and decency."[16] In New York the Reverend John Mason warned the American people against electing a President who "disbelieves the existence of an universal deluge."[17] Upon Jefferson's inauguration, it was reported, pious New England housewives buried their Bibles in their gardens to keep them from confiscation.

Assaults upon Jefferson continued to mingle economics with godliness. A parson, significantly named the Reverend Cotton Mather Smith, charged that Jefferson had robbed a widow and her fatherless children of an estate of £10,000, entrusted him as executor. The President calmly replied that his sister was the only widow whose estate he had ever administered, and that so far as he knew she had no complaints. In the days of Jefferson's Vice-Presidency the Reverend Jedidiah Champion of Litchfield, Connecticut, had prayed with fervor for President Adams, and added "O Lord! wilt Thou bestow upon the Vice-President a double portion of Thy grace, *for Thou knowest he needs it.*" But after Jefferson's accession to the highest office, the Reverend James Abercrombie of Philadelphia declared that on account of the incumbent's atheism he was "very reluctant to read the prayers for the President of the United States, prescribed in the Episcopal ritual." Whether it were better for God to give, or withhold, His grace from Mr. Jefferson was a puzzling question.

Jefferson received scores of anonymous letters about his religion, as his private papers show. They were far more numerous during his first than his second term, by which time most people saw the absurdity of burying their Bibles. A typical letter signed "A. B." and written on January 25, 1801, tells Jefferson he is rumored to be "a kind neighbour" and "certainly a Great Man," but, says the writer, "I am afraid of your Religion & your Politicks." He confesses he is not a pious man himself, but fears that if

[16] S. C. Carpenter, *Memoirs of the Hon. Thomas Jefferson* (printed for the purchasers, 1809), II, 93.

[17] Dr. John Mason, *The Voice of Warning, to Christians, on the Ensuing Election of a President of the United States* (1800), p. 11.

Christianity is uprooted in the United States "oaths will be nothing, and no one will be safe in his person or property." Probably the writer had never read Swift's dry remarks on abolishing Christianity in England. Another letter, signed "a poor Afflicted Sickly bruised Reed," written May 2, 1801, exhorts Jefferson to look to the Bible for wisdom, to pass more severe laws against swearing and Sabbath-breaking. A letter from "a Youth of fifteen," on March 10 of this same year, admits the alarm felt by those "who have some Regard for Religion, Liberty, and good Order," at Jefferson's efforts to destroy "the Constitution which was framed by our forefathers." That a man so near the fountainhead of our national life as Jefferson should have been accused of laying violent hands upon the "forefathers" is a fact worth noting.

The dwindling of such letters during Jefferson's second term sprang, in part, from a rather curious situation. The great mass of his followers were humble rather than rich, farmers rather than city folk. Tidings of Jefferson's deism reached them faintly. More surely they knew he had eased their tax burdens, and was opening to them a vast new frontier for settlement. In other words, he was their friend. And it was among these people, Baptist and Methodist, that a great wave of revivalism surged during the early years of Jefferson's Presidency—the Gasper River, Holly Springs, Red River, Flemingsburg, and other camp-meetings which excited nationwide comment. From the loneliness of back country and frontier they discovered the gregarious warmth of revivals. By the light of flickering lanterns, beneath the tents of Zion, in the muddy waters of a hundred inland rivers, men and women were washed in the blood of the Lamb. A generation later, in the backwoods of the Lincoln country, Herndon found them hugging each other and singing in ecstasy that was half religious, half sexual—

> I have my Jesus in my arms,
> Sweet as honey, strong as bacon ham.

At Newburgh, New York, *The Recorder of the Times,* August 29, 1804, like many another rural newspaper, remarked the incontestable fact that in Mr. Jefferson's "wise and virtuous administration" God Almighty has "poured out his spirit among the people in a manner before unknown in America." It was a mighty rebuke to Dr. Timothy Dwight and his chilly pew-holders. In fact, it became common for the rank-and-file Jeffersonians—radical in politics, conservative in religion—to deny as calumny any doubts of their President's piety.[18] To many, Jefferson's stand against "priestcraft" struck a chord of Protestant sympathy loud enough to be heard above the thunders of Congregational and Episcopal pulpits. One of the worst poems ever written to praise an American hero, called *The Pudding proved by eating of it,* printed in Monroe County, Virginia, in 1804, declares:

> His States' Work doth not depend on any Clergy Whim,
> His Bus'ness hath naught to do with a Priest-Craft System:
> His religious Opinions is but between his God and him.
>
> . . . .
>
> Better have Deist President that is of mild command,
> Than a Christian one, that is for an overbearing hand.

The great mass of Americans, then as later, refused to pay attention to the handful of militant freethinkers who tried to claim Jefferson, or to the small band of parsons who refused to bury the hatchet. Even today a few conservative Virginia dames—born and bred in a socio-economic stratum whose prejudices are well-nigh immortal—think of Tom Jefferson as the freethinker and dangerous radical, who made the Episcopal Church in Virginia "just like any other church." But in the main, Jefferson's reply in old age to a prying individual—"Say nothing of my religion. It is known to my God and myself alone"—has been respected by his average hero-worshippers.

Some charges made against Jefferson early and late by his enemies—that he chattered like a French monkey, loved flattery, and practiced vivisection for cruelty in the name of science—were such distortions of a silent, dignified, kindly man that they had not enough vitality to live. Even Washington Irving's portrait of "William Kieft" in his *Knickerbocker's History* in 1809—dressed

---

[18] G. A. Koch, *Republican Religion: The American Revolution and the Cult of Reason* (1933), p. 137. Dixon Ryan Fox, *The Decline of Aristocracy in the Politics of New York* (1919), Chap. I, gives an excellent review of Jefferson the infidel as seen through Federalist eyes.

in "cocked hat and corduroy small-clothes" and mounted on "a raw-boned charger," who invented carts that went before horses and weathercocks that turned against the wind, who lived in "a sweet sequestered swamp" on an estate "commonly known by the name of Dog's Misery," and who punctuated counsels of state with thunderous blasts of his nose blown into a red cotton handkerchief—is funny, but even more unrecognizable than Maxwell Anderson's picture of Peter Stuyvesant as Franklin Delano Roosevelt. *The Jonnycake Papers* later burlesqued such caricatures by recalling that "Tom Jefferson . . . was nothing but a mean-spirited, low-lived fellow, the son of a half-breed Indian squaw, sired by a Virginia mulatto father, as was well known in the neighborhood where he was raised wholly on hoe-cake (made of coarse-ground Southern corn), bacon and hominy, with an occasional change of fricasseed bullfrog, for which abominable reptiles he had acquired a taste during his residence among the French at Paris." Such hostile nicknames as "Thomas the Magician" or "Thomas Conundrum," seeking to suggest political skulduggery, never caught on. The public indeed had decided that Jefferson's was white magic.

The rankest canard which flew about Jefferson was that his taste ran to colored mistresses. It seems to have been invented in the North, where to some Federalists the fact was perhaps incredible that a Southern gentleman might own a hundred female slaves without claiming a *droit de seigneur.* In *The Portfolio,* issued in Philadelphia in October, 1802, one finds this lyric about the President of the United States:

A SONG

Supposed to have been written by the Sage of Monticello.

Et etiam fusco grata colore Venus.—Ovid.
"And Venus pleases, though as black as jet."

Tune: "Yankee Doodle."

Of all the damsels on the green,
On mountain or in valley,
A lass so luscious ne'er was seen
As Monticellian Sally.

> *Chorus:* Yankee doodle, who's the noodle?
> What wife were half so handy?
> To breed a flock of slaves for stock,
> A blackamoor's the dandy.
>
> What though she by the glands secretes;
> Must I stand shil—I, shall—I?
> Tuck'd up between a pair of sheets
> There's no perfume like Sally.

The little poet Tom Moore, visiting Washington in 1804 and presented at the White House by the anti-Jeffersonian Merrys, was irked by the tall President's failure to take special note of the greatest living Irish bard. To the joy of Federalists he published his verse epistle to Thomas Hume, describing the chieftain in Washington who

> retires to lash his slaves at home;
> Or woo, perhaps, some black Aspasia's charms,
> And dream of freedom in his bondmaid's arms.

James Fenimore Cooper's old schoolmaster "cracked his jokes daily about Mr. Jefferson and Black Sal, never failing to place his libertinism in strong relief against the approved morals of George III."[19] The rumor has no known basis in fact. Jefferson, so scrupulous to answer charges which had a grain of truth, never troubled to quash this story.

Yet it had a long subterranean life. During the campaign of 1860 enemies of Abraham Lincoln, trying to damage him with the liberal as well as the Southern vote, claimed he had said Jefferson was a slaveholder who "brought his own children under the hammer, and made money of his debaucheries." Also that one of Jefferson's dusky daughters "was sold some years ago at public auction in New Orleans, and was purchased by a society of gentlemen who wished to testify by her liberation their admiration of the statesman who 'dreamt of freedom in a slave's embrace.' " Lincoln branded this supposed speech of his "a base forgery."[20]

---

[19] James Fenimore Cooper, *Gleanings in Europe: England* (1837), pp. 264–265.
[20] Carl Sandburg, *Lincoln: The Prairie Years* (1926), II, 369.

"Old Martin," who for many years rang the campus bell of the University of Virginia, proudly boasted that he was a great-grandson of Thomas Jefferson. Although some of the Jeffersonians of Charlottesville thought he might have been a wild oat sown by one of the statesman's "fast" Randolph grandsons, one suspects the projection in time of an old legend. The University founded by Jefferson has always been very proud of him, never prone to apologize for either his real or imaginary vices. In fact it is a roosting place for the more fantastic rumors about him—such as, that he laid out its serpentine walls while drunk, and that he built a row of small houses back of the pavilions to serve as collegiate brothels. Quite without truth, it is sometimes said that in the charter of the University of Virginia Jefferson provided for licensed prostitution, upon the theory that such an outlet was better for young bullocks than vice without regulation. As recently as 1930 Mr. John Cook Wyllie of the University Library received a series of inquiries, asking for a copy or photostat of the charter, from the Public Library of St. Louis. After some coyness it came out that a patron of the St. Louis Public Library had been greatly upset by hearing this ancient rumor.

The remaining charges against Jefferson's morals stem from the year 1802 and the vilification of a Scotchman named James Thomson Callender. The facts are ironic. Callender, who had fled his own land after libeling the British government, was first thought by the credulous Jefferson to be a misunderstood, mistreated democrat. So Jefferson gave him secret patronage. This journeyman of slander soon began to attack the Federalist party, Adams, and Hamilton. His snapping at Hamilton's heels forced that statesman to clear himself of suspected unfaithfulness to public trust, at the expense of revealing his adultery with Mrs. Reynolds—a brave but most humiliating disclosure by Hamilton. The Jeffersonians were gleeful. Attacks upon President Adams, however, sent Callender to a Richmond jail for nine months. Upon Jefferson's inauguration Callender was pardoned and his fine of two hundred dollars was remitted. But a delay in the return of this money so angered Callender that he turned against Jefferson, and bedaubed him with the same mud with which he had spattered

Hamilton. In 1802 in the Richmond *Recorder* he printed charges against Jefferson whose stain can never be quite forgotten by those otherwise disposed to hate the third President. Callender was a maudlin drunkard who often threatened to commit suicide, and in 1803 was found drowned in three feet of water in the James River; but his work lived long after him. A swarm of pamphlets took up the charges, newspapers printed sniggering allusions to them, and early in 1805 they were aired upon the floor of the Massachusetts legislature by Congressman John W. Hulbert.

The charge of cowardice in Revolutionary days, and Jefferson's alleged statement that belief in God was "of no social importance," were spiced with accusations of sexual error, in the Callender-Hulbert libels. Jefferson admitted the truth of only one charge—that as a young man he had made improper and unsuccessful advances to Mrs. John Walker, wife of a lifelong friend and neighbor. This memoir of his dead life must have caused exquisite pain to the sensitive aristocrat. It was singular to find him writhing upon the same barb, driven by the same hand, which had pierced Hamilton. Jefferson penned a confession "that when young and single I offered love to a handsome lady—I acknoledge [*sic*] its incorrectness," and circulated it among his intimate friends and cabinet officers, with denial of the other charges.[21] Jefferson had the misfortune at this time to become involved with the talkative, none-too-sympathetic Lees, Henry Lee serving as go-between for Jefferson and the unhappy husband—who in 1806 requested in Jefferson's hand a statement of "his, & his lady's entire exculpation" for publication if the scandal ever reappeared.[22] It is safe to say, as Douglas S. Freeman remarks, that Jefferson was no hero in the eyes of the Lee family or the idealistic Robert E. Lee; they and related Virginia families have tended to look upon Jefferson with contempt.[23] Americans at large, however, have long forgotten this

[21] Worthington C. Ford, *Thomas Jefferson Correspondence* (1916), p. 115.

[22] Henry Lee to Jefferson, dated "Belvoir 8th Sepr 06," in the Jefferson Papers, Library of Congress, but apparently not listed in the *Catalogue of the Papers of Thomas Jefferson,* published by that Library.

[23] Douglas S. Freeman, *R. E. Lee* (1935), I, 115.

episode, buried among the rotten timber of Callender's libels. It is probable that a score of modern Virginians have heard about Jefferson's mythical taste for octoroons to one who has heard the real story of poor Mrs. John Walker.

Critical students of Jefferson have long been troubled by an aspect of his personality which makes less inflammable tinder for scandal, but comes closer to the real man. It is akin to the only serious blemish of Franklin, a pliant expediency. Were it not for the stalwart example of Washington, cynics might conclude that the greatest heroes of the early republic were men who succeeded because of their resemblance to Sam Slick. Washington alone towered above the fogs of opportunism, and did all his work without recourse to occasional backstairs stratagems. He alone had a scrupulous code beyond that of the practical politician, and deservedly is the greatest hero of our early republic. Franklin and Jefferson generally contrived to compromise issues without compromising themselves, but here and there they slipped a trifle. Clearly below them, in a descending scale, were men like Patrick Henry—who, as Jefferson knew, was a rather shady individual— and Robert Morris, so-called "financier of the Revolution." (Although Morris is still in patriotic favor, with hotels and credit associations named for him, it is now clear, as Professor Abernethy remarks, that the Revolution financed Robert Morris, and that he embraced the cause of independence as a heaven-sent speculative opportunity.[24] But remarkably few, indeed, are the unworthies who have slipped into the fold of American hero-worship.)

The deeps of Jefferson's character are not easy to plumb. In the first place, he was a very amiable gentleman. He liked to please people. In the days of his Ministry to France he obliged a large circle of friends and acquaintances by shopping for them: even Mrs. John Adams wrote asking him to buy her daughter "two pairs of corsets," somehow assuming that Mr. Jefferson without being told would know the right size. Jefferson came close to being a born victim of that American phrase, "let George do it." He was a

[24] T. P. Abernethy, *Western Lands and the American Revolution* (1937), p. 173 *et passim*.

natural committeeman, and if destiny had not drafted him for a higher role he would have made the ideal Vice-President. He wished to say what people wanted to hear, and (despite his authorship of a great document of defiance) he dreaded to provoke criticism, offense, personal friction. The rigors of debate had no appeal for him. Although he might collect gossip about his enemies with the calmness of research, he was reluctant to make aggressive use of it. Only when goaded did he fight back; even then he was quick to offer the olive branch. One of his most characteristic utterances was the statement of his First Inaugural, "We are all republicans—we are all federalists."

In his talk and his letters Jefferson usually let others set the topic and tone, often restating their opinions with his own greater literary finesse. Once this habit brought him to the brink of political ruin. This was at the time of his flowery outburst, in the Latin vein, to Mazzei on April 24, 1796, during Washington's administration and pointed at the President, about those Americans "who were Samsons in the field and Solomons in the council, but who have had their heads shorn by the harlot England." Jefferson was deeply shocked when this letter bounced back in the public eye, and did all he could to unsay it.[25] A little later, proof reached Washington that Jefferson's nephew living at Monticello had forged a letter of flattery, in disguised handwriting under the fictitious name "John Langhorne," hoping to trap Washington into private utterances which might be used against him politically. Whether Jefferson had a hand in this naïve ruse cannot now be proved, in black and white, but Washington himself and some of his later partisans have so believed.[26] Most people know nothing

[25] Cf. Chinard, pp. 312–313.
[26] Fitzpatrick, *George Washington Himself,* p. 504; Beveridge, *John Marshall,* II, 375 and n. A late word on the subject, giving Jefferson the benefit of the doubt, is Manning J. Dauer, "The Two John Nicholases," *American Historical Review,* January 1940, pp. 338 ff. No historian, I believe, has yet pointed out that among the Alexander Hamilton Papers in the Library of Congress is a letter from Washington's correspondent, John Nicholas, dated Richmond, August 4, 1803, offering Hamilton his services as a secret informer against "J" (plainly Jefferson): he adds that "being long intimately & personally acquainted with certain characters & their secret movements, I trust I can render my share of service."

of this incident, and the biographers of Jefferson strangely do not mention it—though they like to tell how Jefferson, one later spring, placed upon the bust of Washington at Monticello a wreath of immortelles a French admirer had sent the philosopher to wear on his own birthday.

Jefferson the man was easy to know, but impossible to know well. Many called him "a trimmer." Sometimes it appeared that he steered a circuitous course, catching the prevailing winds as he went along, to reach in the end a wholly honorable port. John Quincy Adams, naturally inclined to overstate the case, said that Jefferson had "a memory so pandering to the will that in deceiving others he seems to have begun by deceiving himself."[27] More sympathetically, one must say that Jefferson had been forced to learn the arts of expediency. As a young Governor, his scrupulosity over legal points had been the prime reason for a failure he never forgot. Later he was prone to believe that the end justified the means. In his most important decision, the Louisiana Purchase —in which he privately admitted that he had "done an act beyond the Constitution" in not waiting for the cumbersome machinery of democracy—certainly the result was splendid, and vindicated by all patriotism and good sense. Justifying his highhanded methods in the Burr conspiracy, free to admit that democracy is too slow in crises, Jefferson the President wrote (in words so alien to Jefferson the Governor): "Should we have ever gained our Revolution, if we had bound our hands by manacles of the law?"[28] It was significant that President Roosevelt, in his message to Congress on September 3, 1940, apropos of the "swap" of fifty old destroyers for eight naval bases for defense of the Western Hemisphere, should have buttressed himself with the precedent of Jefferson's "unconstitutional" bargain with Napoleon—calling his exchange "the most important action in the re-enforcement of our national defense that has been taken since the Louisiana Purchase." The American people, it appears, approved both.

Jefferson's was a complex brain—the brain of a dreamer and idealist, trained by experience into a shrewd, adaptable, hard-

[27] J. Q. Adams, *Diary,* January 11, 1831.
[28] Jefferson to Dr. James Brown, October 27, 1808.

headed politician—and it let him see all sides of a subject. His very penetration bred contradictions, and led him sometimes into passing inconsistency. (He has been quoted for and against states' rights and the right of secession, for and against restricted immigration, for and against the spoils system, for and against a big navy and preparedness.) Though some of these contradictions are more apparent than real, it must be admitted that Jefferson's intellect—far from being a single-track mind like Washington's— was a whole switchyard. But the most vital fact remains to be added. Jefferson's devotion to the United States, above all other interests private or public, selfish or partisan, was superbly consistent. There he never wavered. Hamilton's intrigues with the British Crown in 1792, which carried him perilously near to treason,[29] have no counterpart in the Jefferson pattern. Only to political dogmas or exclusive economic interests did Jefferson fail to show a fixed loyalty. There he allowed himself to blow hot and cold, depending upon occasions.

Of course the average American on the basis of his vague knowledge, in early times as well as today, could not be expected to rationalize all these things. He was simply disposed to accept Jefferson as "the People's friend," and this trust was not ill placed. Jefferson's contribution to the United States, as statesman and President, was not an airtight or even very logical political system. It was chiefly a faith—faith in the long run in the dependability, wisdom, and honesty of the common literate individual, as represented in his day by the agrarian majority. Woodrow Wilson said: "The immortality of Thomas Jefferson does not lie in any one of his achievements, but in his attitude toward mankind." This verdict, whether endorsed by a great modern liberal or by the man in the street, is the core of the Jefferson cult.

IV

Through the long sunset years between Jefferson's retirement in 1809 and his death in 1826, he became an oracle and patriarch. He was one of the last surviving symbols of the Revolution, the

[29] Samuel Flagg Bemis, *Jay's Treaty* (1923), Chap. V.

sage on the hilltop, who (as a visitor wrote in 1816), after "having filled a seat higher than that of kings, succeeds with graceful dignity to that of the good neighbor." A typical English visitor to America, Isaac Candler, grew bored with being told that Jefferson was "the most learned man in the world," and with hearing Jefferson's opinions on art and literature quoted to end all discussion. (The mantle of versatility was already being cast about the shoulders of great Americans.) Jefferson's growing financial embarrassments were neglected by his native state, but brought generous gifts from citizens of New York, Philadelphia, and Baltimore. In June, 1826, Jefferson declined on the score of health an invitation to become the city of Washington's guest of honor on the fiftieth birthday of the Declaration of Independence. His reply, traced with a feeble hand, but stating with his old fire the conviction that "the mass of mankind has not been born with saddles on their backs," was published immediately as a broadside. It was his last pastoral charge. Shortly after noon of that Fourth of July—the date upon whose prime validity Jefferson had so long insisted—the statesman breathed his last. Every schoolboy knows that John Adams, expiring on the same day in Massachusetts, faintly murmured, "Thomas Jefferson still survives." Many Americans felt a sentiment thus expressed by a Virginia newspaper: "In this most singular coincidence, the finger of Providence is plainly visible! It hallows the Declaration of Independence as the Word of God, and is the bow in the Heavens, that promises its principles shall be eternal." But at least one jealous Jeffersonian, who lived in Albemarle County, thought that John Adams' death on the same day "was a damned Yankee trick."[30]

In death, as in life, Jefferson remained second to Washington. Daniel Webster, in his great joint eulogy on Jefferson and Adams at Faneuil Hall in 1826, exclaimed: "Washington is in the clear upper sky. These other stars have now joined the American constellation; they circle round their center, and the Heavens beam with new light." It was plain that none could rival the glory of Washington, who had fought for and won the liberty that Jefferson

[30] For the newspaper quotation, *The Norfolk* (Virginia) *Herald*, July 10, 1826; for the comment, Randolph, p. 421 n.

and Adams had phrased. The first to hold highest office and the first to die, Washington was divorced more completely than they from sections and parties. It was also clear that to the country at large Jefferson was a greater hero than Adams. His single deeds—from the Declaration to the Louisiana Purchase—had been more splendid, and his policies had struck deeper root. The Adamses have always served America well, but their vanity, coldness, and knack of doing the gracious thing "in the ungracious way" have kept them in a class inferior to the heroes—the worthies.

It was Jefferson's good luck, and the nation's, that his loyal pupils Madison and Monroe for sixteen years carried on his will and testament. The liberalisms of later men, who in various ways tried to revive the faith of Jefferson—Jackson, Lincoln, Woodrow Wilson—were uprooted more quickly by falling into hostile hands. Jeffersonianism enjoyed a long fruitful summer of increase; it became a name and philosophy of rich American associations. Even the Whigs, Jackson's enemies and Webster's friends, who had taken all there was to salvage from the shipwreck of the anti-Jefferson Federalists, in 1841 after their Log Cabin campaign, as a New York newspaper noted, "have of late years repeatedly declared themselves true Jeffersonian Democrats."[31] Henry S. Randall, in a devoted three-volume life of Jefferson in 1858, remarked that although Jefferson was still secretly assailed "by class and hereditary hate," yet no orator dared publicly attack the two greatest Americans, Washington and Jefferson, "the one who was the Sword of his country, and the other the Pen."

Walt Whitman—who had younger brothers named Thomas Jefferson and Andrew Jackson Whitman—spoke of the two agrarian statesmen as "the sainted Jefferson and Jackson." In youth the poet of "the Divine Average" had hailed Jefferson as "the Columbus of our political faith," and in old age still cherished him as "among the greatest of the great."[32] With the storm of Civil War darkening, Jefferson, as author of the affirmation that all men are created free and equal, began to receive fresh honor in the North. The new Republican party, dressing its ranks for a great crusade,

[31] *The New World* (New York), September 25, 1841.
[32] Newton Arvin, *Whitman* (1938), pp. 14–15.

looked to Jefferson the idealist. Lincoln, replying on April 6, 1859, to an invitation to a Jefferson birthday rally in Boston, was moved to grave mirth by the shifting of old party lines. He told the story of two drunks who got into a fight: each fought himself out of his own coat and into that of the other fellow. Lincoln remarked that Jefferson's land, the South, now held that personal liberty was nothing in comparison with property rights, while "Republicans, on the contrary, are for both the man and the dollar, but in case of conflict the man before the dollar." That was Jeffersonianism. "The principles of Jefferson are the definitions and axioms of free society," Lincoln added. "All honor to Jefferson—to the man who, in the concrete pressure of a struggle for national independence by a single people, had the coolness, forecast, and capacity to introduce into a mere revolutionary document an abstract truth, applicable to all men and all times."

Jefferson as hero waned somewhat after the Civil War. New idols like Lincoln and Grant tended to dim the galaxy of the Revolution. The unity symbolized by the amended Constitution now appeared more precious than the ringing defiance of the Declaration. Jefferson's memory had neither its Weems nor its John Hay: his very character was too deep an enigma for conventional biography. Orators, novelists, and poets seemed to pass him by; even Monticello grew shabbier, more neglected, with each passing year. His liberalism fell upon deaf ears in the era Vernon Parrington has called "the Great Barbecue." Only here and there were men to whom Jefferson was a magic spirit. The most ardent of them was Henry George, shocked over land-grabbing in the West and the growing slums of Eastern cities. Henry George believed in Jefferson's God—the Author of Nature who had created the earth for men to till, and to exercise the gift He had given them of life, liberty, and the pursuit of happiness. George conceived the single tax as an offshoot of Jefferson's philosophy, as a safeguard against exploitation of the soil. But he was in the minority.

The Democratic party, reviving slowly after the Civil War, made Jefferson its patron saint; but the national leadership of Jefferson's region, the South, had been shattered. The dominant party, the

Republicans, had forgotten Jefferson since Lincoln's day. A semi-liberal like Theodore Roosevelt (who shared the historical loyalties of his Federalist friend Lodge) detested Jefferson. The only thing he could approve was the Louisiana Purchase; in all else Jefferson was a weakling. Roosevelt's most blasting damnation of Bryan was a comparison with Jefferson—well-meaning, shallow, cheap, vacillating, possessing "Jefferson's nervous fear of doing anything that may seem to be unpopular with the rank and file of the people." Thus he wrote to Taft on September 4, 1906. Indeed, Jefferson was out of fashion with more simon-pure liberals than Roosevelt. One of the most powerful books of that decade, Herbert Croly's *The Promise of American Life* in 1909, offered stinging epithets about "Jefferson's intellectual superficiality and insincerity." Even in his champions Jefferson was unfortunate: in the muckraking era, William Randolph Hearst took up "Jeffersonian democracy" as his favorite shibboleth.

Wilson had marked intellectual sympathy for Jefferson, but no warm personal admiration; he once told Colonel House that Alexander Hamilton "was easily the ablest" statesman of the early republic.[33] After the Great War, Jefferson was often quoted on "entangling alliances," approved as an isolationist and lover of peace. In view of Red Russia, little was said of Jefferson the radical. Upon another tack, in 1928, it was asserted direfully that the election of a Catholic President would "roll back the progress of Democracy of Jefferson and Jackson."[34]

V

Jefferson did not come into his own until the New Deal. Whether consciously or not, he has been built up to offset Lincoln, as a symbol of the Democratic party, and to give the new liberalism its sanction by tradition. The great Jefferson Memorial now being completed in Washington, the reawakened cult at Monticello, the

[33] Colonel House's diary, April 15, 1914; quoted by Dumas Malone, "Jefferson and the New Deal," *Scribner's* Magazine, June 1933.

[34] Quoted with disapproval in an editorial in *The New York World*, September 6, 1928.

three-cent stamp, the new Jefferson nickel, and the massive face which Gutzon Borglum has carved upon Mount Rushmore—all proclaim that he is our newest federal god in the highest degree. Some of these tributes might have come at all events; together, they show an unmistakable drift.

Franklin D. Roosevelt as candidate for President, at St. Paul in the spring of 1932, declared that Benjamin Franklin, Jefferson, and Theodore Roosevelt were the three great Americans who knew best the cross-currents of our folk life, the hopes and fears of the common people—"and of these three Jefferson was in many ways the deepest student. . . . His, after all, was the essential point of view that has been held by our truly great leaders in every generation." (The exclusion of Lincoln was perhaps a political one, since he, rather than the "progressive" Theodore Roosevelt, was embedded so deeply in Republican myth.) A few months later in San Francisco, making his notable speech on progressive government, Franklin D. Roosevelt ranked Jefferson first on the roll call of American liberals, followed by Theodore Roosevelt and Woodrow Wilson. As President, on July 4, 1936, at Monticello, he glowingly praised Jefferson's "consecration" to social justice and to "the freedom of the human mind." Mr. Roosevelt has quoted George Washington a little gingerly, even on so safe a subject as popular education, lest he be contradicted by other passages "from the somewhat voluminous writings and messages of the First President"[35]—but of Jefferson's mind, which many regard as more perilously self-contradictory, Mr. Roosevelt has always spoken with assurance. In a more personal view, the parallel between the master of Monticello and the squire of Hyde Park, another gentle radical, is too good to miss. In July, 1937, it was reported that a portrait of Jefferson painted by the Polish patriot Kosciuszko, and carried at that time from the Polish Embassy to the White House, bore a striking resemblance to Mr. Roosevelt. Certainly the thirty-second President feels at home in the milieu of the third. At the University of Virginia on June 10, 1940, the day of Italy's entry into the War, the President welcomed an occasion to speak his mind in "this university founded by the first great

[35] F. D. Roosevelt, *Public Papers and Addresses* (1938), V, 80.

American teacher of democracy." That Thomas Jefferson is Mr. Roosevelt's political hero one can hardly doubt, or that his ideals have tinged the philosophy of the New Deal.[36]

Claude G. Bowers, admirer and biographer of Jefferson, was made Ambassador to Spain by President Roosevelt in 1933. From Madrid, to the Democratic campaign of 1936, Mr. Bowers contributed his book, *Jefferson in Power: The Death Struggle of the Federalists.* It described the career of a liberal aristocrat through eight years of serene triumph, winning the people's love, engaging in vast public works, and readily crushing his enemies who had "fought with far-seeing cunning from behind the protecting shield of the Supreme Court." Mr. Bowers pointed his moral by saying, "the story is offered as a warning to all succeeding political parties and politicians that public opinion cannot be defied with impunity." (Dissenters remarked that Mr. Bowers had nothing to say about Jefferson's dictum that "the best government is that which governs least.") While Mr. Bowers, here and elsewhere, implies that Jefferson would applaud the New Deal, Mr. James Truslow Adams in *The Living Jefferson* (1936) states that Jefferson would have hated it. Needless to say, both men agree with Jefferson.

The enemies of Jefferson are dead, or in hiding. Nowadays no such words are uttered publicly as those of Bishop Henry Codman Potter, "shepherd of the Four Hundred," at the Washington Inaugural Centennial of 1889 in New York: "We have exchanged the Washingtonian dignity for the Jeffersonian simplicity, which was in truth only another name for the Jacksonian vulgarity." Under the new liberalism, the Federalist heirlooms of the Republican party have been locked away in the cupboard. Since Andrew Mellon was called "the greatest Secretary of the Treasury since Alexander Hamilton," the name of Jefferson's bitterest enemy has scarcely been heard in American politics. Republicans, like the Whigs of Webster's day, now invoke "sound Jeffersonian principles." Nobody can raise many votes with sound Hamiltonian principles.

Conservatives may also claim the hereditary honors, as it were,

[36] Charles M. Wiltse, *The Jeffersonian Tradition in American Democracy* (1935), pp. 261–267.

in having among their ranks the lineal descendants of Jefferson, the Coolidges of Boston. This family presented Jefferson's writing desk to the nation in 1880, has served on the trusteeship of Monticello and the new federal memorial, and takes unfailing pride in Jefferson's memory. Thomas Jefferson Coolidge, banker and member of the Somerset Club, served as Undersecretary of the Treasury early in the New Deal, but it was apparent that he was no scourge of the vested interests. Harold Jefferson Coolidge in 1937 published a slim volume called *Thoughts on Thomas Jefferson: Or What Jefferson Was Not.* He there pays his respects to " 'Jefferson Clubs' whose leaders are politicians of the type of 'Al' Smith, 'Jim' Farley, or James M. Curley. These are the men who talk most about Jefferson." Mr. Coolidge, one gathers, is a little irritated, knowing that by any other name the wild Irish rose would smell as sweet.

Today three great shrines to Jefferson are being repaired or built.* The first is Monticello, where Jefferson lavished ingenuity over windvanes and double-action doors and experimented with new seeds and cuttings, and where, as he wrote, "all my wishes end." Thousands of pilgrims, in Jefferson's later years, called to pay their respects; the sage's hospitality to them helped to drive him bankrupt. After his death Monticello fell into strangers' hands; less reverent visitors, seeking souvenirs, broke open the high iron gates and chipped pieces from Jefferson's obelisk. At its lowest ebb the estate was bought by a Jewish commodore in the Navy, Uriah Levy. His nephew, Jefferson Monroe Levy, a New Yorker who had made millions in Canadian Pacific Railway and had a taste for politics, inherited it and took some pride in possession. In 1923 he sold Monticello for half a million dollars to the newly formed Jefferson Memorial Foundation—which immediately turned it into a national shrine. Only 19,414 visitors came in the first year, and the outlook, with a staggering mortgage,

*The author wrote in 1941. Since that time the restoration of Monticello has been completed, the Jefferson Memorial built in Washington, D.C., and "Jefferson National Expansion Memorial," in St. Louis, Missouri, largely completed, though on a different plan from the one described in the following pages [ed.].

was not bright. But through the following years popular interest in Jefferson quickened; new biographies were printed, orators invoked Jefferson more warmly, magazines published articles on Jefferson and the New Deal. Last year [1940] more than a hundred thousand visitors paid a half dollar each for admission to the shrine—even though Monticello is more remote from large cities and major highways than are Mount Vernon, Franklin's grave, the Hermitage, or Grant's tomb. Chairman of the Foundation and most enterprising of Jeffersonians is Mr. Stuart Gibboney, a direct descendant of Patrick Henry, veteran of the Spanish-American War and the Boxer uprising, and New York attorney for Angostura Bitters. Mr. Gibboney, a good friend of the Jefferson Coolidges, takes pleasure in sending them—with something of a twinkle in his eye—copies of their great ancestor's more inflammatory utterances.

Jeffersonians have long regretted the lack of a great federal shrine, comparable to the Washington Monument and the Lincoln Memorial. Through the efforts of Mr. Gibboney and the Foundation, aided by sympathy from the Democratic party, Congress in June, 1934, created a Jefferson Memorial Commission. Its choice of a site is significant of Jefferson's new hero-rank. When the Lincoln Memorial was built to complete an axis running from the Capitol through the Mall, and past the Washington Monument to the river bank, it was seen that at some future date the general cruciform plan would be finished by an intersecting axis drawn from the White House through the Washington obelisk to the tidal basin, where hundreds of cherry trees bloom in the spring. This site, long awaiting some memorial to match Washington's and Lincoln's, is that of the new $3,000,000 shrine to Jefferson. A circular temple of white marble, in the Palladian style of dome and colonnade that Jefferson introduced to America, will house a heroic standing figure of Jefferson yet unmade. President Roosevelt broke ground in December, 1938, and in November, 1939, laid the cornerstone, saying, on the latter occasion: "He lived as we live, in the midst of a struggle between rule by the self-chosen individual or the self-appointed few, and rule by the franchise and approval of the many. He believed as we do, that the average opinion of mankind is in the long run superior to the dictates of the self-chosen."

The third project is in St. Louis. The state of Missouri has always had a special affection for Jefferson. Even though he narrowly missed having a state as namesake, when Jefferson Territory was rechristened Colorado, in Missouri Jefferson has received more official honors than in his native Virginia. Jefferson, it is not forgotten, bought from Napoleon the inland empire of Upper Louisiana, of which St. Louis was the capital, and described this commonwealth as "choice country with room enough." The St. Louis Exposition of 1904 was held to celebrate this Purchase and to honor Jefferson. Missouri's capital is Jefferson City, and the statesman's statue rises above the capitol steps. In 1883 the University of Missouri asked for, and received from the Jefferson heirs, the original tombstone discarded from Monticello; it has been ever since the most prized possession on that campus. (Some years ago, President Richard H. Jesse of the University of Missouri caused a furore among loyal Missouri Jeffersonians when, at a dinner of the Knife and Fork Club of Kansas City, he mentioned the old darky who claimed descent from Jefferson, and other "intimate" rumors which Jesse as a Virginian was disposed to believe.) From Missouri Jefferson has received many miscellaneous tributes: In 1856 the legislature commissioned the state's best artist, George Caleb Bingham, to copy the Stuart portrait of Jefferson for the Senate chamber of the Capitol. In Missouri oratory, Jefferson's name has always carried something of the same finality as Webster's in Massachusetts or Lincoln's in Illinois; Senator George Graham Vest—greatest of Missouri spellbinders and best known for his "Tribute to a Dog"—once exclaimed, "For myself, I worship no mortal man living or dead; but if I could kneel at such a shrine, it would be with uncovered head and loving heart at the grave of Thomas Jefferson."[37] In 1931 Jefferson's

[37] George Graham Vest, *Thomas Jefferson: An Address* (St. Louis, 1885), p. 24. For the Jesse incident, letter to the author from Mr. C. B. Rollins of Columbia, Missouri, April 24, 1940; for the Bingham portrait, *Missouri Historical Review,* January 1938, pp. 196 ff.

birthday was made a legal holiday in Missouri. The Jefferson Highway, joining Canada and Louisiana, runs the length of the state, where an extensive new park has been reserved in Jefferson's honor.

In Jefferson's lifetime the city of St. Louis, in 1824, sent him an honorary membership in her Agricultural Society.[38] Later the city set up a Thomas Jefferson Museum. Pilgrimages from St. Louis to Monticello have been popular. In October, 1901, "the Jefferson Club of St. Louis" (organized in 1892, and soon counting six thousand members) invited "all those persons who believe in the principles and teachings of Thomas Jefferson" to go to Monticello on a chartered train and set up a block of Missouri granite near his tomb. On Jefferson's birthday in 1939 some six hundred Missourians, headed by their Governor, called at Monticello. Early in the Depression, when P.W.A. and W.P.A. funds were flowing, St. Louis conceived a monster project to honor Jefferson the expansionist. Her politicians persuaded Congress to appoint a commission—which recommended that a tract of eighty acres, in the slums along the St. Louis waterfront, be bought and cleared as the site for a $33,000,000 "Jefferson National Expansion Memorial," with a great park, fountains, a dome-capped temple, and in the center a huge granite shaft. Today, in the colder light of economy, the project "is down to about $9,000,000, and the city of St. Louis is paying part of the cost," as Representative Cochran reported in 1939. Even so, the project was attacked by Congressman Schafer of Wisconsin: "The New Deal has strayed far from the fundamental principles and policies of government expounded and practised by Thomas Jefferson. Our New Deal friends, no doubt, ease their consciences by spending millions of dollars to erect a great memorial in honor of the man whose principles and policies

---

[38] Jefferson MSS., Massachusetts Historical Society, Jefferson to Robert Simpson of St. Louis, February 14, 1824, saying characteristically: "It's [*sic*] object, agriculture, is certainly the first in human life and houshold [*sic*] manufactury is it's genuine companion & handmaid. I wish to them both all possible prosperity, and to the state in which the society is placed all those blessings which it's soil, climate, & government so richly promise it."

they have repudiated."[39] A park has taken the place of the slums, but the fate of the Memorial as planned is still uncertain.

At all events the cult of Jefferson marches on. He has attracted the worship of more statesmen and political thinkers than of artists, dramatists, and poets. The absence from the halo of Thomas Jefferson of Washington's military glory, Jackson's rugged picturesqueness, or Lincoln's tenderness and pathos, is responsible no doubt for the slower growth of his legend. Jefferson's greatest deeds—the Declaration of Independence, the abolition of class privilege in Virginia, the Louisiana Purchase, the fostering of secular education in America—grew increasingly less dramatic and pictorial. By no homely incident, no single gesture, can the maker of myths evoke for every man the essence of Jefferson. His appeal is more reflective, more intellectual. Doubtless this has handicapped the lovability of the man. In art, even Jefferson's arch-enemy Hamilton has fared better—in romantic novels of which Gertrude Atherton's *The Conqueror* is best, in John Drinkwater's play *Hamilton,* and in statues usually found among the marts of trade and finance. But, with his lack of glitter and "theater," and his quiet life unmarked by Hamilton's aura of martyrdom, Jefferson is beyond question the greater American symbol. The drafter of documents and policies that stand beside the wellspring of our national life, Jefferson remains (as his most scholarly biographer Gilbert Chinard calls him) "the apostle of Americanism." He is the first great democrat, the people's friend. The stature of no traditional figure has grown taller than his, in the last generation. His fame is slow-ripening but solid. Undoubtedly, as John Adams said, Thomas Jefferson still survives.

---

[39] *Congressional Record,* March 14, 1939, in regard to the Interior Department Appropriation Bill for 1940, pp. 3839–3841. See also President Roosevelt's Executive Order of December 21, 1935, respecting the Memorial. Other data in letter to the author from Mr. Daniel Cox Fahey, Jr., Executive Officer of the Memorial, January 19, 1940.

❂

What Is Still Living in the Political Philosophy of Thomas Jefferson?

I believe . . . that there exists a right independent of force.

—THOMAS JEFFERSON

Many nations have traced their history back to a fabled Golden Age, to the beginning of created things, when, as Hesiod says, "men lived like Gods, free from toil and grief." Our own history can likewise be traced, through its European origins, back to that mythical time. But we commonly think of it as beginning more recently, somewhat abruptly, in the clear light of day, with the settlement of Jamestown, the landing of the Mayflower, and the founding of Massachusetts Bay colony. Men did not then live like gods, or free from toil and grief; but there were in those days men of heroic stature, men around whom myths have gathered, and whom we delight, with good reason, to honor. The beginning of our history as an independent nation is still more recent, and still more open to critical inspection in the still brighter light of the eighteenth century; and yet this is for us still more truly the time of our Golden Age, and of our ancestors of heroic stature. Among the founders of our federal republic (to name only the most distinguished) were Washington, Franklin, and John Adams, Alex-

Reprinted from *Proceedings of the American Philosophical Society,* Vol. LXXXVII, No. 3 (1944), pp. 201–210, by permission of the American Philosophical Society.

41

ander Hamilton and John Jay, Robert Morris and James Wilson, Richard Henry Lee, James Madison, and Thomas Jefferson. No doubt we are apt to magnify these "Fathers" beyond their just merits. Their just merits were, nevertheless, sufficiently great; for it would be difficult to find, in the history of any other country, or in the history of our own country at any other time, within a single generation, as many statesmen in proportion to the population equally distinguished for learning, probity, and political intelligence. And of these ten men, none exhibited these qualities to better advantage or more lasting effect than Thomas Jefferson.

Jefferson, like Franklin, attained an international eminence; like Franklin he was familiar with all of the ideas of his time, contributed something to its accumulated knowledge, and was identified with its most notable activities and events. There was indeed scarcely anything of human interest that was alien to his curious and far-reaching intelligence. Nevertheless, his name is for us inevitably associated with a certain general idea, a certain way of regarding man and the life of man, a certain political philosophy. The word that best denotes this political philosophy is democracy. More than any other man we think of Jefferson as having formulated the fundamental principles of American democracy, of what we now like to call the American way of life.

Any significant political philosophy is shaped by three different but closely related influences. The first is what Alfred North Whitehead has taught us to call the "climate of opinion"—those unconsciously accepted presuppositions which, in any age, so largely determine what men think about the nature of the universe and what can and cannot happen in it, and about the nature of man and what is essential to the good life. The second is more specific: it derives from the political conflicts of the time, which dispose groups and classes to accept a particular interpretation of current ideas as a theoretical support for concrete political measures. The third is still more specific: it derives from the mind and temperament of the individual who gives to the philosophy its ordered literary form. Whatever is original in the philosophy is usually contributed by the individual who gives it this form. Whatever value it has for its own time depends largely upon the extent to which it can be used to illuminate or resolve the particular political issues of that time and place. But its value for other times and places will depend upon the extent to which the fundamental presuppositions on which it rests have a universal validity—the extent to which they express some essential and enduring truth about nature and the life of man.

The political philosophy of Thomas Jefferson was not in its fundamental principles original with him. It was his only in the sense that he gave to ideas widely current, and genuinely entertained by him, a Jeffersonian form and flavor. Nowhere is this peculiarity of form and flavor so evident as in the famous Declaration of Independence, but Jefferson did not claim that the ideas themselves were in any way novel. Some years later his old friend John Adams, a little irritated (as he was apt to be on slight provocation) by the laudation of Jefferson as the author of the Declaration, protested to Pickering that there "is not an idea in it but what had been hackneyed in Congress for two years before."[1] To this Jefferson replied that it was not his purpose "to find out new principles, . . . to say things that had never been said before, but to place before mankind the common sense of the subject," and to harmonize the "sentiments of the day, whether expressed in conversation, in letters, printed essays, or the elementary books of public right."[2] This was indeed Jefferson's merit, and the high value of the Declaration for his own time, that it expressed in lucid and persuasive form ideas then widely accepted, and thereby provided a reasoned justification for renouncing the authority of the British government. But the Declaration purports to have a higher value than that; for in providing reasons for renouncing the authority of a particular government at a particular time, Jefferson took occasion to formulate the universal principles that, as he believed, could alone justify the authority of any government at any time.

These principles are formulated in a single paragraph. We are

---

[1] Charles Francis Adams, ed., *Works of John Adams,* II (Boston, 1850), 514.

[2] Paul L. Ford, ed., *The Writings of Thomas Jefferson* (New York, 1892–1899), VII (1896), 304, 407.

all familiar with it, having read it or heard it read many times. But it will always, and certainly at no time more than now, bear repeating; and I will therefore repeat it once more, not precisely as it appears in the Declaration, but as Jefferson first wrote it in the original draft.

We hold these truths to be sacred and undeniable; that all men are created equal and independent; that from that equal creation they derive rights inherent and inalienable, among which are the preservation of life, and liberty, and the pursuit of happiness; that to secure these rights governments are instituted among men, deriving their just powers from the consent of the governed; that whenever any form of government shall become destructive of these ends, it is the right of the people to alter or to abolish it, and to institute new government, laying its foundation on such principles and organizing its powers in such form, as to them shall seem most likely to effect their safety and happiness.

This statement contains the sum and substance of Jefferson's political philosophy, which may be reduced to four fundamental principles: (1) that the universe and man in it is governed by natural law; (2) that all men have certain inherent natural rights; (3) that governments exist to secure these rights; and (4) that all just governments derive their authority from the consent of the governed. These principles, made explicit in our federal and state constitutions, are still the fundamental principles of our political system; and on this anniversary occasion, when we are fighting a desperate war to safeguard the political system that Jefferson did so much to establish, it is indeed appropriate for us to ask: What is still living in this political philosophy? In order to answer this question, I will break it down into two more specific questions. First, what did Jefferson understand by natural law and natural rights, and what form of government did he think best suited to secure these rights? Second, to what extent is his conception of rights and government still valid for us?

The doctrine of natural law and natural rights, as Jefferson understood it, was revolutionary only in the sense that it was a reinterpretation, in secular and liberal terms, of the Christian theory of the origin, nature, and destiny of man. As commonly understood in the eighteenth century, it was perhaps never better stated than by the French writer Volney.

Natural law is the regular and constant order of facts by which God rules the universe; the order which his wisdom presents to the sense and reason of men, to serve them as an equal and common rule of conduct, and to guide them, without distinction of race or sect, towards perfection and happiness.[3]

For Jefferson as for Volney, God still existed. But for them God the Father of Christian tradition had become attenuated into God the Creator, or First Cause. Having originally created the world for a beneficent purpose and according to a rational plan, the Creator had withdrawn from immediate and arbitrary control of human affairs to the dim recesses where absolute being dwells, leaving men to work out their own salvation as best they could. But they could work out their salvation very well because the Creator had revealed His beneficent purpose, not in Holy Writ, but in the open Book of Nature, which all men by the light of reason could read and interpret. "Is it simple," exclaimed Rousseau, "is it natural, that God should have gone in search of Moses in order to speak to Jean Jacques Rousseau?" To Rousseau, to Jefferson and Volney, it seemed more natural that God should have revealed His beneficent purpose through His works; from which it seemed self-evident that the whole duty of man was to discover progressively, by studying His created works, the invariable laws of nature and of nature's God, and to bring their ideas, their conduct, and their social and political institutions into harmony with them.

From this conception of natural law Jefferson and his fellows derived the doctrine that all men are created equal and are endowed by their Creator with certain natural and imprescriptible rights. Many otherwise intelligent persons have thought to refute Jefferson by pointing out that all men are in fact not equal. With the same ingenuity and poverty of imagination one might refute St. Augustine's doctrine of the brotherhood of man by pointing out that all men are in fact not brothers. All men, St. Augustine would

---

[3] *Oeuvres* (second ed.; Paris, 1826), I, 249.

have replied, are brothers in the sight of God; and Jefferson's doctrine of equality comes to the same thing—that all men are equal in the possession of a common humanity, and if they are not in fact equal, and have not in fact the same rights and privileges, the highest morality, both for the individual and for society, is to act always on the assumption that all men should be accorded, so far as is humanly possible, the same opportunities and considera- tion. To act on this assumption would be, both for individuals and for society, to do the will of God and to live the good life.

In this respect—in respect to the primary values of life—the natural rights philosophy of Jefferson was essentially at one with the Christian faith; but in respect to the means best suited to realize these values, it differed sharply from current official Chris- tian teaching. It denied that man is naturally prone to evil and error, and for that reason incapable, apart from the compulsion of Church and State, of arriving at the truth or living the good life. On the contrary, it affirmed that men are endowed by their Creator with reason in order that they may progressively discover what is true, and with conscience in order that they may be disposed, in the measure of their enlightenment, to follow that which is good. It was perhaps the dominant quality of Jefferson's mind and tem- perament, as it was of so many men of his time, to have faith in the worth and dignity, the rational intelligence and good will, of the individual man; and it was for this reason that, in considering the means for achieving the good life, they relied so confidently upon the negative principle of freedom of the individual from social constraint—freedom of opinion, in order that the truth might prevail; freedom of occupation and of enterprise, in order that careers might be open to talent; and freedom from arbitrary political control, in order that no man might be compelled against his will.

These freedoms were precisely what Jefferson meant by "lib- erty" as one of the inalienable rights of man, and it was through the fullest enjoyment of these freedoms that the "pursuit of happiness" would be most likely to end in happiness for the greatest number of men. And so we arrive at the central idea of the natural rights philosophy in respect to the proper function of government—the happy idea that the best way to secure the inalienable rights of man is just to leave the individual as free as possible to enjoy them, and that accordingly no form of government can secure them so well as the one that governs least. This idea was so engaging that anyone with an unbounded faith in the natural goodness of men, and an equal faith in the validity of formal logic, might easily push straight on to the conclusion reached by Proudhon—the conclusion, namely, that "property is theft," that all governments exist to condone it, and that men will never be free and happy until all governments are abolished.

Jefferson had not sufficient faith either in the native goodness of men or in formal logic ever to reach that conclusion. He had more faith in the goodness of men than many of his contemporaries— more, for example, than John Adams; but less than some others— less, for example, than Samuel Adams or Thomas Paine. He had a logical mind, and relied upon it, but logic was not for him a "systematic way," as has been said, "of going wrong with confidence"—not, that is to say, a device for manipulating empty concepts in the void in vain, but a means of reaching sound practical conclusions on the basis of knowledge and common sense. History and political experience, rather than the logic of political theory, convinced Jefferson that men had been governed too much, and above all too arbitrarily, by kings claiming divine right, and that among the institutions that obscured the native goodness of men by depriving them of equal rights none was less defensible than a hereditary aristocracy enjoying privileges that were unearned and exacting a deference that was unmerited. It seemed to him self-evident, therefore, that the people could govern themselves better than kings and aristocrats, whose powers and privileges rested upon the accident of birth, could do it for them. Not that the people could govern themselves with perfection, or without difficulty. All forms of government, he was aware, had their evils, and of popular government the principal evil, he said, was "turbulence; but weigh this against the oppressions of monarchy, and it becomes nothing."[4]

The evils of government by the people were even less than

---

[4] *Writings of Thomas Jefferson* (Ford ed.), IV (1894), 362.

nothing when compared with its virtues, its chief virtue being that "it is the only form of government that is not eternally at open or secret war with the rights of mankind."[5] But what, in concrete instances, did Jefferson mean by "the people" who have a right to govern themselves? The people, in this sense, might mean all the people in the world, or all the people in Virginia, or all the people composing a particular race or sect. Practical statesman that he was, Jefferson took the world, politically speaking, as he found it, divided into groups that by tradition and community of interest regarded themselves, and were commonly regarded, as "nations." For purposes of government, all such nations might at any time "assume, among the powers of the earth, the separate and equal station, to which the laws of nature and of nature's God entitle them." Thus nations as well as individuals had their natural rights—the right of political self-determination. But how was this self-determination to be effected, how was the consent of the governed to be obtained? Any nation is composed of individuals, and individuals necessarily differ in their opinions and their interests; and it seemed to Jefferson self-evident that the only practicable way of reconciling these differences was by majority vote. Even a monarchy with all of its trappings, or an aristocracy with all of its privileges, if really supported by a majority vote, would be a "just government" because it would rest on the "consent of the governed."

Not that majority vote conferred on the majority of the moment any fundamental right not shared by the minority. It was merely a practical device imposed upon individuals bound by their nature to live together, and aiming to live together with the maximum degree of harmony and good will, and Jefferson justified it by saying that this rule once disregarded, "no other remains but force, which ends necessarily in military despotism."[6] There is, of course, no more fundamental or obdurate problem in political philosophy than that of the conflicting interests of the one and the many—the difficulty being to reconcile the desirable liberties of the individual with the

[5] *Ibid.*, V (1895), 147.
[6] *Ibid.*, X (1899), 89.

necessary powers of society; and Jefferson was not more successful than other philosophers in providing a satisfactory solution of it. His solution, such as it was, is presented in a letter to Dupont de Nemours,[7] some portions of which I venture to quote, because in it he states briefly and categorically, and better perhaps than anywhere else, the chief tenets of his political faith.

I believe with you that morality, compassion, generosity, are innate elements of the human constitution; that there exists a right independent of force; that the right to property is founded on our natural wants, in the measure with which we are endowed to satisfy these wants, and the right to what we acquire by those means without violating the similar rights of other sensible beings; that no one has a right to obstruct another exercising his faculty innocently for the relief of sensibilities made a part of his nature; that justice is the fundamental law of society; that the majority, oppressing an individual, is guilty of a crime, abuses its strength, and by acting on the law of the strongest breaks up the foundations of society; that action by the citizens in person, in affairs within their reach and competence, and in all others by representatives, chosen immediately, and removable by themselves, constitutes the essence of a republic; that all governments are more or less republican in proportion as this principle enters more or less into their composition; and that government by a republic is capable of extension over a greater surface of country than any other form.

The right of national self-determination, and republican government based upon popular suffrage and majority vote—these were Jefferson's fundamental ideas as to the form of government best suited at any time and in any country to secure the natural rights of man. Turning then from the proper form of government to its function, we find that Jefferson would confine its activities within narrow limits. In the passage just quoted, and in Jefferson's writings generally, we can note his disposition to believe that man is naturally good but that men are prone to evil; or, translating it into political terms, that citizens in the mass are to be trusted but that citizens elected to office need to be carefully watched. I have quoted Jefferson as saying that the chief evil of republican govern-

[7] *Ibid.*, X (1899), 24.

ment is "turbulence"; but he did not really think so. Indeed, he said that a little turbulence on the part of the people now and then would do no harm, since it would serve to remind elected officials that their authority was after all only a delegated and limited franchise from the people. What Jefferson really believed is that political power is inherently dangerous, and that accordingly the chief evil in any form of government is that there may be too much of it. From this it followed that in devising a republican government the chief aim should be to avoid that danger by dispersing power among individual magistrates, separating it in respect to function, and otherwise limiting it by applying the grand negative principle of checks and balances. Fundamentally, Jefferson agreed with Thomas Paine, that whereas society is the result of men's virtues, government is the result of their vices, and therefore a necessary evil: necessary in order to preserve order, protect property, and guarantee contracts; evil because inherently prone to magnify its authority and thereby impair the liberties of the individual.

Jefferson's ideal of democratic society and republican government could best be realized in a small agricultural community, such as he was familiar with at Monticello, composed of a few men of substance and learning like himself and his friend James Madison, and otherwise chiefly of industrious, upstanding yeoman farmers; making altogether a community of good neighbors, in which everyone knew who was who, and what was being done and who was doing it. The affairs of such a community, being easily within the "reach and competence" of the people, could be managed by them with the minimum of officials, exercising the minimum of authority, and attended with the minimum of palaver and ceremonial display. Unfortunately, this ideal community could not live to itself; and since this was so it was necessary for the people, in managing the affairs of the wider region, to delegate their authority to representatives. This departure from the ideal was the beginning of danger; but there was no help for it except to prepare for the danger in good time by electing representatives for very short terms and limiting their powers to very specific matters.

The broad principle would then be that the wider the area the less safe it would be to entrust representatives with power; from which it followed that representatives from the counties to the state capital of Virginia could be safely entrusted with more power than could be safely entrusted to the representatives from Virginia to Philadelphia. That the states must remain united, Jefferson fully realized; but he was convinced that the several states must retain their sovereign powers, and at first he thought the Articles of Confederation very nearly the ideal constitution for such a union. When experience proved that a "more perfect union" was necessary, he approved of the Constitution of 1787, but insisted, as a guarantee against too much power in the hands of a government far removed from the people, that a bill of rights should be incorporated in the Constitution, and that the powers therein granted to the federal government should be strictly and narrowly interpreted.[8] As it happened, Jefferson's grasp of political realities was destined to override this principle. As President, he pushed through the purchase of Louisiana in spite of the fact that in so doing he was exercising an authority which he believed the Constitution did not confer upon him.[9] That perverse circumstances should have made Thomas Jefferson the man to usurp power from the people is ironical enough, and it troubled his political conscience not a little; but he could reflect that he tried, although in vain, to get a constitutional amendment to authorize the act, and that in any case his conscience was clear since he had acted solely for the public good.

Closely associated with Jefferson's fear of the open usurpation of political power, was his fear of the secret and more insidious influences by which men become debased and corrupted. Republican government, he was aware, could not well succeed unless the majority of citizens were independent, honest, and reasonably intelligent. Intelligence could be sufficiently trained and directed by

[8] *Ibid.,* V (1895), 41, 42, 45, 81.
[9] Jefferson to R. R. Livingston, April 18, 1802, *ibid.,* VIII (1897), 143. This is the letter in which Jefferson made his famous statement that if France took possession of New Orleans, "we must marry ourselves to the British fleet and nation." Today we are again marrying ourselves to the British fleet and nation, and for essentially the same reasons given by Jefferson in justification of his statement.

education—schools for the people and colleges for the leaders. But honesty and independence depended far less upon precept than upon the conditions in which men lived. The best conditions were those of country life. "Cultivators of the earth," Jefferson said, "are the most virtuous and independent citizens."[10] Vice and political corruption flourished, as he thought, chiefly in cities and the industrial communities that produce cities. In cities, where people were mostly unknown to each other, unscrupulous individuals could push their selfish interests under cover of the general indifference; and industrial communities, making so much of impalpable and evanescent forms of wealth, opened the door to speculation for unearned profit, stimulated greed, and rewarded conspicuous but useless luxury: provided all the conditions, in short, for the rise of a corrupt and politically influential "money power." Jefferson regarded a limited commerce and industry as necessary adjuncts of agriculture, but he had the farmer's settled antipathy to banks and their dubious financial manipulations. "The exercise, by our own citizens, of so much commerce as may suffice to exchange our superfluities for our wants," he cautiously admitted, "may be advantageous to the whole"; but he was profoundly convinced that it would be fatal for us "to become a mere city of London, to carry on the commerce of half the world at the expense of waging eternal war with the other half." Capital invested in agriculture and useful manufactures was productively employed; but "all of the capital employed in paper speculation is barren and useless, producing, like that on a gaming table, no accession to itself"; and as for banks, they are "a blot left in all our constitutions, which, if not covered, will end in their destruction."[11] Jefferson was never weary of pointing to England as the most ominous example of a nationa rapidly losing its freedom by the unchecked multiplication of such evils; and he was convinced that the United States would suffer the same loss if it did not profit in time by that example.

Such in brief was Thomas Jefferson's political philosophy—his conception of human rights, and of the particular form of govern-

10 *Ibid.*, III (1894), 279.
11 *Ibid.*, X (1899), 28.

ment best suited to secure those rights. What then is still living in this philosophy? To what extent is Jefferson's conception of rights still valid for us? To what extent is the form of government recommended by him well adapted for securing the rights, whatever they are, that need to be secured in our time?

Any careful study of Jefferson and his ideas is apt, sooner or later, to leave one with the general impression that he was more at home in the world of ideas than in the world of men and affairs. He had little of Franklin's salty zest for life in the rough, little of his genial, tolerant acceptance of men as they are, and none of his talent for being comfortable in crowds and hobnobbing with persons of every station, from kings to scullions in the kitchen. Jefferson was a democrat by intellectual conviction, but by temperament and training a Virginia aristocrat—a man of cultivated tastes and preferences, with a fastidious aversion from what is vulgar and boisterous, passionate and irrational and violent in human intercourse. One may say that he felt with the mind as some people think with the heart. John Adams said that his writings were characterized by "a peculiar felicity of expression."[12] They were indeed—perhaps a little too much so. In reading Jefferson one feels that it would be a relief to come, now and then, upon a hard, uncompromising, passionate sentence, such as: "As for me, give me liberty or give me death." What one expects to find is rather: "Manly sentiment bids us to die freemen rather than to live as slaves." Jefferson's ideas had also this felicity, and also perhaps a little too much of it. They come to birth a little too easily, and rest a little precariously on the aspirations and ideals of good men, and not sufficiently on the brute concrete facts of the world as it is. Jefferson was no visionary, and in his policy in respect to the purchase of Louisiana he exhibited a masterly grasp of international political realities; but it is characteristic of him that, in respect to the Embargo, he should have taken the position that our neutral rights, since they were in theory equally violated by France and England, should be impartially defended against both countries, even though England alone was able to do us any injury in fact; characteristic also that the high intention of

[12] C. F. Adams, ed., *Works of John Adams*, II, 514.

his method of defending those rights was to attain the object by humane and peaceful means, and its signal effect to inflict a greater material injury on the United States than it did on the countries by which our rights had been violated. One suspects that with a little more humane feeling and a great deal more passion in his make-up, Jefferson would have been an out-and-out nonresistance paci-fist; as it is he presents us with the anomaly of a revolutionist who hated violence, and a President of the United States who was disconcerted by the possession of political power.

If Jefferson was more at home in the world of ideas than in the world of men and affairs, it follows, more or less as a consequence, that, as a political philosopher, he was a better judge of ends than of means. In all that relates to the fundamental values of life, both for the individual and for society, in all that relates to the ideal aims that democratic government professes to realize, his under-standing was profound. But in respect to the means, the particular institutional forms through which these values and ideal aims were to be realized, he was often at fault, if not for his own time at least for the future. And when he was at fault, he was so partly because he conceived of society as more static than it really is; partly because he conceived of American society in his time as some-thing that could, by relatively simple political devices, be kept relatively isolated and with slight changes be preserved in its rela-tively Arcadian simplicity. But his chief limitation as a political philosopher (and one should in fairness remember that it was the chief limitation of most political thinkers of his time) was that he was unduly influenced by the idea that the only thing to do with political power, since it is inherently dangerous, is to abate it. Jefferson did not sufficiently recognize the harsh fact that political power, whether dangerous or not, always exists in the world and will be used by those who possess it; and as a consequence of this failure he was too much concerned with negative devices for obstructing the use of political power for bad ends, and too little concerned with positive devices for making use of it for good ends.

This gives us, in general terms, the answer to our questions. In respect to fundamentals, Jefferson's political philosophy is still valid for us; in respect to what is more superficial—in respect to certain favorite institutional forms—it is outmoded. In elaborating this general answer I can note only the salient points.

None of Jefferson's ideas are so irrelevant to our needs as those about banks and speculation, cities and industrial communities— not because there is not much truth in what he had to say about them, but because his hope that the United States might be kept a predominantly agricultural society was entirely misplaced. During Jefferson's time there was occurring, insidiously and without blare of trumpets, a revolution of which he was unaware, or the profound significance of which at all events he quite failed to grasp. I refer of course to the Industrial, or more properly the Technological, Revolution occasioned by the discovery and application of steam power, electricity, and radiation. It is now obvious that this was one of the two or three major revolutions in the history of civilization. Within a brief span of years, by giving men unprecedented power over material things, these discoveries have transformed the relatively simple agricultural societies of the eighteenth century into societies far more complex, more integrated, and at the same time more mobile and swiftly changing than any ever known before—formidable, blank-faced leviathans that Thomas Jefferson would have regarded as unreal, fantastic, and altogether unsuited to liberty and equality as he understood those terms. That Jefferson did not foresee this momentous revolution is no discredit to him; no one in his time foresaw it more than dimly. But the point is that the societies created by this revolution are the societies in which we live, and in connection with which we have to consider anew the nature of human rights; and it is now obvious that the favorite doctrine of Jefferson and of his time, the doctrine of *laissez faire* in respect to economic enterprise, and therefore in respect to political policy also, can no longer be regarded as a guiding principle for securing the natural rights of men to life, liberty, equality, and the pursuit of happiness.

The doctrine of *laissez faire,* as it was understood by Jefferson and the early nineteenth-century social philosophers, rested upon the assumption that if each individual within the nations, and each nation among the nations attended to its own interests, something not themselves, God or Nature, would do whatever else was necessary for righteousness. Or, better still, as Professor Edward H. Carr has put it in his recent book, the doctrine was based on the assumption that from the unrestrained pursuit of individual self-interest a "harmony of interests" would more or less automatically emerge.[13] In the political realm this meant that the function of government should be limited in principle to the protection of life and property, the enforcement of contracts, the maintenance of civil order, and the defense of the country against aggression. In the economic realm it meant that the free play of individual initiative, stimulated by the acquisitive instinct, would result in the maximum production of wealth, and that the competitive instinct, operating through the price system, would result in as equitable a distribution of wealth as the natural qualities and defects of men permitted. In the international realm it meant that the strict attention to national interest and power by each sovereign state, restrained by the recognized rules of international law, would tend to create a balance of interests and of power which would serve, better than any other method, to promote international commercial exchanges and cultural relations and to preserve the peace.

It is now sufficiently clear that this doctrine of *laissez faire*—of letting things go—however well adapted it may have been to the world in which Jefferson lived, is no longer applicable to the world in which we live. In a world so highly integrated economically, a world in which the tempo of social change is so accelerated, and the technological power at the disposal of individuals and of governments is so enormous and can be so effectively used by them for antisocial ends—in such a world the unrestrained pursuit of self-interest, by individuals and by states, results neither in the maximum production or the equitable distribution of wealth, nor in the promotion of international comity and peace, but in social conflicts and global and total wars so ruthless as to threaten the destruction of all interests, national and individual, and even the very foundations of civilized living. In our time the right to life, liberty, and the pursuit of happiness can be secured, not by letting

[13] Edward H. Carr, *The Conditions of Peace* (New York, 1942), p. 105.

things go and trusting to God or Nature to see that they go right, but only by deciding beforehand where they ought to go and doing, so far as possible, what is necessary to make them go there. The harmony of interests, if there is to be any, must be deliberately and socially designed and deliberately and cooperatively worked for. To bring this harmony of interests to pass is now the proper function of government; and it will assuredly not be brought to pass by any government that proceeds on the assumption that the best government is the one that governs least.

The history of the United States for the last hundred years confirms this conclusion, and nullifies for us Jefferson's favorite idea that the function of government should be reduced to a minimum, that sovereign rights should be retained by the states, and that the powers of the federal government should be strictly and narrowly interpreted. Decade by decade the states have gradually lost their sovereign powers, and the federal government, by virtue of a liberal interpretation of the Constitution and of amendments to it, has assumed powers that have been used to limit the freedom of some individuals in order to protect the freedom of others. This extension of power and expansion of function on the part of the federal government has been brought about, in spite of the inertia of traditional ideas and the pressure of interested groups, by the insistent need of regulating the activities of powerful corporations which, although regarded in law as private enterprises, are in fact public utilities, and which therefore enjoy irresponsible power which they are sometimes unwilling but more often unable to use for the public good. It is in this respect that the engaging word "liberty" now appears in a guise unknown to Jefferson and his contemporaries. In the eighteenth century the obvious oppressions, for the majority of men, were those occasioned by arbitrary governmental regulation of the activities of the individual; so that liberty could be most easily conceived and understood in terms of the emancipation of the individual from social constraint. But in our time the principle of free enterprise has created a situation in which the obvious oppressions, for the majority of men, are those that arise not from an excess of governmental regulation but from the lack of it; so that liberty can now no longer be understood in terms of political and economic *laissez faire,* but only in terms of more and more intelligent social regulation of economic enterprise. Jefferson and his contemporaries, as James Bryce has well said, "mistook the pernicious channels in which selfish propensities had been flowing for those propensities themselves, which were sure to find new channels when the old had been destroyed."[14] The selfish propensities with which we have to deal are the same as they were in Jefferson's time; but since the channels—the institutions and customs—in which they flow are different, the remedies must be different also.

In this respect—in respect to his idea of the proper function of government—the philosophy of Jefferson is now outmoded. But this is after all the more superficial aspect of Jefferson's philosophy; and if we turn to its more fundamental ideas—the form of government as distinct from its function, and the essential rights to be secured as distinct from the specific means of securing them—we find that Jefferson's political philosophy is as valid for our time as it was for his.

That the republican form of government—that is to say, government by elected representatives and magistrates—is the best form Jefferson was convinced, because, as he said, it "is the only form of government that is not eternally at open or secret war with the rights of mankind." The republican form of government, which Jefferson helped to organize under the Constitution of 1787, still exists essentially unchanged; and today we accept it with even less qualification and divided loyalty than obtained in Jefferson's time. We accept it for many reasons, no doubt—because it has on the whole worked so well, because we have become habituated to it, and because there is nothing in our political traditions to provide us with a model of any other form. But we also accept it for the same fundamental reason that Jefferson accepted it—from the profound conviction that it is the only form of government that is not at war with the natural rights of mankind, or at all events with those familiar rights and privileges which we regard as in some sense natural because from long habituation they seem to us so imprescriptibly American.

[14] James Bryce, *Modern Democracy* (New York, 1921), I, 14.

Recent events have greatly strengthened this conviction. Some twenty years ago we were in a mood to ask whether the representative system of government might not be, if not at open, at least too often at secret war with the rights of mankind. That was a mood induced by comparing the democratic practice with the democratic ideal, with the inevitable if perhaps salutary result of magnifying the defects and minimizing the virtues of the democratic system as a going concern. But for ten years past we have been permitted, have indeed been compelled, to reappraise the democratic system with all of its defects in the light, not of the democratic ideal, but of the practical alternative as exhibited for our admiration in Germany and elsewhere; and the result of this reappraisal has been to make it clear that the defects of our system of government are after all, in comparison, trivial, while its virtues are substantial. Indeed, the incredible cynicism and brutality of Adolf Hitler's way of regarding man and the life of man, made real by the servile and remorseless activities of his bleak-faced, humorless Nazi supporters, has forced men everywhere to re-examine the validity of half-forgotten ideas, and to entertain once more half-discarded convictions as to the substance of things not seen. One of these convictions is that "liberty, equality, fraternity," and "the inalienable rights of man" are generalities, whether glittering or not, that denote realities—the fundamental realities that men will always fight and die for rather than surrender.

It is in defense of these rights, and of the democratic or republican form of government, that we are now fighting a desperate war; and we justify our action by the very reasons advanced by Jefferson—that the democratic form of government is the form best suited to secure the inalienable rights of man. We may be less sure than Jefferson was that a beneficent intelligence created the world on a rational plan for man's special convenience. We may think that the laws of nature, and especially the laws of human nature, are less easily discovered and applied than he supposed. We may have found it more difficult to define the rights of man and to secure them by simple institutional forms than he anticipated. Above all, we have learned that human reason is not quite so infallible an instrument for recording truth as he believed it to be, and that men themselves are less amenable to rational persuasion. Nevertheless, in essentials the political philosophy of Jefferson is our political philosophy; in essentials democracy means for us what it meant for him.

Democracy is for us, as it was for him, primarily a set of values, a way of regarding man and the life of man. It is also for us, as it was for him, a set of concrete institutions devised for the purpose of realizing those values. We understand, as he did, but rather more clearly than he did, that the concrete institutions are bound to change: they have changed in many ways since Jefferson's time, they are changing now, and they will change even more in time to come. But we may believe, as Jefferson did, that the essential values of life are enduring; and one reason for believing so is that the values which we cherish are those which Jefferson proclaimed, and which for more than two thousand years the saints and sages of the world have commonly regarded as the ideal end and ultimate test of civilized living. If we were to write a modern declaration of the democratic faith, it might run somewhat as follows:

We hold these truths to be self-evident: that the individual man has dignity and worth in his own right; that it is better to be governed by persuasion than by force; that fraternal good will is more worthy than a selfish and contentious spirit; that in the long run all values, both for the individual and for society, are inseparable from the love of truth and the disinterested search for it; that the truth can be discovered only in so far as the mind of man is free; that knowledge and the power it confers should be used for promoting the welfare and happiness of all men rather than for serving the selfish interests of those individuals and classes whom fortune and intelligence have endowed with a temporary advantage; and that to secure these high aims in the life of man no form of government yet devised is so well adapted as one which is designed to be a government of the people, by the people, and for the people.

To this declaration of the modern democratic faith Thomas Jefferson would, I feel sure, have subscribed without qualification. And it is in this sense, the most important sense of all, that his political philosophy, and still more the humane and liberal spirit of the man himself, abides with us, as a living force, to clarify our aims, to strengthen our faith, and to fortify our courage.

JOHN DOS PASSOS

✪

A Portico Facing the Wilderness

At eight o'clock a fine April morning in 1782, one of the general
officers of Lafayette's staff, who was taking advantage of the
unaccustomed peacefulness of the spring after Yorktown to make
a little tour on horseback of the hilly country of Virginia, set out
from the inn where he had passed not too comfortably the night, to
follow the wagonruts up the forested valley to Monticello. He was
the Chevalier de Chastellux, a military gentleman of philosophic
tastes, with an enthusiasm for landscape and travel and the habit
of jotting down what he saw and heard in his notebook every
evening.

As he rode he was surprised by the sharp heat of the morning
sun and the backwardness of the season. The trees were barely
coming into leaf. He pulled up his horse from time to time to
admire the abundant singing and the pert behavior of the mocking-
birds. When the trail came out on a clearing he began to see blue
mountains ahead of him through the light haze of green of the
budding twigs. He rode on and on without seeing a house. The trail
got more and more tangled in dense thickets that cut off the view
of the mountains, and was made confusing by crisscrossing paths.
The Chevalier had just about lost his bearings when he caught
sight of a man on horseback ahead of him. The rider turned out to
be an Irishman who had settled in the western part of North
Carolina.

Full of lively curiosity about things American, the Chevalier, so
he put down in his notes, had his way made short by the Irishman's conversation, and furthermore was reassured about the road
to Mr. Jefferson's house. The Irishman had been wounded in the
war and still carried a British musket ball in his hip, which, the
Chevalier noted, in no way affected his high spirits. He had settled
on the extreme frontier beyond Catawba. Farming there was subsistence farming. The settlers had to raise or shoot their own meat,
to weave their own cloth and to cobble their own shoes. Until their
appletrees grew up enough to bear, or they could afford to import
a still, their only drink was water or milk. Their tools were the
broadax and the saw. The main thing they lacked, the Chevalier
was surprised to hear, was nails: everything else they made for
themselves. They built fences and shingled their houses without a
single nail. Of course whittling wooden pegs took time, and labor
was scarce and high in those parts, as one could imagine. The only
cash crop was horses. It didn't cost anything to drive their horses
to market because they grazed them as they went. On this present
trip alone, the Irishman said, he had covered a good four hundred
miles in the saddle.

"While the conversation," so the Chevalier wrote down in his
notes, "went on briskly, we were reaching the foot of the mountains. We recognized without difficulty the house of Mr. Jefferson
on one of the summits: because it can truly be said to shine alone
in its retreat. He built the house and chose the site himself; to tell
the truth, although he was already the owner of considerable lands
in the vicinity, in such a desert there would have been nothing to
hinder him from setting himself up wherever he chose. But nature
owed it to a Sage and to a man of taste to furnish him on his own
inheritance with the spot where he could best study her ways and
enjoy her beauties. He named this house Monticello, surely a very
modest name, for it is placed on a really high mountain, but a
name that announces the attraction the Italian tongue holds for the
proprietor, and especially the Fine Arts of which that country was
the cradle and of which she is still the asylum. From now on I
needed no guide; I said goodby to my Irishman; and after having
climbed more than a half an hour up a fairly convenient path, I

arrived at Monticello. This house, of which Mr. Jefferson was the architect and on which he did much of the work with his own hands, is built with considerable elegance in the Italian style, not however without some defects; it consists of a large square pavilion, into which one enters by two porticos ornamented with columns. The ground floor is principally occupied by a great high-ceilinged drawingroom which will be decorated in absolutely antique style: above the drawingroom is a library of the same shape; two little wings that have only a ground floor and an attic flank this pavilion and probably communicate with the kitchens, servants' quarters, etc., which will form on each side a sort of subbasement surmounted by a terrace. It's not to enter into a description of the house that I subscribe these details but merely to prove that it is far different from those one usually sees in these parts; so that one may truly say that Mr. Jefferson is the first American who has consulted the Fine Arts in the matter of putting a roof over his head. But I want to put my time in on the man himself: I should paint a man not yet forty years of age, tall of stature, with a refined and friendly countenance, in which the evidence of wit and learning could take the place of any possible external charms; an American who, without having ever left his country, is a Musician, a Draftsman, a Geometer, an Astronomer, a Physicist, a Jurisconsult and a Statesman: an American Senator who sat two years in the famous Congress, author of the revolution of which they never speak here without respect unfortunately mixed with too many regrets; a Governor of Virginia who filled this position of difficulty during the invasions of Arnold, of Phillips and of Cornwallis; finally a Philosopher retired from the world and its business, because he loves the world only so far as he can flatter himself that he is being useful, and because the education of his fellowcitizens has not yet developed to the point where they will stand for enlightenment or brook contradiction. A gentle and amiable wife, some pretty children he brings up with great care, a house to beautify and great possessions to improve, science and art to cultivate; this is what is left of Mr. Jefferson, after having played a distinguished role on the theatre of the New World, and this is what he prefers to the situation of Minister-Plenipotentiary in Europe. The visit I was making him was not unexpected; long since he had invited me to come to spend several days in the bosom of his society, that is to say of his mountains. All the same I found his first greeting unsmiling and even cold; but I hadn't spent two hours with him before I felt as if I had lived with him all my life; walks, the library, and especially conversation;—always varied, always interesting, always sustained by the satisfaction two people feel, who in communicating one to another their feelings and their opinions, find themselves always in accord, and able to understand each other with half a word,—made four days pass like four minutes. This conformity of sentiments and opinions on which I insist because it's something for me to be proud of, (and we sometimes have to let our egoism show itself) this conformity I say, was so perfect, that not only were our tastes similar, but also our predilections: those predilections that dry and methodical spirits make fun of as *fad* and which men of sensibility and animation glory in as *feeling*. I can remember with pleasure that one evening when we were chatting over a bowl of punch after Mrs. Jefferson had gone to bed, we fell to talking of the poems of Ossian. It was an electric spark that passed rapidly from one to the other: we reminded each other of the passages in these sublime poems that had most struck us and entertained with recitations of them my travelling companions, who fortunately knew English well and were capable of appreciating them but who had never read them. Before long we got the idea that the book itself ought to take part in the toast, we went to fetch it and it was placed beside the punchbowl. One thing and another had already led us pretty far into the night, without our noticing how late it was. Other times it was Physics or Politics or Art that was the subject of our conversations; for there is nothing of the sort that has escaped Mr. Jefferson, and from his youth up he seems to have set his mind, like his house, on an elevated place from which he could contemplate all the universe."

From accounts of members of the family and of later visitors we can form a pretty fair picture of how the amiable Chevalier passed his time at Monticello. The first meal of the day, served around nine, was an eighteenth-century breakfast, with broiled meats and the cold joints from the day before, washed down with cider and beer and plenty of hot coffee. Jefferson, who had been up writing and reading since daybreak, would meet his guests at the table. After breakfast the company couldn't help stepping out on the terrace to look for a moment at the great view of the valley of the Rivanna and the blue ridges beyond the gap above the little village of Charlottesville. Jefferson sometimes would say that the only thing he regretted was that there was not a body of water in the foreground or perhaps a volcano in the distance. Then he would take his guests around to the other end of the house to point out the little conical hill which was the only thing that broke the flatness of the leafy plain sweeping to the horizon to the south. He used to tell them this little hill was just about the size and shape of the pyramid of Cheops and describe the peculiar forms the mirage sometimes made it take on.

Landscape was one of the great pleasures of Jefferson's life. In planning his gardens and planting his hilltop he had put much thought into how best to open out and emphasize the features he liked best in the view. The type of landscape that appealed to him was the landscape of the first burst of English romanticism. Oaks were "venerable and antient," evergreens were "gloomy," vales were "solitary and unfrequented," walks were winding, gardens naturalistic. His garden was the parklike English garden of the romantic school where all the planting was supposed to look as if it had grown there of its own accord. It was a taste that went with grottoes, and the sudden reversal of the color of the word Gothic, and with the enthusiasm for the imaginary Celtic epics of Macpherson's Ossian, which Jefferson as a young man had shared with the fashionable reading public of the time to such a point that he wrote a friend in Scotland to get him, no matter at what cost, a copy of the original manuscript and a grammar so that he could study the poems in Gaelic. No wonder the fashionable Chevalier de Chastellux was surprised and pleased to find his host so versed in the *dernier cri* of cosmopolitan sensibility. It was like coming on a reader of James Joyce in an African rubber plantation.

After the view had been admired there were the gardens and the park to visit, possibly astride one of the blooded horses that

Jefferson raised and cared for with the passionate pride in a good
horse and an easy seat in the saddle that he shared with his
Virginia neighbors. Undoubtedly the Chevalier was again surprised
by the number of European fruits and vegetables and by his host's
knowledge of their names in French and Italian as well as in
botanical Latin. Some years before a young Italian named Mazzei
had come to a neighboring plantation with a number of Italian
gardeners and vineyard hands, and immediately Jefferson's little
garden notebook had filled up with the names of Italian vegetables.
From then on zucche, broccoli, savoy cabbage, sorrel, peppers and
Italian squashes and marrows of all kinds were part of the yearly
sowings in the kitchengardens that were terraced into the south
slope of the hill. From Mazzei too Jefferson had learned the newest
technique for grafting and budding fruittrees. Besides strawberries
and currants, and asparagus for which Monticello was famous, he
planted a great variety of fruits in orchards on the slopes of the hill
and in rows instead of hedges between the wheat and cornfields in
the valley. Even before his marriage, when as a young man he was
laying out his countryseat on the scale of a Roman emperor's villa,
he had planted appletrees, pears, peaches, nectarines, apricots,
quinces, medlars, pomegranates, figs, plums, cherries and walnuts.
To all these he had added rows of vines planted out in the Italian
style, put in according to Mazzei's instructions, and olivetrees and
bitter oranges as an experiment. His neverending and daily task
was to induce the listless darky slaves, whom he treated with
fatherly and indulgent patience, and the overseers who could keep
their minds only on cash crops, to keep all these trees properly
pruned and weeded. Possibly some of the fruittrees were still in
bloom the April day of cloudflecked blue skies, full of the endless
chirruping of songbirds in a variety so amazing to Europeans,
when Chastellux was shown around.

After the gardens came the park. There the morning sunlight,
hot even in April, was cooled a little, if not yet quite cut off, by the
various greens and the pink and bronze fuzz of buds just coming
into tiny leaf on the great forest trees Jefferson had left where he
found them. Perhaps on the way he had silently pointed out to his
visitor the enormous oak on top of the hill under which Dabney

Carr, his brother-in-law and the great friend of his boyhood, the father of the little nephews and nieces he was raising in his own family, lay buried, and where the family burying ground, so indispensable a part of a Virginia plantation, had already sprouted a few small fresh stones. In the park was an enclosure where some red deer lived, as well as peacocks, guineafowl, rabbits, squirrels, pheasants, partridges and pigeons. Jefferson would point out that he was hoping to get hold of a buck elk or a buffalo to give the place more interest and to prove to European visitors that Buffon was wrong in his theory that animals tended to run smaller in the Western than in the Eastern Hemisphere.

Back at the house, they went upstairs to the library, where Jefferson brought out his favorite edition of Palladio, printed with magnificent plates by Leoni in London in 1715, or the poems of Collins or Shenstone, or volumes of Shaftesbury and Bolingbroke and Locke and Algernon Sidney. If the talk turned to novels he would point to *Don Quixote* and to Sterne's *Sentimental Journey* as his favorites. Among the classics it was Homer he never tired of. By that time the colored butler was tapping on the door to announce with a flourish that the ladies were in the drawingroom waiting to be taken in to dinner. Mr. Jefferson would have to put off till later the explanation of his meteorological instruments and of the records he was keeping of the weather and of his theory of how the prevailing winds were affected by the progressive clearing of the forests as the settlers hewed their way west.

After four days of this typical Monticello entertainment, after having ridden one afternoon into Charlottesville with Mr. Jefferson to dine with a French colonel who was drilling a newly recruited regiment there and who had a young black wolf for a pet, Chastellux and his retinue rode off across Rockfish Gap to visit the famous natural bridge up in the Valley. It had turned out that the bridge and the canyon below it was the property of his host, who considered it one of the most beautiful spots on earth; Mr. Jefferson had explained that he would have to deny himself the pleasure of accompanying the amiable Chevalier on the excursion on account of the delicate health of his wife.

Although Chastellux was never allowed to know it, he visited

Jefferson during one of the unhappiest periods of his life. From the moment of Cornwallis' surrender at Yorktown early in the previous autumn the Revolutionary War was won; but Jefferson looked back on his own public career with a stinging sense of failure. Negotiations for peace were under way. The existence of the new nation he had done so much to launch was assured. But he had retired, he honestly believed forever, from public life under circumstances infinitely distressing to a man so touchily sensitive to the opinion of his neighbors as he was in those days.

In spite of his many warm friendships he had always been a solitary man, somewhat haughty and retiring in his relations with the world. After the backbiting of the legislature and the rough lessons of his Governorship he had come home to the retreat he had picked for himself as a boy, that he had planned and built every inch of, and to his wife Patty he so tenderly loved, and to his little girls, and to the compact home group so tightly knit by the extraordinary ardor of family feeling that characterized the isolated households of the Virginia landowners of the time. He had come back to projects for building and farming and to the doglike flattery of his houseservants, and to his books and his music and his draftingboard and the delightful work of planning and completing his halffinished mansion according to his own adaptation of classical architectural style into what he felt a free man's house should be. In Virginia it was the letdown period after a great accomplishment when everybody starts to show his worst side. Jefferson had come home seeking a refuge and that refuge he had found made bitter by the most painful daily anxiety any man can feel. His children had never been very strong. His little son was dead. And now Patty whose health was so frail was going to have another baby. The fear that she would not live through another birth was always in the background of his mind.

He had come to that period in his life, which seems to come to most men around their fortieth year, when all the blank checks of youth have been cashed and a man has to face himself as an adult, the way he's going to be until he dies; that is the point from which a man of ability either goes on to mature and to take his place for better or worse in the world, or else drops back into the great army of might-have-beens.

Up to those years of the Governorship Jefferson's career had been brilliant and easy. The eldest son of an energetic farmer, who had risen from what the Virginians in those days spoke of as the "overseer class," to marry a Randolph and to become a great landowner, he had had every advantage the colony could offer a young man growing up. Shadwell where he was born had only been settled a few years before, so the country he was raised in still had the freshness and freedom of the frontier, and as has so often happened on the American frontier, contained a high proportion of vigorous and welleducated men and women.

His father was a surveyor and mapmaker; he had finished Byrd's survey of the North Carolina line; through him must have come that taste for exact figuring and laborsaving inventions. His mother's people, the highfalutin' Randolphs, were almost a caricature of the British county family transplanted to Virginia. As a child he grew up in the cozy hotbed of flattery and indulgence from Negro servants that so often brought out the worst in white people, but at least inculcated into their very bones the assurance that a white man was the paragon of animals. In Jefferson, as in not a few similar men of aristocratic upbringing, selfrespect was so strong it became a feeling of respect for all mankind. His family and friends in early life were people who felt they were equal to, if not a little better than, any man on earth. They were willing to do other men the courtesy of considering them as highly as they considered themselves. It was the type of leveling that comes from a sense of complete personal security. In young Jefferson's case there was, besides the spur to ambition that lay in the need to prove to the world that a Jefferson was as good a man as any nameproud Randolph of the lot, perhaps an underlying suspicion that he was as much kin to the people who weren't Randolphs as to those who were.

His father's death when he was fourteen threw him on his own early. As eldest son he immediately was sole arbiter of all the daily decisions of the life of a series of estates, of his mother's household affairs and of those of his small brothers and sisters. It's characteristic of him that in the first letter of his we have handed down, written when he was about seventeen, he's politely but firmly suggesting to his guardian, Colonel Harvey, that the time has come for him to go to college at Williamsburg. Bossing a farm and a lot of household servants under the isolated conditions of pioneer life trained those Virginians early in making their own decisions. Their daily horseback riding, alone, was an education in applying their will to their environment.

At Williamsburg Jefferson had the great good luck to fall in with a little group of remarkable men. Dr. Small the Scotch professor of mathematics at William and Mary was the bosom friend of George Wythe, a Virginian of wealth and broad classical culture, who was the great liberal lawyer of the time. The pair of them were the special cronies of Governor Fauquier, a courtly beau of the Augustan school, a man of good education and sound taste in the fads and fashions of St. James's Park and the pumproom at Bath and the Whig country houses of England, who spread round him in the provinces some of the religious skepticism, the harsh commonsense, the predilection for the fine arts, and the craze for gambling of the London wits of Queen Anne's day. Governor Fauquier was very fond of music; so, as young Jefferson had scraped a fiddle from boyhood, and Dr. Small had taken an immediate fancy to him as a favorite pupil, he soon found himself part of Fauquier's amateur orchestra and a frequent diner at the "Governor's Palace," as the brick mansion that represented the House of Hanover at Williamsburg was called. The lanky redheaded lad from the foothills became, while still in his teens, the habitual fourth at the Governor's little exquisite dinners. There he imbibed, instead of the taste for three bottles of port and cards and foppish behavior that might have been expected, the enthusiasm that possessed him all his life for music and architecture, for light wines, good conversation and for getting to the bottom of a subject.

The first subject he tried to get to the bottom of was the English law. He studied Common Law under George Wythe, who saw it, as the long line of English liberal lawyers back through Coke and Littleton had seen it, as a charter of liberties, rather than as a rule for protecting privilege. He worked so hard at it that he even gave up his horses. Not that he lacked any of the passion for horseflesh and hard riding of his contemporaries, or their taste for foxhunting and cockfighting and brawling and drinking and dancing, and other entertainments in which the young men at Williamsburg sowed their wild oats; but he found he couldn't spare the time. To get his reading done he had to cut down his exercise to an hour's run each evening. Before long he was studying Anglo-Saxon in order really to understand the origins of the Common Law. Like the men of Commonwealth days he caught early the bias for their imagined free previous England of the Teuton tribes as against the Latinized authoritarian England of the Norman conquest.

Meanwhile he remained good friends with a wild young man of Irish extraction he'd met in his foxhunting days, a great drinker, fiddler and hunter, who managed to give a slender body of legal learning expression in an amazing flow of natural eloquence. Later Jefferson wrote of him with a kind of awe that he spoke as Homer wrote. Although Jefferson's studies began early to interfere with his pleasures Patrick Henry stayed with him whenever he came to Williamsburg. At twentyfour, Henry had managed to go bankrupt as a storekeeper and had gotten himself admitted to the bar after a few weeks' study. Although he was older than Jefferson, it was probably from Jefferson's talkative friendship that he picked up what little education he had. The young men had in common the good nature that comes from physical strength and health and an enthusiasm they could hardly have explained even to themselves for the word Liberty.

Jefferson was just twentytwo when he stood in the doorway of the House of Burgesses to which Henry had only recently been elected, and heard him read his resolutions against the Stamp Act and defend them with the speech that brought the smoldering opposition of the colonies to George Third's imperial schemes to a blaze in the proposition: no taxation without representation. "Caesar," Henry roared in his summing up, "had his Brutus, Charles the First his Cromwell and George the Third . . ." Young Jefferson's breath must have caught in his throat. There were shouts of "Treason" from the speaker and the more con-

servative burgesses . . . "may profit by their example." As the
uproar continued he finished boldly, "If this be treason make the
most of it."

Jefferson himself was no orator, but his learning and methodical
habits seem to have made him much respected and even to have
brought him in some cash when he began to practice law before
the Virginia bar. Looking over his notebooks tends to raise the
suspicion that perhaps he didn't collect many of his fees. A lawyer
at that time spent a good deal of time jogging around on his nag to
the county courts with his briefs in his saddlebags. Clients were
scattered far and wide and nobody had much hard money. Most of
Jefferson's cases, however, were in Augusta and Albemarle counties, so much of his work must have been done at home. This gave
him time to superintend the farming at Shadwell. His courage in
saying what he thought and his intoxication with free institutions
soon made him a leader among the "associators" who met in the
Apollo room of the Raleigh Tavern at Williamsburg to implement
their defiance of the British cabinet with a boycott on British
goods.

As a youngster he'd been popular with the girls on account of
his lively dancing and fiddling and the breakneck riding he was
already famous for; he'd courted a number of young ladies but had
never quite come to the point of popping the question because he
was obsessed with the notion that he wanted to take a great trip
around the world, to England and Italy and Greece, before settling
down. As it turned out the most travel he managed to get was a
tour of Annapolis, Philadelphia and New York the summer before
he was admitted to the bar. A Virginia landowner was lord of all
he surveyed, but he was dependent on his agent in England for
cash; and if his tastes were as expensive and his interests as varied
as young Jefferson's, he was usually in the red on his tobacco
account. Besides, Thomas Jefferson had the responsibility of his
mother's estates and the care of his younger brothers and sisters to
tie him down further.

He was established as a rising lawyer and had served a term in
the House of Burgesses (where one of his first acts had been to
introduce a bill, which was promptly defeated, to make it possible

for planters to free their slaves) when, in June, 1770, he wrote to
his agent in London to ship him a Forte-piano "in a case of fine
mahogany, solid not veneered, the compass from Double G to F in
alt, and plenty of spare strings; and the workmanship of the whole
very handsome and worthy of the acceptance of a lady for whom I
intend it" . . . "By this change (in the goods drawn against
consigned tobacco) I shall be brought into debt" . . . and to
discharge it he would ship to Mr. Adams, the agent, the first
tobacco he got to warehouse in the fall. The lady for whom the
piano was intended was a musical young widow with whom Jefferson had often played duets, daughter of a popular lawyer who was
master of The Forest on the James River. Her name was Martha
Skelton.

When they were married on New Year's Day 1772 they drove
away from The Forest in a light snow that turned into a blizzard as
they advanced, headed for the hill which had been his favorite
lookout and place of rumination from boyhood and which he
already called Monticello. Since his mother's house at Shadwell
had burned Jefferson had been living up there alone in the little
brick building that accents one of the ends of the flat U that the
terraced wings of the mansion cut out on top of the hill. The bride
and bridegroom had to leave their chaise with friends at Blenheim
in the valley because the snow was too deep. They rode up through
the silent forest on horseback. When they got to Monticello they
found that the Negroes had all turned in. Their little house had
only one room. Jefferson put the horses in the stable below and
made up a fire in the brick fireplace. On a shelf behind his books
he found a bottle of wine, and he and Patty drank it together in the
solitude and the snow before going to bed.

His wife's father was well off and she was expecting that a considerable portion would come to her when he died. Jefferson's own
part of his father's estate seemed ample and he was making money
as a lawyer. Even if his account stood in the red with his agent in
England, he was a rich man; he had determined to build himself a
seat as fine as any Roman villa of his classical reading. Beside his
passion for the Common Law, there had been growing up in

Jefferson a strong practical interest in architecture. For years the most prized book in his library had been the magnificent 1715 London edition of Leoni's translation of Palladio's *Four Books*. That and Gibbs' handbook seem to have been his only school, along with the occasional houses of some pretensions to style he had seen in Williamsburg or Annapolis or on such Virginia estates as Mount Airy. Out of a few plates and plans, and some basic idea of a dignified order for the life of man in his head, and probably some discouraging advice from a few practical masons and brick-layers, he invented his own peculiar version of the Palladian style. Thus he became the originator of the colonnaded type of brick building which for some reason we describe as "colonial," although these houses were all built under the republic.

In a letter written later in his life Jefferson said that architecture was the most important art to study in a young country because "it shows so much." He might have gone on to say that it showed everything. The manner of building and decorating buildings in any particular country or at any particular time shows you more directly than anything else the truths and shams of the society involved. Architecture is the one art that cannot be faked. The arts that use words, sounds, colors are infinitely deceitful, but a build-ing is there. You can look at it from all angles, you can walk around in it, you can use it. Inevitably it will tell you what kind of life the people who built it lived, and hoped to live, and whether their claims to such and such a standard of civilization were false or sound.

Jefferson was a man who felt and expressed one branch of the English culture of his time with peculiar intensity. It was a culture of the gentry. The peculiar circumstances of landowning in Vir-ginia made each gentleman a little monarch on his estate and built up every latent tendency to selfreliance and independence he had in him. In England the gentry had already been institutionalized by the sycophancy of the life of the court and of fashionable London. The Virginians were too far away to get to court and lived more like the English landowners of the early seventeenth than of the eighteenth century. Along with the somewhat perfunctory religios-ity of their Anglican Church (the Virginia church was the Low

Church of the early English reformation; the churches had no
steeples and used communion tables instead of altars), their first
schooling was in the classics and especially in that selection of the
classics that expressed the stoical philosophy of the country gentlemen of the late republic and early empire of Rome. In England the
leading men of the republican cast of mind had been wiped out in
one of the most successful bloodpurges in history: whatever
energies their descendants possessed found expression in building
themselves careers in the institutions that were the basis of the
maritime empire. In America the great estates kept out of bank-
ruptcy just long enough to give a group of men of brains whose
bent had been formed by them the leeway they needed to put all
their energies into public service: the establishing of the republic
that was heir to the whole line of English libertarian thought.
When Jefferson turned his mind, reinforced by the innate mechanical skill necessary for the work, on building, it was immediately
the Greco-Roman tradition that appealed to him. It was the
natural style for an English republican to turn to. Typical of
Jefferson's thoroughness and eagerness to get to the bottom of
things was his working his way through Gibbs's more or less
perfunctory builder's handbook, to the sources in Palladio and
Vitruvius.

Palladio was an architect who worked in Vicenza and in the
Venetian hinterland during the late sixteenth century. With less
taste and originality, perhaps, he revived the aims of Brunelleschi
and Bramante, builders of the earliest Florentine Renaissance,
which were to get back to architecture as it had been actually
practiced by the Romans of the time of Augustus. Palladio went
around measuring the Roman remains, studied the Roman text-
book that had come down under the name of Vitruvius and
embodied what he considered the Vitruvian laws of proportion and
procedure in his own manual, his famous *Four Books*. These
influenced all the architects of Europe during the period of reaction to the rhetorical style that developed from Michael Angelo's
intensely personal use of the antique elements, the style we now
call "the baroque." Palladio's measurements of the ancient buildings were all a little off, and indeed researchers tell us that Vitru-

vius's were too, but the *Four Books* contained an excellent set of plates and a very clear exposition of the classical rules for using the Greek orders as applied to Roman domed, vaulted and arched buildings of brick and rubblework. The palaces he built for the small nobles of Vicenza, who must have been a race of four-flushers too big for their boots, bristle with theatrical effects and archaeological bombast. That part was not of much use to Jefferson. But Palladio had also built and illustrated in his work a set of country villas for the practical businessmen of Venice who had estates along the Brenta, in which he tackled exactly the problem a Virginia landowner had to face, the problem of giving unified style and elegance to the complicated buildings of a farm.

Basic in Palladio's theory was the idea of the module. The module was the unit of measurement; say, the diameter of a column. If the diameter of the columns were so much, then they must be so many modules high, so many modules apart, and the unit must be embodied, according to a mathematical scheme, in every detail of the building. Here was a rule that appealed immediately to a man with a mathematical turn of mind and some training in music. An amateur needed a shortcut of this kind that allowed him to figure out his effects according to rule, because he had no practical apprentice's experience in building to start on. Jefferson didn't stick to his measurements any more than Palladio or Vitruvius had, but the system gave him a sense of a building as a whole and gave his work that proportion and musical order that is his personal stamp on a house. In my own opinion, no architect has ever done better in the Palladian style than Jefferson did in his houses at Monticello, Bremo, Poplar Forest or the big front room at Farmington.

His design for the state capitol at Richmond (in its original form that can still be seen in the plaster model) is in a slightly different class, as are the designs he made at the end of his life for the buildings of the University of Virginia. As soon as he got to Europe he went right to the bottom of the classical revival by going to look at the ancient buildings themselves. For the Virginia state capitol he adapted the actual Maison Carrée at Nîmes just as it had come down from the time of Augustus. In making the model he had the help of the meticulous drawings and of the advice of the antiquarian painter Clérisseaux and of the technical skill of his draftsmen and stuccoworkers. But the idea and the invention were Jefferson's, who thus produced the first of a long line of designs, developed later by Latrobe in this country, that went deliberately back to classical originals (in Latrobe's case to the Greek) and set the course of American architecture for fifty years.

We know what kind of buildings Jefferson built; they are still standing; but nothing in his writing tells us in so many words why he wanted to build that way. At Bremo on the James, not far from the house Jefferson designed for his younger friend, the eccentric and philanthropic General Cocke, are the general's own previous efforts in the "picturesque" style of Queen Anne, so we know it was not inevitable that a Virginia gentleman in the late eighteenth century should turn to the antique when, as Chastellux quaintly put it, "he consulted the fine arts in the matter of putting a roof over his head." The current type of building of the houses Jefferson saw as a boy, the true "colonial," was a much less emphatic style that had sifted into England from the Italian Renaissance originals through Inigo Jones and Sir Christopher Wren and into America through practical builders' handbooks. Jefferson was in personal matters the least articulate of men, it is probable that he never expressed his deepest feelings even to himself in other than legal and political phraseology, but it becomes fairly obvious as you read through his letters, and become familiar with the sort of thing he left unsaid in them, that his architecture was the most direct and personal expression we have of the turn of his mind, the frame for the sort of life he wanted to live and wanted his fellow-citizens to live. Monticello and the Declaration of Independence are two key achievements of the same man and they are not incompatible.

In the first place the buildings Jefferson designed are admirably contrived to give full scale to the human figure. His country houses are manorial mansions in the sense the English country houses were, but with the feudal factor left out. Jefferson hated flunkeys and personal service, and spent a great deal of his time working out contraptions that would let him live at ease without them. No footmen threw open the glass doors of his drawingroom, they were arranged so that they both opened simultaneously at a touch. To run a big place like Monticello, to clean, to keep the fires going, to fetch water, to make the beds and empty the slops, he had to have a mass of servants, but every effort was taken in planning the house to keep them at least out of sight. In his dumbwaiter and his little elevator for bottles of wine and the rotary servingdoor between kitchen and diningroom he planned for General Cocke at Bremo he was heading towards the modern mechanized house where the householder and his family can do all the work themselves. He wanted a house where a free man could live in a society of equals. Already he had seen the possibility, which is even more teasing and tantalizingly near today, that, with the growth of mechanical invention, the productive work of the world can be made so light that the men who do it can be free and equal to those who organize and exploit production. It was for the free men of the future republic, when Negro slavery would have been done away with, when every citizen's son should have as good a chance for an education as any other and as much of an opportunity to show what he had in him, when every man could have his farm and his garden and his house, it was for the free men of the vast westward continent of the future that Jefferson planned the white porches with their careful modulation of columns and windows and pediments and their severely simplified ornaments "from the antique." Even today, with all the certainty under our skins of a world so heartbreakingly different, it is hard to stand on one of those porches, looking out at the sweep of landscape rich in great trees which the columns frame, without feeling a lift of the spirits.

In the years since he had sat a somewhat stiff fourth at Governor Fauquier's little dinners Jefferson's architecture and his gardening had been, with some music thrown in, the main pleasure and occupation of his life at home. He managed to turn a hobby into a career of invention and accomplishment that would have made him important in early America as an architect, if he'd never done anything else. But all the while he was carrying on a difficult and wearing public life of negotiation, committee meetings and close work on the law books. With a few friends who thought as he did he was trying to turn the Old Dominion into something like a modern democracy.

In the fall of 1776 he had refused re-election to the Continental Congress and accepted a seat in the Virginia legislature instead, because he wanted to be home with his family and because he felt his first allegiance was to his own state. Immediately he set to work, using all his prestige as signer of the Declaration of Independence and leader of the new national government, to liberalize the laws and administration. Virginia was still organized like an English county under the Walpole squirarchy; dissenting ministers could not preach without running the risk of being put in jail, Unitarians could not testify in court, a Quaker stepped across the state line at his peril, property went to the eldest son under entail, every man had to pay his tithe to the established church: all the bloody laws under which great British landowners had kept tenants and daylaborers and, in Virginia, slaves and bondservants in subjection for centuries were on the statutebooks. With George Wythe and the conservative leader John Pendleton he sat on a committee to humanize the code of law. It meant months of close detail but in the end the delegates accepted their work.

Then Jefferson's troubles began. He introduced a bill for complete religious toleration and church disestablishment. It was only passed years later after a strenuous fight by Jefferson's friends led by his young neighbor James Madison. He did manage to get through a bill repealing the laws of entail, a measure he hoped would break up the big estates and keep landholdings small, but the landowners were already getting balky. In the matter of slavery he had been so completely unsuccessful before that he and his friends thought it better to wait; his plan was to tack on some conservative bill an amendment to regulate slavery to the effect that all Negroes born after a certain date should be free. He did induce the delegates to prohibit further importation of slaves.

His greatest disappointment was that he could not argue the legislature into passing three bills for public education he had prepared. This scheme was the key to his whole plan for democratic selfgovernment and its failure did more than any other single factor to ruin his hope of turning Virginia into a democratic agrarian commonwealth. The plan was that the counties should be divided into wards and that each ward should support a free school for all children, to be paid for by local taxation and superintended by a local school board. Over these was to be established a set of regional colleges or high schools for the further education of the brightest students, and William and Mary was to be turned into a state university to which the star students in the colleges should have their way paid. People of means were to be allowed to send their children to the public schools too by paying for them, but the system would make it sure that no child of ability should lack the best education the state could offer. Associated with it was a plan for a state library.

The Virginians had none of that enthusiasm for education the New Englanders had inherited from their Puritan forebears, who had been truly people of the Book. The delegates would not be convinced, so the one measure failed that could have given a self-governing base to Virginia and the whole South and could possibly have saved those states the lost years of ruined plantation economics and guttering gentility that ended in the smashup of their whole system in the Civil War. At the end of his life Jefferson did manage to embody part of his great plan in the University of Virginia, but he himself knew and always said, that the lack of primary selfgovernment in the counties and of primary education would be the ruin of Virginia democracy. Up to his death he dinned it into the ears of his followers that without the wards as a popular unit to correspond to townmeeting in New England, self-government would fail in Virginia.

Patrick Henry, rapidly degenerating into a selfsatisfied conservative, had been a fizzle as the commonwealth's first Governor. As the second Governor, Jefferson managed to do an immense amount of useful work, but he retired from the office with even less credit than his old friend.

He had been chosen Governor on the first of June 1779. It was the blackest time in the whole war. In Europe the surrender of Burgoyne at Saratoga and the subtle diplomatic webs that Franklin sat weaving like a genial gray-worsted spider in Paris were stacking the cards against England; but in America French help had not yet taken effect.

The economic situation was desperate. Continental paper and the paper of the various states had been inflated to the vanishing point. Hard cash couldn't be laid hold of. Farming and commerce had been ruined by the blockade.

Washington was sitting in his camp up the Hudson watching the British force in New York. He was already committed to the Fabian policy, temporarily at least so disastrous, of not scattering his troops even if it meant leaving his native state open to the enemy. The British had command of the sea, and on land their armies ravaged wherever they pleased.

In the South things were bad indeed. Charleston had fallen. General Gates, the hero of Saratoga, had let himself be whipped at Camden.

From the minute Jefferson was sworn in as Governor he was busy helping the Continental forces by stripping his own state of levies and military supplies to send them north to Washington and Lafayette and south to Nathanael Greene in the Carolinas, where that longfaced Rhode Islander was sourly pulling together strings Gates had left untied. Jefferson had confidence in Washington's master plan, but it took time. Farmers laughed at Virginia currency, so supplies and horseflesh had to be impressed. Governor Jefferson had gotten in wrong with the clergy by advocating disestablishment, with the conservative landowners by the repeal of the laws of entail and by all this talk about educating the poor and freeing the slaves; now he had to superintend the forcible seizure of the goods of his own constituents. He worked doggedly supplying the armies and seconding Washington's grand strategy in every way he could. It didn't make him popular with the farmers.

Things were already quite bad enough when, in the winter of his second term, a British force under Benedict Arnold, whose treason had been one of the worst blows the Continental cause had suffered, sailed up the James and made a sudden landing at Westover, just seven miles below Richmond. The capital had been recently moved to the mill village of Richmond above the falls for security from just such raids. Jefferson rode around until his horse fell dead under him directing the removal of stores. He was not a military man and strictly left the military command to the professionals, but he had to do what he could. Some munitions he managed to save, but Arnold entered Richmond unopposed and destroyed a foundry for cannons and an arms depot, and did a great deal of damage before he sailed off down the river again with a fair wind.

British raids continued. Towards spring, Cornwallis, who had shaken off Greene's army that was supposed to keep him in the Carolinas, marched up the coast to Petersburg. The Virginia legislature fled to Charlottesville. The delegates had barely gotten settled in the Charlottesville taverns when they had to run again with Tarleton's dragoons right on their coattails. The seat of government was moved breathlessly to Staunton in the Valley, but Jefferson and the speakers of the two houses were almost nabbed at Monticello by a British detachment. Meanwhile Colonel Lynch had handled a near insurrection in Montgomery County so roughly that his name became a proverb; the Virginians were penniless, their farms were ruined, they had seen their cattle driven off by the British and by their own elected officials and all they had in return was saddlebags full of paper money that wouldn't buy anything, and they were sore. The legislators were still in a funk from their narrow escape at Charlottesville. Grumbling and recrimination increased every day. Jefferson had already refused a third term and suggested the appointment in his stead of the man he had put at the head of the militia, General Nelson.

There was a painful irony in the fact that, after Jefferson had been the scapegoat for all the worst of it, the tide turned in that same summer of '81. The Virginia campaign of Washington and Rochambeau, backed by the blockade of the Chesapeake by De Grasse's fleet, brought about the surrender of Cornwallis' army in Yorktown by October. Suddenly it was all over. The states were free and independent.

During the dark days young George Nicholas had jumped to his feet in the legislature to demand an enquiry into Governor Jefferson's conduct during the British raids. By the time the enquiry came off things were sunny again, animosities had faded and

Nicholas made such handsome amends that he and Jefferson continued fast friends all their lives. The legislature tendered Mr. Jefferson a vote of thanks. But it did not make up for the slights he had undergone nor for the sense of failure he felt at not having been able to accomplish the reforms he had felt most important. Things were not made any better by the fact that he was in a bad way for money. He had had heavy expenses during the war. His salary as Governor had been in almost worthless paper and Cornwallis had amused himself by destroying the house and the crops and carrying off the slaves at Elk Hill, one of the best farms that had come to him through his wife. At Monticello the British had done no damage, though they had given his butler a bad scare, so it was to Monticello he retired, with that sense of relief that every Virginian felt in getting back to his own acres after an excursion into the world.

He had left the field and gone to skulk in his tent, but he was no man to skulk in idleness. While he was Governor he had found time to draft a plan for modernizing the government buildings at Williamsburg. A century and a half later the architects of the recent reconstruction used his drawings as the basis of their work. While he was laid up after a nasty fall from a horse, he wrote his *Notes on Virginia* in answer to some enquiries of the Marquis de Marbois, an attaché of the French Legation in Philadelphia, who was collecting information about the geography, economic social and political, of the new states. Jefferson had been so much impressed by the set of the public mind against him and his ideas that he did his best to keep the book from being published in America; for fear, as he said, that his remarks on slavery would do more harm than good; that they would tend to deepen the prejudices of his fellowcitizens rather than argue them away.

Jefferson had reached that barrier that every original mind eventually encounters in dealing with the generality of men. In the end he was to take the Boyg's advice to Peer Gynt: "Go roundabout," but for a while he was stopped dead.

It is part of the nature of consciousness, of how the mental apparatus works, that free reason is only a very occasional function of people's "thinking" and that much of the process is made of reactions as standardized as those of the keys on a typewriter. Some sets of words, in any given situation, are positively charged and give sensations of pleasure and approval, while others are negatively charged with sensations of disgust and disapproval. The verbal apparatus through which people keep in touch with the social and political organization under which they live is particularly full of inhibiting machinery. The process of getting people to accept political changes or novelties, even those from which they will immediately benefit, has broken the hearts of innovators since history began. "I have found," Fred Taylor, the management engineer who first methodically rationalized factory work, wrote in 1909, "that any improvement is not only opposed but bitterly and aggressively opposed by the majority of men."

Socrates tried tricking people out of prejudice by asking them questions. Somewhere in *Mein Kampf* Hitler exclaims with naïve surprise on how much it is constantly necessary to deceive people for their own good. Habit, selfinterest, fear of change, and purely automatic reflexes of negation are hurdles every reformer (be his work good or bad) has to reckon with.

It is the discovery of this barrier that breeds the hasty cynicism and low estimate of mankind that is at the inner core of the average successful politician. If he manages to get past it at all, he ends up too often with the state of mind of a confidence man who has found it's as easy to pass bad checks as good ones. The surprising thing, I suppose, is that men are bred at all who are able to climb that barrier in their fellowmen where so much that is fresh honest inventive hopeful stops dead, and who having climbed it keep some of their first honesty of purpose. Perhaps the survival of the race itself demands the handing down from generation to generation and the occasional emergence of the type of mind that can't shake off a feeling of responsibility for other men, the type of mind in which the qualities grouped under the tag "the parental bent" are dominant.

Anyway it is plain that among Virginians who took the side of Independence during the Revolutionary War, this parental bent was very strong. There was something about the secure family life, the daily work of keeping a plantation going, even perhaps their patriarchal relations with their Negroes, that produced a race of men who were skillful enough in the art of inducing their fellows to take action to be effective and who still were unwilling to use their ascendancy for their own selfish ends. Washington, who was certainly not a brilliant man in other ways, owed his pre-eminence to the dominance of that quality in his makeup. It wasn't only the Virginians; because the small town printer and merchant Franklin had it to an immense degree. It was strong in the Adamses for all their crotchets and vanities. Even Hamilton had it. But it was particularly compelling in Monroe, Madison and Jefferson. In reading the letters and documents of the period you get the feeling that it was particularly from the Virginians that emanated the intellectual and moral tone that gave such stature to the men who governed the United States during our first twentyfive or thirty years of being a nation.

When Jefferson came home sore and smarting from his exoneration by the legislature, he had not yet found how to dodge the automatic veto of prejudice and habit. He was bitterly disillusioned. He was determined to fill his life entirely with the routine of his farm and his home, with raising his children and his nephews and nieces, and his crops and his fruittrees and his horses and his gristmill, and his projects for building and the endlessly diverting daily meticulous study of the climate and the plants and the animals of his own Albemarle County. But it was not on the books that Jefferson should be a private man. The center of all that rich family world was his wife, whose health was never off his mind when he was forced to be away from her. In September 1782 she died.

ROBERT R. PALMER

✪

The Dubious Democrat

Thomas Jefferson in Bourbon France

Thomas Jefferson, the second United States Minister to France, remained in that country from 1784 until September of 1789, two months after the fall of the Bastille. The author of the Declaration of Independence saw at first hand the collapse of the monarchy by whose aid American independence had been established, and the revolutionary of 1776 was an eyewitness, and even a participant, in the greater revolution of 1789. These activities of Jefferson, inviting as they do a comparison of the American and French revolutions, and raising the whole conundrum of American relationships to Europe, have long offered an intriguing and now ancient subject, on which it yet always seems possible to say more. My own knowledge is more of Europe than of Jefferson. If the following impressions have any value or novelty, it is because the author is no Jefferson expert, but has simply sat down, with a point of view derived from the study of European history, to a fresh reading of Jefferson's letters from France—both his letters to personal friends, and his official communications to John Jay, the American Secretary of State under the Articles of Confederation. The new edition of *The Papers of Thomas Jefferson,* pre-

Reprinted with permission from *Political Science Quarterly,* Vol. LXXII, No. 3 (September 1957), pp. 388–404.

pared by Julian P. Boyd and his aides with an abundance of useful annotation, is in fact just now approaching the year 1789.[1]

The title that I have ventured upon requires a word of explanation. To call Jefferson a "dubious democrat" is a pretty alliteration, but "democrat" is an anachronism, and "dubious" is ambiguous. Jefferson did not call himself a democrat, and the word itself was then new, first coming into accepted use to describe some of the Dutch Patriots about 1787, a sense in which Jefferson employed it himself. If we nevertheless call Jefferson not only a democrat but a dubious one, at the time of his sojourn in France, we fall into a double meaning. We imply either that he was a questionable democrat or that he was a skeptical one. Either it is we who doubt the extent of his democratic principles, or it is he, a good enough democrat, who took a doubtful view of what he saw happening in France. There is a little of both these meanings in what I have to say.

One day in Paris, in February, 1787, Jefferson wrote a letter to his old friend, John Adams, the American Minister in London. They had been closely associated in the American Revolution, in which they had both been on the committee to write the Declaration of Independence, and their political ideas were still much alike, as may be seen in their opinions of the constitutions of Virginia and Massachusetts, their respective native states. The political estrangement of a few years later had not yet come. Jefferson had not yet been stigmatized as a Francophile nor Adams as an Anglomaniac; nor was Jefferson yet thought the pre-eminent father

[1] Julian P. Boyd and others, eds., *The Papers of Thomas Jefferson,* Vols. XI–XIII (Princeton, 1955–1956). See also Dumas Malone, *Jefferson and the Rights of Man* (Boston, 1951), pp. 180–237; Gilbert Chinard, ed., *The Letters of Lafayette and Jefferson* (Baltimore and Paris, 1929); O. Vossler, *Die amerikanischen Revolutionsideale in ihrem Verhältnis zu den europäischen: Untersuch an Thomas Jefferson* (Munich, 1929), of which there is a digest in the *William and Mary Quarterly,* XII (July 1955), 462–471; Durand Echeverria, *Mirage in the West: A History of the French Image of American Society to 1815* (Princeton, 1957); and my article, "Notes on the Use of the Word 'Democracy,' 1789–1799," *Political Science Quarterly,* LXVIII (June 1953), 203–226. The present article originated as a paper delivered at the Society for French Historical Studies in February 1957.

of American democracy, or Adams looked back upon, perhaps mistakenly, as a deep philosopher of conservatism.

Jefferson had two things to say in his letter. He told his colleague of what had happened at Versailles the day before, the meeting of the Assembly of Notables called by the minister Calonne to deal with the crisis of the French finances. He also commented on Adams' new book, *The Defense of the Constitutions of the United States,* of which Adams had sent him a copy, and which he had just finished reading, as he said, "with infinite satisfaction and improvement." He thought it would do "much good in America," and took immediate steps to have it translated into French. A few days later he went off on a three-month tour of the South of France. His insatiable curiosity turned to the vine, the olive and the fig, to the mysteries of fossil sea shells, Roman ruins and the shifts in the Mediterranean coastline since the building of Aigues-Mortes, to the wages of farm laborers and the hardness or softness of peasants' beds, to the habits of nightingales in Touraine, the introduction of the steam engine at Nîmes, and the precise width of the Languedoc canal at the bottom. Meanwhile he was out of touch with Versailles, where the Assembly of Notables met during his absence.

The point is that when the King of France upon Calonne's advice convened the Assembly of Notables, and when John Adams wrote his *Defense of the Constitutions of the United States,* there was one idea that they had in common, and one that this acute and tireless observer, Thomas Jefferson, seems much less fully to have shared. This was the idea that a strong independent executive might be a good thing for the people.

The drift of Adams' book was to justify, by a survey of Europe, the separation and balance of governmental powers in America, that is of executive, judiciary, and upper and lower houses of legislation; and it was this separation and balance that won Jefferson's approval. For Adams, the main purpose of such separation was to preserve executive independence, and the purpose of executive independence was to prevent public bodies from degenerating into privileged oligarchies. "If there is one certain truth to be collected from the history of all ages," said Adams, "it is this: that the people's rights and liberties . . . can never be preserved without a strong executive." He saw what has become the commonplace of our history textbooks: that an alliance of kings with burghers and peasants, over the centuries, had put down the feudal classes. "What is the whole history of the barons' wars but one demonstration of this truth? What are all the standing armies in Europe, but another? These were all given to the kings by the people, to defend them against aristocracies." And he concluded, in modern vein, indeed disconcertingly like a latter-day Democrat, that the executive (whom he preferred to have popularly elected) was "the natural friend of the people, and the only defense which they or their representatives can have against the avarice and ambition of the rich and distinguished citizens."[2]

It is a curious speculation to wonder what Adams would have thought of Calonne and the Assembly of Notables, if he rather than Jefferson had been the American Minister to France. For Calonne called the Assembly because he believed that the rich and distinguished citizens were evading taxes. In his opening speech to the Assembly he denounced the "abuses of pecuniary privileges."[3] He proposed to use the executive authority of the French Crown to impose a kind of equality before the law. In his complex program to save the French monarchy by reforming it, in what Miss Wilma Pugh once called Calonne's New Deal, there were two principal proposals: to introduce a new kind of land tax payable in proportion to income by persons of all legal classes alike, cleric, noble and commoner, without privilege or exception; and to introduce certain representative consultative bodies, called provincial assemblies, whose members should qualify as landowners, and be elected by landowners in general, with no regard to the legal system of three estates. Calonne was perfectly aware that he was attacking privilege and aristocracy at their foundation. His plan for provincial assemblies came directly from the thinking of Turgot, Mira-

2 John Adams, *Defense of the Constitutions of the United States,* Charles Francis Adams, ed., *Works of John Adams,* IV (Boston, 1851), 290, 355, 585.
3 *Discours prononcés par S.M. Louis XVI, Msgr. l'archevêque de Narbonne et M. de Calonne à l'Assemblée des Notables le 22 fevrier, 1787* (Versailles, 1787), p. 23.

beau and Dupont de Nemours.[4] As for the tax reforms: "Privileges will be sacrificed, yes, as justice demands and as our needs require. Would anyone prefer to put an even heavier load on the unprivileged, the people?"[5] If there was ever a case of the executive defending the people against certain pretensions of aristocracy, in Adams' formula, this last effort of the expiring Bourbon monarchy was such a case.

But Calonne's program met with insuperable resistance in the Assembly of Notables. He and his successor had to abandon the land tax and the principle of equal representation in the new provincial assemblies. There presently followed what we know as the aristocratic resurgence and the Revolt of the Nobles. On this phenomenon historians have come to agree. Albert Mathiez and Georges Lefebvre have described it, and all the great G's of contemporary learning on the French Revolution, Gottschalk and Gershoy in this country, Goodwin in England, Göhring in Germany, Godechot in France, agree in telling the same story, that the privileged classes in the Assembly of Notables blocked the plan for equality of taxation and equality of representation put forward by Calonne.

I do not know what John Adams would have thought of all this. He was in England, and in his letters and diary he made no significant comment on events in France. It seems likely that the crusty New Englander, who inveighed against the maneuvers of "aristocratical gentlemen" even at Geneva, would have had some sardonic reservations on the aristocracy of France. We do know what Jefferson thought. He thought very well of the Assembly of Notables. When the Assembly first met, he blamed the French for their levity toward it; [6] for a great many witticisms were in circula-

<hr/>

[4] P. Jolly, *Calonne, 1734–1802* (Paris, 1949), p. 166.

[5] *Collection des mémoires presentées à l'Assemblée des Notables. Première et seconde division* (Paris, 1787). Published by Calonne about March 30, 1787, and widely circulated, to strengthen his case in the Assembly of Notables by an appeal to public opinion. See an unpublished dissertation at Princeton University by Ralph W. Greenlaw, "The French Nobility on the Eve of the Revolution," pp. 22–23.

[6] Jefferson to Abigail Adams, February 22, 1787, *Jefferson Papers* (Boyd ed.), XI, 174. "The people at large view every object only as it may furnish

tion, chiefly turning on the select composition of its membership, which, beginning with seven princes of the blood and thirty-six dukes and peers, proceeded through the whole array of legalized status to include, in 144 members, only four who were altogether of the Third Estate. Jefferson showed no disposition to be critical on this score. He thought the Notables "the most able and independent characters in the kingdom."[7]

Calonne had explicitly raised the question of privilege. The word "privilege" never occurs in Jefferson's letters until much later in the controversy, until December, 1788. And when the provincial assemblies proposed by Calonne did meet, in altered form, a few months later, when, instead of being elected as landowners by landowners, they represented the three estates of clergy, nobility and commoner, with some of their membership designated by the King, and the rest co-opted, Jefferson made no comment on the change that the plan for provincial assemblies had undergone. The assemblies "will be of the choice of the people," he wrote to John Jay, long enough after his return to Paris to have learned what had happened. And he told Adams that "the royal authority has lost, and the rights of the nation gained," as much in France in three months, by peaceable change of opinion only, as in England during all the civil wars under the Stuarts. He thought only old people opposed the change. The revolution, so to speak, was over.[8]

It is no news to report that Jefferson, while in France, took a fairly conservative view of the beginnings of the French Revolution. The problem is to examine the quality and content of this so-called conservatism. The problem is to explain why Thomas Jefferson, of all people, was so insensitive to the case for equality of taxation, equality of representation, and equality of citizenship in France.

It is possible that if he saw no issue of privilege, the politically conscious French public still saw no such issue either. It may be

puns and bons mots. . . . When a measure so capable of doing good as the calling of the Notables is treated with so much ridicule, we may conclude the nation desperate. . . ."

[7] Jefferson to John Jay, June 21, 1787, *ibid.,* XI, 489.

[8] Jefferson to Jay, *ibid.,* XI, 490; to Adams, August 30, 1787, *ibid.,* XII, 68.

that the archbishops and *grands seigneurs* who led the attack on
Calonne acted as the accepted leaders of the country, and in the
country's interest. Many of the objections of the Notables to
Calonne's tax program were perfectly valid. The Notables preferred a continuation of the old *vingtième* to his new land tax, but
the *vingtième* was legally payable by both nobles and commoners;
and if there were *de facto* inequalities in its incidence, arising from
underassessment, I am not sure that these were much greater than
with the land tax in England—at least I would like to see some
comparative research on this subject. The tax privileges most hotly
defended by the Notables, and those which Calonne most vigor-
ously attacked, were actually, as Ralph Greenlaw has pointed out,
the privileges of certain provinces, by which provinces as a whole,
and in theory all classes in those provinces, carried a lighter share
of the national tax burden. To Jefferson such privileges or liberties,
depending on old agreements, might well seem like states' rights
within a kind of federal system, and as such perfectly defensible
against the Crown.

Before judging what he thought, we must ask what it was
possible for him to know. We must distinguish between what could
be seen by contemporaries and what can be seen by historians. The
issue was not entirely invisible in 1787. In the past, to be sure, the
Bourbon monarchy, in its frequent clashes with the privileged
orders, had been highly secretive, and had yielded all the advantages of publicity to spokesmen for the aristocracy and the clergy.
But in 1787 Calonne appealed to the public. He himself published,
during the sessions of the Assembly, the main substance of his
differences with it. Moreover, Dupont de Nemours, with whom
Jefferson was in close contact, had been a secretary to the Assembly, and drew up a detailed report of one of its most critical
sessions. Dupont was a partisan of Calonne's program, and,
though his confidential report was not published, Jefferson could
easily have learned from him what went on. Others of Jefferson's
circle, Condorcet and Morellet as well as Dupont, friends and
supporters of the late Turgot, were outspoken believers in equality
of taxation and in provincial assemblies meeting without regard to
legal estate. There were men in France in 1787 who distrusted the

lead taken by the prelates and the great nobles. Jefferson was not one of them.[9]

The truth seems to be that Jefferson's idea of what was happening was taken almost entirely from his good friend the Marquis de Lafayette, who played an active part in the Assembly of Notables, as in other later events. Professor Gottschalk, in his great work on Lafayette, allows that his hero in the troubled months of 1787 was somewhat naïve, that he only very slowly came to see the character of the aristocratic resistance to proposed reforms, and that in his patriotic and idealistic outbursts he served as a cat's-paw for the privileged interests.[10] At any rate, when Calonne announced that the monarchy was bankrupt, Lafayette and the Assembly refused to believe him. When he revealed the amount of the deficit, which was of old standing and greatly increased by the American war, they attributed it to his own maladministration, insisting that there had been no deficit in Necker's time a few years before. When Calonne desperately asserted that the government's income must be immediately raised, and that certain loopholes and privileges in the tax structure must be stopped, they retorted that economies in expenditure would suffice. They accused Calonne of scandalous waste, graft and corruption, and denounced the monstrous prodigality of the royal court. Lafayette, in high-minded indignation, did as much as any man to draw this red herring of alleged personal dishonesty and courtly extravagance across the trail marked out by Calonne for structural reform. The trouble in this view was not in the legal and social organization of France, but in the misconduct of an overgrown and arrogant government.

[9] See notes 3 and 5 above. Dupont's report, written in June 1787, was published by P. Renouvin, *L'Assemblée des Notables de 1787: la conférence du mars, texte publié avec introduction et notes* (Paris, 1920). The Abbé Morellet, who had translated Jefferson's *Notes on Virginia* the year before, observed in July 1787 to the Earl of Shelburne that the Parlement of Paris demanded "the Estates-General, the most false and vicious representation that any nation ever had, instead of letting us form and develop provincial administrations in which the deputies would become true and perfect representatives, much better than yours." *Lettres de l'abbé Morellet à Lord Shelburne* (Paris, 1898), p. 245. See also Jolly, pp. 183, 205.

[10] L. R. Gottschalk, *Lafayette Between the American and the French Revolution (1783–1789)* (Chicago, 1950), pp. 279, 297 *et seq.*

This was doctrine that a Virginia gentleman could readily understand. Powerful government was what Jefferson feared; monarchy was his bugaboo; it was resistance to tyrants that expressed the will of God. "You are afraid of the one—I, of the few. . . . You are apprehensive of Monarchy; I, of Aristocracy."[11] So John Adams wrote to him, diagnosing the difference between them. It is true that Jefferson shortly revised his opinion of Calonne, finding "him less wicked, and France less badly governed, than I had feared."[12] It was in the nuance, the emphasis, the first impulse, more than in the considered judgment, that he differed from Adams.

It does appear that Jefferson at the moment, in mid-1787, was not very apprehensive of aristocracy in France, or in Europe either. He was aware of the troubles then raging in Holland and Belgium. These, he said in August, 1787, were the places where "we have at present two fires kindled in Europe." What we call the reforms of Joseph II in Belgium, which included religious toleration and reduction of the costs of justice, Jefferson described as innovations of a whimsical sovereign.[13] He knew that the incipient Belgian revolution was led by nobles and priests, but was untroubled by this knowledge. In the Dutch provinces the attempted Patriot revolution had reached its climax and was soon to be suppressed by Great Britain and Prussia. Jefferson, who sympathized with the Patriots, described how they were composed of two groups, the Moderate Aristocrats and the Democrats. When the two disagreed, it was the Democrats that he blamed for their unreasonableness.[14] The Dutch Democrats were middle-class burghers who had formed themselves into militia companies, held a National Assembly of such companies, protested at the subservience of the House of Orange to Great Britain, talked of equality of rights for persons of diverse religions, protested at the hereditary monopolizing of office in certain families, repudiated

[11] Adams to Jefferson, December 6, 1787, Boyd, XII, 396.
[12] E. M. Sowerby, *Catalogue of the Library of Thomas Jefferson,* II (1953), 425, citing a letter of October 18, 1787; Boyd, XII, 247.
[13] Boyd, XI, 672, 679, 685.
[14] *Ibid.,* XI, 696.

the three-estates system in Utrecht, and believed that they were imitating the American Revolution. Jefferson thought them very immoderate.

At the same time he reported of France that "the constitutional reformations have gone on well," and that the provincial assemblies would probably soon bring "a revolution in the constitution."[15] Lafayette had been designated by the King as one of the noble members in the assembly of Auvergne; and this assembly had hardly met when it began, with Lafayette's enthusiastic agreement, to demand the revival of long obsolete liberties of the province, which is to say more powers for the clergy and nobility of Auvergne. In these demands, echoed by most of the other provincial assemblies, historians nowadays see signs of the aristocratic resurgence, the attempt of some in the privileged orders, as Göhring says, to turn France into a *Ständestaat*, a status state. For Jefferson they seemed to be a liberal movement to check the Crown.

In the next year, 1788, we can detect a new dimension in Jefferson's ideas, corresponding to that "widening of political notions" which Gottschalk finds in Lafayette. The summer of 1788 saw the high tide of the aristocratic resurgence, or what we have learned to call the *révolte nobiliaire*. Jefferson's friends Dupont and Condorcet were becoming more radically antinoble. So was another in Jefferson's circle, Philip Mazzei, an Italian whom Jefferson had known for years in Virginia, and of whom he was now seeing a good deal in Paris. Mazzei now made a living by writing bulletins to the King of Poland. That dignitary was receiving stronger medicine from Mazzei than the American Congress ever got from Jefferson. "Aristocratic tyranny is struggling against despotism and monarchy. The pretext is the good of the people, to which, however, the aristocracy here, as it is everywhere else, and always has been, is far more opposed than the monarchy is."[16] Jefferson never talked this way about aristocracy. At most, he thought the Parlement of Paris rather obstinately selfish.

---

[15] Jefferson to Jay, August 6, 1787, *ibid.*, XI, 697–698.

[16] R. Ciampini, ed., *Lettere di Filippo Mazzei alla corte di Polonia* (Bologna, 1937), I, 7. Despatch of July 28, 1788.

He did now admit, in the middle of 1788, as Lafayette now did, that the royal reforms were good in substance, but bad in manner. If the King alone has power to reform France, he says, the government is a despotism.[17] He no longer simply sees liberty against tyranny, but a choice of values. Nor, incidentally, do I think that John Adams or any American at the time would have chosen otherwise than as Jefferson did: as between reforms, and even justice, at the hands of an irresponsible and bureaucratic monarchy, however well-intentioned, and a measure of political liberty through elective and representative bodies, even though unequal, Jefferson unhesitatingly chose the latter. We begin to read in his letters of a possible convocation of the Estates-General. Jefferson thinks this a promising step toward a fixed constitution, limitation of the Crown and reduction of expense. Equality of representation seems not to enter his mind; he thinks it will be best if the Estates meet in two houses, one representing the people, the other made up of nobles elected by nobles, as, he observes, is done in Scotland.[18] If such a body meets, issues a bill of rights, puts the King on a civil list, and takes care that it shall meet periodically in the future, quite enough will be accomplished. "I think it probable," he wrote to James Monroe in August, 1788, "this country will within two or three years be in the enjoyment of a tolerably free constitution, and that without its having cost them a drop of blood."[19]

His ideas continued to develop at deliberate speed, not an inch ahead of average opinion in France, and well behind a good deal of it. Like others, he was dismayed when the Parlement of Paris, in September, ruled that the coming Estates-General must meet as in 1614, in three separate houses—clergy, nobles and commoners. The Parlement, he said, here revealed "the cloven hoof."[20] Now

[17] Jefferson to Carmichael, June 3, 1788, Boyd, XIII, 233; to Cutting, July 24, p. 405; to Madison, July 31, p. 441.
[18] Jefferson to Washington, May 2, 1788, *ibid.*, XIII, 126. For Jefferson's persistent belief that the French would be wise to model their government on England rather than on America, see Malone, *Jefferson and the Rights of Man*, pp. 181, 220.
[19] Boyd, XIII, 489.
[20] *Ibid.*, p. 642.

for the first time he began to use the word "privilege," to tell his American correspondents that there were privileged classes in France, and that they paid less than their share of taxes—as Calonne had said publicly almost two years before.[21] But where others, sensing an aristocratic bid for power, moved on like the Abbé Sieyès to denounce the aristocracy in bitter terms, and to demand equality of representation in the sense of vote by head in a single chamber, Jefferson, still in agreement with Lafayette, hoped for a compromise between nobility and Third Estate. Sieyès, Condorcet and Mirabeau were already chiding Lafayette as an "aristocrat"; I see no reason why they should not have thought the same of Jefferson also.[22] Of the coming Estates-General Jefferson was content to expect very little. If they "do not aim at too much they may begin a good constitution," he told Madison in November. What he meant was that they should obtain, at their first session, only certain rights over taxation and rights to register laws but not take the initiative in legislation, in addition to the assurance of periodic future meeting.[23] The King himself a few weeks later offered more than Jefferson thought the Estates could prudently ask. Nor did his talks with Lafayette about declarations of rights represent any very radical departure. "All the world is occupied at present in framing, every one his own plan, of a bill of rights," he wrote as early as December, 1788.[24]

He remained confident for a while that a moderate constitutional "revolution" could be peaceably effected by men of good will, and by men, it must be admitted, occupying a fairly com-

[21] Jefferson's first use of the term "privilege" seems to be in letters to Paine, December 23, 1788, Andrew A. Lipscomb and Albert Ellery Bergh, eds., *The Writings of Thomas Jefferson* (Washington, 1903), VII, 246; to Price, January 8, 1789, p. 256; to Jay, January 11, p. 264. The expression "privileged orders" was denounced as a neologism too much favored by the Third Estate in one of Louis XVI's messages of June 1789 to the Estates-General; see Mazzei's report in Ciampini, p. 146.

[22] See Gottschalk, p. 416; Ciampini, pp. 51–56.

[23] *Writings of Thomas Jefferson* (Lipscomb and Bergh ed.), VII, 184. Same view expressed to Jay, November 19, 1788, *ibid.*, p. 191; to Washington, December 4, p. 227; to Price, January 8, 1789, p. 258.

[24] Jefferson to Dr. Currie, December 20, 1788, *ibid.*, VII, 239; to Madison, January 12, 1789, p. 268.

fortable place in society—"all the honesty of the kingdom," as he put it, "sufficiently at its leisure to think; the men of letters, the easy bourgeois, the young nobility."[25] When a serious working-class riot broke out at a wallpaper factory, just at the moment to jeopardize the harmony of the Estates-General, Jefferson was thrown into an agitation most unusual with him; one is reminded of Luther excoriating the peasants. He called the rioters "wretches" bent only on mischief, "abandoned banditti," whose repression was "unpitied."[26] To the last possible moment he kept his faith in the moderation of the aristocracy, repeatedly declaring, in the first months of 1789, that the clergy would cause the trouble in the coming Estates-General, but that the majority of the nobility might reach an understanding with the Third Estate.[27] He still hoped, at the very opening of the Estates-General, on May 6, 1789, as a means of resolving all difficulties, that the two privileged classes might be persuaded to sit together in one house, the unprivileged in another.[28] This was by no means what was wanted by Frenchmen classified against their will as Third Estate.

His political education, like everyone else's, became dizzily rapid in the next few weeks. He found that the bulk of the Catholic clergy, whom perhaps even ardent admirers of Jefferson would not claim that he well understood, were prepared to take sides with the Third Estate; and that the bulk of the nobles, in whom he had placed his hopes, were less enlightened than he had supposed. He now discovered, seemingly for the first time, that a great many country nobles did not share the affable liberality of the Marquis de Lafayette—that they still entertained, as he put it, "a disposition to keep distinct from the people, and even to tyrannize over them."[29] He readjusted his ideas with alacrity, but no faster than

[25] Jefferson to Price, January 8, 1789, *ibid.*, VII, 254.

[26] Jefferson to Carmichael, May 8, 1789, *ibid.*, VII, 336; to Jay, May 9, p. 342; to Madison, May 11, p. 354. Contrast the far more understanding account of these Reveillon riots given by Mazzei to the King of Poland, Ciampini, pp. 125–127, 136.

[27] Jefferson to the Count de Moustier, March 13, 1789, *Writings of Thomas Jefferson* (Lipscomb and Bergh ed.), VII, 304; to Madison, March 15, p. 313; to Paine, March 17, p. 316; to Humphreys, March 18, p. 321.

[28] Jefferson to Lafayette, May 6, 1789, *ibid.*, VII, 334.

[29] Jefferson to Madison, May 11, 1789, *ibid.*, VII, 355.

many others. In the very letter of May 6 in which he expressed the hope of compromise to Lafayette, he also urged him, should compromise fail, to repudiate the instructions of his noble constituency and join with the Third Estate before he lost their confidence. By May 20 he was agreeing with the radicals of the Third Estate, or rather with the predominant opinion forming in that body.[30]

On June 17, 1789, the Third Estate took its decisive revolutionary action, passing the point of no return. By a five-to-one majority it declared itself a National Assembly, the only competent representative body, representing not social orders but a nation; it again invited persons from the other two orders to come and merge into this single body; and it arrogated sovereign power to itself, to the extent of gratuitously authorizing all existing taxes, thus implying that it might withdraw authorization and instigate a taxpayers' rebellion. Two days later the clergy joined. The next day came the oath of the Tennis Court. The King mildly resisted, then appeared to accept, then began secretly to prepare the dissolution of the Assembly by armed force. The country trembled with excitement. There was rapturous praise for good King Louis, and an almost religious belief in the dawning of a new era.

Jefferson remained cool and collected. His mind moved with events, but his feelings were scarcely involved in his judgments. "A tremendous cloud hovers over this nation," he reported to Jay on June 17. He gave a sober analysis. If the King, he said, were to

side openly with the Commons, the revolution would be completed without a convulsion, by the establishment of a constitution, tolerably free, and in which the distinction of Noble and Commoner would be suppressed. But this is scarcely possible. The King is honest and wishes the good of his people; but the expediency of a hereditary aristocracy is too difficult a question for him.[31]

This is substantially the judgment of most historians today. Jefferson had moved a long way since 1787. He no longer saw a Whiggish clash between King and people. He now saw a clash

[30] Jefferson to Crevecoeur, May 20, 1789, *ibid.*, VII, 368.
[31] Jefferson to Jay, June 17, 1789, *ibid.*, VII, 379–380.

between King and people because the King now supported the aristocracy. Hereditary legal aristocracy was revealed to him as the issue, the stumbling block, the one thing which the commons would not accept, and which the King would not and could not abandon. In short, this was the French Revolution, not the English Revolution of 1689.

Jefferson now felt an optimism qualified by prudent fears. The Assembly, he told Thomas Paine three days before the episode of the Bastille, had by their sagacity and fortitude come into "undisputed possession of sovereignty. The executive and aristocracy are at their feet; the mass of the nation, the mass of the clergy, and the army are with them; they have prostrated the old government, and are now beginning to build one from the foundation."[32] Now that all France seemed to want a radical rebuilding, Jefferson wanted it for them, too. Now that sweeping change seemed to be possible, with nation, clergy and army behind it, he thought it possible also, or at least worth trying. Materials were at hand for a "superb edifice," he said. But he had his doubts: the Assembly might be too large to do business; it was composed of Frenchmen, that is, "more speakers than listeners"; bread shortages, by causing popular violence, might bring division among the leaders; troublemakers of the Left might stir up an agitation around the Duke of Orleans; the discomfited aristocrats might organize counterrevolution.[33] All eventually happened much as he feared. Meanwhile, in September, 1789, he went home.

What can we conclude? First of all, Jefferson was no visionary. He conducted no apostolate in Europe for the principles set forth in the Declaration of Independence. He engaged in no proselytism; when he gave advice, he was usually more conservative than those who sought his opinions. He had no idea, at this time, that America might be a model for Europe; it was the British government that he thought the French ought to imitate. The existence of

[32] Jefferson to Paine, July 11, 1789, *ibid.*, VII, 405.
[33] Jefferson to Shippen, March 11, 1789, *ibid.*, VII, 291–292; to Carmichael, August 9, p. 434; to Jay, August 27, p. 442; to Madison, August 28, p. 447; to Rutledge, September 18, p. 466.

the independent United States, simply as a fact, was a subversive influence on the old order in Europe, but Jefferson did nothing to make it more so. He saw Europe and America as quite different societies. Until events taught him otherwise, he accepted the social order in France, the legalized inequalities, as natural and permanent features of the French landscape, like old churches and chateaux. He had no feeling of impending revolution; he was much more concerned in 1787 with the probabilities of European war, and the fires which he saw kindled were in Holland and Belgium.

He was no optimist. Or, rather, he was optimistic because he expected little. He would have been satisfied if the political crises in France had stopped at any point after the middle of 1787. Repeatedly he predicted that all might turn out well, that the French would soon have a "tolerably free constitution" without bloodshed. He wanted for the French "as much liberty as they are capable of managing," but until June of 1789, if then, he did not think they could manage very much. As for equality, that is civil and legal equality, or equality of representation in elected bodies, he believed in it in principle, of course, and had tried to get more of it written into the constitution of Virginia in 1776; but even in Virginia he had failed, and he expected little from Europe. He lacked class consciousness, being a gentleman rather than an aristocrat, and had little awareness of it in others. There is nothing in his writings of that angry irritability, that sense of downright outrage, or of having been imposed upon flagrantly, that runs through John Adams' account of European patriciates in his *Defense of the Constitutions,* or which animates the Abbé Sieyès's eloquent diatribe, *What Is the Third Estate?* This latter work, which created a stir at the end of 1788, seems to have made no impression on Jefferson. He could with difficulty think of revolution as something demanded from below, by the lower or even the middle classes, or those hitherto excluded from public life. He thought of revolution as something to be arranged by persons already active in political affairs.

Yet he could be realistic in his observations, and was certainly no enthusiast or doctrinaire. His reports are notable for their unimpassioned analysis, the reverse of the ideological, the work of a predominantly intellectual type of man, who sought calmly to weigh the forces at work, and to make reasonable forecasts of the future. It is this practical purpose that we must keep in mind when we speak of his political moderation. If he disapproved of the Dutch Democrats, and thought them dangerously extreme, it was largely because he thought that extremism would provoke reaction, weaken the Patriot coalition, and ruin the Patriot cause. If he thought the French would have a good constitution if they aimed at very little, if as late as the end of 1788 he thought the Estates-General should insist on nothing more than some control of taxation and a right to register proposed laws, it was because he thought that to ask more would consolidate the opposition to any change at all. We can comment on his moderation, if we like, and even on his timidity, at a time when many Frenchmen were getting into a mood to fight, but we cannot easily dismiss his judgment. He was perfectly right in foreseeing that conservative opposition, aroused by revolutionary demands, would make peaceable reformation impossible.

Jefferson's views before he left France must be described as tepid. When he embarked at Le Havre, in September, 1789, he was well to the right of the majority in the National Assembly. His hopes for the future were troubled with forebodings. Why then, after his return home, in the great crisis of 1793, did Jefferson emerge as the leading sympathizer with the French Revolution— the great American "Jacobin"? That he was, as his enemies now said, a visionary, a doctrinaire, a facile optimist, a naïve enthusiast for human perfectibility, or even much of a democrat, as democracy was already understood in Europe, I do not believe.

There may have been three reasons why our dubious democrat became the great American Jacobin. Indeed, the same three reasons may explain why many Frenchmen became Jacobins, properly so called. First, Jefferson did feel that liberty and equality, if and where possible, were desirable states of being. Second, it was his tendency, as with most people, to accept the accomplished fact, to adjust his ideas in correspondence with the rush of events, to doubt the feasibility of a thing before it occurred, and to accept and defend it after it had happened. Like Frenchmen, he thus accepted the French Republic: perhaps a measure of liberty and equality was possible, after all. Third, he saw the conflict in Europe in 1793 as a conflict of real forces. He did not see the issue, as conservatives then did and still do, as a choice between anarchy and order, or between political metaphysics and political wisdom, or between godless human presumption and Christian civilization. He had learned the hard way himself, and even against his natural inclinations, that hereditary aristocracy was the ultimate issue in the French Revolution. He had found France virtually unanimous—nation, clergy and army—against the claims of the nobility in July of 1789. He thought that in 1793 the Revolution was simply opposed by Counterrevolution, and that the Counterrevolution consisted of elements of the old French aristocracy, the Continental monarchies, the European nobilities and patriciates, the wealthy and privileged classes everywhere, the ecclesiastical hierarchies and the Parliamentary oligarchy of Great Britain. No one who has read Jefferson's letters from France could imagine that he thought all the measures taken during the French Revolution to be wise, even those taken at the very beginning. But he compared the wisdom or unwisdom of the French, not with perfect wisdom, but with the wisdom then exhibited by living and actual opponents of developments in France. Given the choice as he saw it, he chose to take sides with the Revolution.

MERRILL D. PETERSON

✪

Thomas Jefferson and Commercial Policy, 1783–1793

On December 16, 1793, just two weeks before he resigned the office of Secretary of State, Thomas Jefferson submitted to Congress his Report on the Privileges and Restrictions on the Commerce of the United States in Foreign Countries.[1] The Report had a curious history. It was made in compliance with a resolution of the House of Representatives in February, 1791. Jefferson worked it up in the ensuing months and planned to present it when Congress convened in the fall; but his colleague in the Treasury Department, Alexander Hamilton, opposed it "violently," thinking the threat of commercial warfare on Great Britain, which the Report carried, would wreck the negotiations then in process with the British Minister. Jefferson agreed to defer the Report.[2] It lapsed into the catalepsy of the British negotiations. A year passed; Jefferson revised the Report and prepared to submit it at

[1] The Report will be found in Paul L. Ford, ed., *The Writings of Thomas Jefferson* (New York, 1892–1899), VI, 470–484. The best study of the background and the circumstances surrounding the Report is Vernon G. Setser, *The Commercial Reciprocity Policy of the United States, 1774–1829* (Philadelphia, 1937), Chap. 4 especially.

[2] The Anas, March 11, 1792, *Writings of Thomas Jefferson* (Ford ed.), I, 186–187.

Reprinted from *The William and Mary Quarterly*, 3rd. Ser., Vol. XXII (1965), pp. 584–610, by permission.

the close of the Second Congress in February, 1793. But the timing troubled him. His recommendations would almost certainly get a better hearing from the Third Congress, more heavily freighted with Republicans, and in the interim the new French Minister would have an opportunity to present the attractive commercial propositions he was thought to be bringing from Paris, thus strengthening the Secretary's case for differential treatment of the commerce of Britain and France. The Republican leadership in the House, prodded by Jefferson, decided not to call for the Report.[3] Edmond Genêt did, indeed, propose a new and liberal treaty of commerce; but the circumstances of European war and American neutrality, combined with the Minister's own monumental ineptitude, put the project out of the way of serious discussion. Urgent problems of neutrality usurped the place previously occupied by the long-range problems of peacetime commerce. A discriminatory commercial policy was one thing in 1792, when the leading maritime powers were at peace; it was another thing in 1793, when they were at war. For it must then, whether founded in treaty or in statute, have the color of an unneutral act. Moreover, the injuries complained of by the United States as a neutral were different from the injuries to American trade in a world at peace. In the waning hours of his ministry, Jefferson must have pondered what to do with his twice deferred Report on Commerce. He finally decided to submit it, without further revision, based upon the conditions of American commerce in the year 1792.

It was a gesture of summation. The Report culminated a decade of unremitting labor to develop a national system of political economy independent of Britain, tied to France, and directed ultimately to a reign of free exchange and pacific intercourse among nations. This was, Jefferson had come to insist, "my system,"[4] and it was directly at odds with the fiscal system of the Secretary of the Treasury. The Report rested on a body of assump-

3 Jefferson to the Speaker of the House, February 20, 1793, Andrew A. Lipscomb and Albert Ellery Bergh, eds., *The Writings of Thomas Jefferson* (Washington, 1903–1904), IX, 31–32.

4 Jefferson to George Washington, September 9, 1792, *Writings of Thomas Jefferson* (Ford ed.), VI, 103.

tions Jefferson had never fully articulated, and only suggested here, but which can be pieced together from his private letters, diplomatic correspondence, and other papers written over a period of years.

The subject, broadly stated, is the relationship of the American economy to the European world. As an agricultural-commercial nation, its internal trade undeveloped, its industrial base exceedingly narrow, the United States must cherish its navigation, penetrate foreign markets, and seek its economic well-being in the transatlantic trading area. Economic policy is inseparable from foreign policy. Trade is a weapon of diplomacy—the only potent weapon in the American armory—to be employed in pursuit of the national interest, including in that term not only the security and independence of the United States but also the widening acceptance of liberal commercial principles in the international community. "Instead of embarrassing commerce under piles of regulating laws, duties, and prohibitions," Jefferson wrote, "could it be relieved from all its shackles in all parts of the world, could every country be employed in producing that which nature has best fitted it to produce, and each be free to exchange with others mutual surpluses for mutual wants, the greatest mass possible would then be produced of those things which contribute to human life and human happiness; the numbers of mankind would be increased, and their condition bettered."[5]

Ideally, trade should be free; in fact it is burdened with monopolies and restrictions injurious to the United States and to the peace and happiness of mankind. In his Report Jefferson described these burdens, nation by nation, and drew up the balance sheet of American maritime commerce. France appeared as America's best friend. With republican France, though she was deeply troubled, the "system of free commerce" might be fairly begun. Britain appeared as the monstrous enemy. She supplied three quarters of American imports, took one half of our exports, re-exported the greater part, prohibited what she pleased, monopolized the navigation, and left everything at the hazard of executive decree. British command of American commerce held the nation on its tether. To

[5] Report on Commerce, *ibid.*, VI, 479.

break this dangerous connection, Jefferson proposed counter prohibitions, regulations, and duties, working reciprocally on all nations but in the necessity of the case working hardest on Britain. The inconveniences attending the introduction of this plan "are nothing when weighed against the loss of wealth and loss of force, which will follow our perseverance in the plan of indiscrimination." "Free commerce and navigation are not to be given in exchange for restrictions and vexations," Jefferson declared, "nor are they likely to produce a relaxation of them."[6] But by granting favors where favors were due, by meeting prohibitions with prohibitions, the United States might, in the course of serving its own interest, bring other nations to the liberal standard.

The sequel to the Report on Commerce is well known. This piece of unfinished business might have attracted little notice but for renewed British violence on the seas. Falling in with the turn of events, the Report set off a great Congressional debate. In January, James Madison, Jefferson's collaborator in this enterprise as in so many others, introduced a series of resolutions based on the Report.[7] France was stamped on their face, the Federalists charged. The movement for commercial discrimination stemmed from the old unreasoning hostility to Britain, revived now solely for political effect. Hamilton's spokesman in the House, William Loughton Smith of South Carolina, decried "the impracticability and Quixotism of an attempt by violence, on the part of this young country, to break through the fetters which the universal policy of nations imposes on their intercourse with each other."[8] Whatever the disadvantages of the British trade, Federalists said, they were more than offset by the rewards in capital and credit, federal revenue, and dependable markets and supplies. But as relations with Britain deteriorated, chances for passage of the resolutions improved. Then, unfortunately for the Republicans, the deterioration was too rapid, bringing the two countries to the verge of war,

---

[6] *Ibid.,* VI, 479, 483, 480.

[7] For the resolutions and debate, see U.S., Congress, 3d Congress, 1st session, in Joseph Gales, comp., *The Debates and Proceedings in the Congress of the United States . . .* (Washington, 1834–1856), IV, 155 ff.; hereafter cited as *Annals of Congress.*

[8] January 13, 1794, *ibid.,* IV, 196.

causing the resolutions to be put aside in favor of an emergency embargo, and leading finally to the mission of John Jay, whose famous treaty consummated the British-centered policy of the Federalists—an astounding defeat for the Jeffersonian system.

The Report of 1793 led nowhere: it was epilogue rather than prologue. Never fairly put to the test, the Jeffersonian policy can only be appraised in the light of antecedent experience. While the underlying principle of this policy had been widely shared by America's leaders, with only shadings of difference, from the Revolution until the inauguration of the Hamiltonian system, no one had been so long or so deeply committed to it as Thomas Jefferson. It had given coherence and direction to all his work and thought on national affairs during the previous decade. How he came to this conception of commercial policy, the difficulties he encountered, the successive phases through which it passed before the eclipse of 1794, is an important but often neglected chapter in the early history of the American nation.

When Jefferson entered Congress in 1783 the prospects of American commerce, perforce of American wealth and power, were very uncertain. From the first, the hopes of the new nation had been tied to the kite of commercial freedom. The United States stood ready to trade freely with all comers who would recognize its independence and enter into liberal treaties. "Our plan is commerce," *Common Sense* had declared, "and that, well attended to, will secure us the peace and friendship of all Europe; because it is the interest of all Europe to have America as a free port. Her trade will always be a protection. . . ."[9] Acting on this calculation, Congress, in 1776, adopted the "plan of treaties."[10] It failed of conspicuous success except in the case of France, where, however, the treaty of commerce was coupled with a treaty of alliance involving political commitments inconsistent with the "commerce

[9] Philip S. Foner, ed., *The Complete Writings of Thomas Paine* (New York, 1945), I, 20.

[10] See the discussions in Setser, Chap. 2, and Felix Gilbert, *To The Farewell Address: Ideas of Early American Foreign Policy* (Princeton, 1961), Chap. 3.

only" principle of the "plan of treaties." That plan, for all the troubles it encountered, was the natural offspring of the union between revolutionary necessity and revolutionary aspiration. Seen in the light of the policies of nations, rather than of their forms of government, the American Revolution announced the dissolution of mercantilism and the liberation of trade, together with a new openness, trust, and pacific temper in all dealings among nations. It was this emphasis on commercial freedom that made the revolutionary event and the simultaneous publication of *The Wealth of Nations* something more than a coincidence; that gave substance to the Earl of Shelburne's abortive project for a commercial union between Britain and the United States at the conclusion of the war; and that conveyed the message of the American Revolution to many enlightened Europeans who, while they valued commercial freedom, either had little use or little hope for republican government.[11]

The "plan of treaties" was the first lineal ancestor of Jefferson's 1793 Report on Commerce. He had no responsibility for it, of course, and had not thought much on commercial questions before he returned to Congress after an absence of seven years; but he was in complete accord with the spirit of the standing policy. With the conclusion of the war, it was thought that nations that had been reluctant to treat with a rebel government would be eager to treat with a legitimate one whose only interest was mutual trade and profit. To take advantage of these friendly dispositions, Congress had appointed a three-man European Commission. Jefferson was soon engaged in drafting a report on their work and revising their instructions.[12] The undertaking had assumed a new impor-

[11] See, in general, Vincent T. Harlow, *The Founding of the Second British Empire, 1763–1793*, I (London, 1952); Richard Koebner, *Empire* (Cambridge, Eng., 1961); and Carl Ludwig Lokke, *France and the Colonial Question: A Study of Contemporary French Opinion, 1763–1801* (New York, 1932).

[12] Report on Letters from the American Ministers in Europe [December 20, 1783], and Instructions to the Commissioners for Negotiating Treaties of Amity and Commerce, May 7, 1784, Julian P. Boyd and others, eds., *The Papers of Thomas Jefferson* (Princeton, 1950–), VI, 393–400; VII, 266–271.

tance. Lacking the old privileges of trade within the empire, the Americans, in 1783, had secured few privileges of trade outside of it, and so they suffered the same colonial dependence as before the Revolution. It became increasingly evident that Britain, though she had lost the colonies, was determined to hold the Americans in commercial vassalage. The Earl of Sheffield demonstrated how easily it could be done.[13] Exploit the feebleness of the Confederacy. Exploit the British merchants' mastery of the American market. Above all, destroy the American carrying trade by imposing the navigation law that had nurtured its growth within the imperial system. The crippling blow fell in July, 1783. An order in council excluded American ships from the British West Indies; and this, together with the restoration of old restrictions in the French and Spanish colonies, closed off the most profitable branch of American trade.[14]

There were several possible lines of attack on the problem, and in different contexts Jefferson advocated all of them. When moral and political considerations were foremost in his mind, he held up the ideal of a hermit nation. "Were I to indulge my own theory," he wrote characteristically, "I should wish them [the Americans] to practice neither commerce nor navigation, but to stand with respect to Europe precisely on the footing of China. We should thus avoid wars, and all our citizens would be husbandmen." He thus expressed his sense of the unique opportunities of American society, which modified the orthodox canons of European political economy. "But this is theory only," he hastened to add, "and a theory which the servants of America are not at liberty to follow."[15] Foreign commerce was a necessity, all the more so if America stuck to its agricultural calling; and he never let the dreamy ideal control his search for a viable system of political

---

[13] Earl of Sheffield [John Baker Holroyd], *Observations on the Commerce of the United States* . . . (London, 1783).

[14] See, in general, Merrill Jensen, *The New Nation: A History of the United States During the Confederation, 1781–1789* (New York, 1950), Chap. 7; and Curtis P. Nettels, *The Emergence of a National Economy, 1775–1815* (New York, 1962), Chap. 3.

[15] Jefferson to G. K. van Hogendorp, October 13, 1785, Boyd, VIII, 633.

economy. A variation on the insular approach looked to the development of internal commerce. The Americans are peculiarly blessed and have no need of foreign commerce, no cause to incur its vices, enmities, and debaucheries, Richard Price counseled in 1784. "They are spread over a great continent, and they make a world within themselves."[16] The English radical was gifted with prophecy. In time the Americans would realize the conception of a great home market—"a world within itself"—but few had as much as a glimpse of it in 1784. Jefferson was a warm advocate of internal commerce; he was thinking a good deal about it at this time in connection with Virginia's efforts to open arteries of trade with the trans-Allegheny West. Yet, like nearly everyone else, he regarded inland commerce as an accessory of foreign commerce.[17] Still another strategy called for the creation of a counteracting system of mercantilist restrictions in the United States. Jefferson was not averse to retaliatory measures of this kind. In the condition of American affairs he did not believe trade should be left to regulate itself, though that was his theoretical preference of course. He helped to draft the Congressional address of April 30, 1784, recommending that the states "vest Congress with so much power over their commerce as will enable them to retaliate on any nation who may wish to grasp it on unequal terms; and to enable them . . . to pass something like the British navigation act."[18] The Confederacy must be strengthened primarily, in his opinion, for the purpose of regulating foreign commerce. But the states held back, preventing a truly national system, and regulation by the states severally raised more problems than it solved. Madison and some other nationalists inclined to believe that so long as the vacuum of commercial power existed in the Confederacy there was really nothing to do but fill it.[19] Jefferson, always sanguine, did

[16] Richard Price, *Observations on the Importance of the American Revolution, and the Means of Making It a Benefit to the World* (London, 1784), p. 62.

[17] See Jefferson to George Washington, March 15, 1784, Boyd, VII, 25–27; and the observations in Joseph Dorfman, *The Economic Mind in American Civilization* (New York, 1946–1949), I, 248–251.

[18] Jefferson to Horatio Gates, May 7, 1784, Boyd, VII, 225.

[19] James Madison to Jefferson, April 25, 1784, and the note on Jay's attitude, *ibid.*, VII, 123, 470.

not—not yet anyway—take this desperate view. Although the front door to commercial regulations was closed, the back door was already opened. In its power to make treaties the United States could act as "one Nation,"[20] and so acting not only develop its commercial system but strengthen the bonds of Union as well. On May 7, 1784, Jefferson was appointed to the European Commission, replacing John Jay. At the same time Congress approved the revised instructions he had had a hand in drafting and would soon convey to the other commissioners, Benjamin Franklin and John Adams, in Paris. These instructions, more explicit than any to precede them, carried forward the liberal policy with some modifications. The plan was founded on the principle of the "most favored nation," which only offered a guarantee against treatment *less* favorable than was accorded another nation. The principle was European, far short of the American objective, as stated in previous instructions, of "the most perfect equality and reciprocity."[21] Although the Commission was authorized to go as far toward the ultimate goal as conditions might permit, it was recognized that the "most favored nation" formula offered the only realistic starting point for negotiations. Mercantilist prejudice and practice, deeply embedded in the European states, had to be reckoned with. Jefferson willingly accepted this concession to expediency, yet was steady in his pursuit of the goal. With respect to the American colonies of European nations, however, trade was to be put on a reciprocal basis if at all possible; at the very least United States ships and productions should be admitted into direct trade with these possessions. This was asking a good deal when scarcely a foreign port in the Western Hemisphere was open to American vessels. Other provisions covered the rights of enemy aliens and neutral carriers in time of war—matters of pacific and humanitarian import under the law of nations, in which Jefferson built on the work already begun by Franklin.

[20] For the use of this phrase, see the Report of December 20, 1783, and the Instructions of May 1784, previously cited, *ibid.*, VI, 394; VII, 267; and Jefferson's Notes for Consideration of the Commissioners, VII, 478–479.

[21] Cf. Instructions of October 29, 1783, with those of May 7, 1784, *ibid.*, VII, 265, 267.

Congress authorized commercial treaties with sixteen European states, as well as the Barbary powers. The decision to pursue this general European plan was of considerable importance. Freedom from British domination was to be found in the widening of markets. A strong minority in Congress, primarily New England men, advocated a different approach, one which would give precedence to a commercial treaty with Britain. The restoration of the British trade to something like its old footing was so vital, in their opinion, that it should not be complicated with other matters infinitely less important; and no doubt some objected to the European plan because it would pivot on France, thereby increasing that nation's influence in American affairs.[22] Jefferson opposed the re-establishment of a partial connection with Britain, even assuming, in the face of mounting evidence to the contrary, the London government was amenable. He was well aware of the importance of a British treaty both for itself and for the over-all plan, for if Britain could be drawn into the paths of progress, other nations would likely follow.[23] But Britain must come on the terms of the European-wide plan. Nor did Jefferson favor a preferential status for France. "Our interest calls for a perfect equality in our conduct towards these two nations," he wrote to Adams in 1785, "but no preferences any where."[24] He envisioned the French treaty not as a new axis of American commerce replacing the discredited British one, but rather as the point of departure for the creation of a far-flung system.

It was an incredibly ambitious undertaking: nothing less than a diplomatic mission to convert all Europe to the commercial principles of the American Revolution. The end in view was a system of purely economic relations with foreign states, which, being based on the exchange of mutual surpluses for mutual wants, need not plunge the United States into the blood-drenched rivalries of the Old World or, alternately, force the country into isolation and penury. Clearly, however, the end could not be reached along

22 See the editorial commentary, *ibid.,* VII, 466–469.
23 Jefferson to Edmund Pendleton, December 16, 1783, *ibid.,* VI, 386–387.
24 Jefferson to John Adams, September 24, 1785, *ibid.,* VIII, 545.

purely commercial lines. In order to overcome mercantilism it was first necessary to play the mercantilist game and exploit trade as a political weapon. Although no threats were issued, it was well understood—Congress had so declared—that nations declining to enter into treaty relations with the United States would be liable to discriminatory regulations in the American market and would, of course, be denied other valuable privileges in peace and in war. How much these considerations could be made to count in the European balance of power depended on the progress of reform at home. In the end, however, every nation, on a rational view of its own interest, must see the advantages of entering the American consortium.

Unfortunately, most of the European courts met the American overtures with colossal indifference. As Jefferson later recalled the experience: "They seemed, in fact, to know little about us, but as rebels, who had been successful in throwing off the yoke of the mother country. They were ignorant of our commerce, which had always been monopolized by England, and of the exchange of articles it might offer advantageously to both parties."[25] In the two years allotted to the Commission, only one European negotiation, with Prussia, on the model treaty drafted by Jefferson, was successfully concluded.[26] (A treaty was also concluded with Morocco, but that is another story.) Frustrated and discouraged, Jefferson began to question the practical wisdom of the system of treaties.

His reappraisal focused on two points. First, since it was "indispensably necessary" to gain access to the West Indies, treaties with the several colonial powers were of first importance. "Yet how to gain it," he reflected, "when it is the established system of these nations to exclude all foreigners from their colonies. The only chance seems to be this. Our commerce to the mother countries is valuable to them. We must endeavor then to make this the price of an admission into their West Indies, and to those who refuse the admission we must refuse our commerce or load theirs

[25] *Autobiography of Thomas Jefferson* (New York, 1959), p. 75.
[26] On the Prussian treaty, see the editorial note and the documents collected in Boyd, VII, 463–493, 615–628, and VIII, 26–33.

by odious discriminations in our ports."[27] The privilege of free trade with the mother countries would be attractive, he thought; but it would be no privilege at all, he came to realize, if every piddling kingdom in Europe could claim it on the ordinary ground of the "most favored nation." The change of tactics met with no greater success. Of the colonial powers only France and Portugal (for a brief time) showed the slightest disposition to lower commercial barriers. Months before their commissions expired, Jefferson and Adams were actually shunning the advances, earlier invited, of nations like Austria. Jefferson expressed the dilemma to John Jay, Secretary of Foreign Affairs: "Our instructions are clearly to treat. But these made part of a system, wise and advantageous if executed in all it's parts, but which has hitherto failed in it's most material branch, that of connection with the powers having American territory."[28]

The second part of the reappraisal concerned the home front. Jefferson had said, more than once, "that my primary object in the formation of treaties is to take the commerce of the states out of the hands of the states, and to place it under the superintendance of Congress, so far as the imperfect provisions of our constitution will admit, and until the states shall by new compact make them more perfect."[29] It is difficult to believe that this was the "primary object," that the treaty-making in Europe was an elaborate shadow-play screening consolidation at home. Yet consolidation was certainly one of Jefferson's calculations. He had written into the Commission's instructions the article declaring the United States to be "one Nation" toward others: an implicit denial of state authority so far as American commerce was covered by treaties. Not only was he a firm friend of national authority in this sphere, but, regarding frequent war as the inevitable price of commercial power, he pleaded for the establishment of an American navy and always underscored the value of trade and navigation as resources of national defense.[30] He began to question, however, whether the

---

[27] Jefferson to James Monroe, June 17, 1785, *ibid.,* VIII, 232.

[28] Jefferson to John Jay, January 27, 1786, *ibid.,* IX, 235.

[29] Jefferson to James Monroe, June 17, 1785, *ibid.,* VIII, 231.

[30] Jefferson to John Jay, August 23, 1785, *ibid.,* VIII, 426–427; Report on Commerce, *Writings of Thomas Jefferson* (Ford ed.), VI, 480.

approach to national strength and dignity by way of the back door was sound. In 1785 several of the states were pushing their own commercial systems; and while Jefferson applauded any retaliatory laws against British monopoly, he also reckoned their damage to the idea of "one Nation."[31] Earlier he had seen the plan of treaties as a means, however imperfect, of arming the Union. Now he stressed the limitations of this plan and wondered if it should not be abandoned for the frontal attack of nationalists like Madison and Jay. "My letters from members of Congress render it doubtful," he wrote Adams, "whether they would not rather that full time should be given for the present disposition of America to mature itself, . . . rather than, by removing the incentive, to prevent the improvement."[32] He was soon advocating coercion of the states, if need be, to strengthen the Confederacy.[33] This greater realism in no way dimmed his vision of friendly intercourse among nations, which drew him on even as he struggled for solutions within the limits of circumstance.

With the failure of the general European plan, Jefferson turned his attention to the development of a Franco-American commercial axis. In part, the change of direction was a natural result of the position he now occupied, Minister Plenipotentiary to France, succeeding Franklin in 1785. But it also stemmed from the conviction, soon firmly implanted in Jefferson's mind, that France held the key to America's commercial problem. The British monopoly could be overthrown, the main avenues of American trade shifted to France and her colonies, if Versailles would abolish antiquated regulations, open the ports to American productions, and pay for them in manufactures, oils, wines, tropical produce, and other articles. France had everything to gain. Her hopes of permanently displacing Britain in the American market as a result of the war had been cruelly disappointed; but the commercial war was still on, in Jefferson's opinion, and France might yet succeed.

[31] Jefferson to John Bannister, August 16, 1785, and to John Adams, November 19, 1785, Boyd, VIII, 393; IX, 42–43.
[32] Jefferson to John Adams, September 24, 1785, ibid., VIII, 545.
[33] Jefferson to John Adams, October 3, 1785, ibid., VIII, 579–580.

The Vergennes ministry hated Britain, a hatred that played into Jefferson's hand, and he did not have to look far in the French capital—to Americanists like Lafayette, to physiocrats like Dupont, to philosophes like Condorcet, even to Vergennes himself —for men of influence who sympathized with the commercial goals of the American Revolution.[34] As for the United States, the infant prodigy needed France's friendship. War was an ever-present danger, especially with Britain. Aside from the economic benefits of a strong commercial union, it would undergird the treaty of alliance. "It will be a strong link of connection," Jefferson said, "the more [so] with the only nation on earth on whom we can solidly rely for assistance till we stand on our own legs."[35] He no longer talked of "perfect equality" of commerce with the two great European powers. To be sure, every improvement in Franco-American relations was so much additional leverage for working on Britain; but neither he, in Paris, nor Adams, in London, had much hope that the British could soon be moved. "Nothing will bring them to reason but physical obstruction, applied to their bodily senses," Jefferson said; and his experience during a visit to England in the spring of 1786 only served to deepen this conviction.[36] Unable to obtain equal terms from Britain, unable as yet to apply that "physical obstruction," the prudent course for the United States was to connect its commerce unequivocally to France.

When Jefferson took up commercial diplomacy at Versailles in the later months of 1785, the French economy was depressed, the mercantile community was still reeling from the disaster of its first peacetime venture in the American market, and the government was hard put to defend the limited concession it had a year earlier made to American trade in the West Indies. The circumstances

[34] Louis Gottschalk, *Lafayette Between the American and the French Revolution, 1783–1789* (Chicago, 1950), is particularly informative on this subject. See also Dumas Malone, *Jefferson and the Rights of Man* (Boston, 1951).

[35] Jefferson to Ralph Izard, November 18, 1786, Boyd, X, 541–542.

[36] Jefferson to James Madison, March 18, 1785, and to R. H. Lee, April 22, 1786, *ibid.*, VIII, 40; IX, 398.

demanded caution all around.[37] In the ministry's view, the Americans seemed irrevocably attached to English merchandise and English commercial practices. Jefferson combatted these ideas, saying "that were national Prejudice alone listened to, our Trade would quit England and come to France."[38] The difficulty, he insisted, was the inability of the Americans to trade directly and make exchanges in the French market. The remedy was no less obvious: the eradication of monopoly and restriction in France. Of course, this was not the whole of the problem. As a Virginian, himself deeply in debt to British merchants, Jefferson knew all too well that the chains of bondage were the invisible chains of credit.[39] The French merchants, not as adventuresome as their British counterparts, unaccustomed to advancing credit and trading on consignment, lacking established connections in American ports, were necessarily at a disadvantage. Diplomacy alone would not slay the hydra of British credit, nor could Jefferson change the conservative habits of French merchants, though he tried. Commercial restrictions were more readily assailed, and Jefferson centered his efforts on opening the French market to direct trade in American productions.

Tobacco, America's leading export, was substance and essence of the entire proceeding. France took large quantities of this commodity but granted a monopoly in its importation to the Farmers-General, the powerful company to which His Majesty's government "farmed out" the collection of several indirect taxes and customs duties, including the lucrative tobacco duty. The Farmers-General was interwoven with the French system of finance—ministers tampered with it at their peril and the peril of

[37] For Jefferson's observations, see the letters to Elbridge Gerry, May 11, 1785, James Monroe, June 17, 1785, and John Adams, November 19, 1785, *ibid.*, VIII, 142–143, 228–229; IX, 42–43. George V. Taylor, "Problems of an Immature Economy: France in the 1780's," a paper read at the annual meeting of the Southern Historical Association, November 13, 1964, in Asheville, N.C., focuses on the industrial crisis which struck in the later months of 1786. I am indebted to this paper and also to suggestions made by Mr. Taylor in correspondence with me.

[38] Jefferson's Report on Conversations with Vergennes [December 1785], Boyd, IX, 139.

[39] Jefferson to Nathaniel Tracy, August 17, 1785, *ibid.*, VIII, 399.

the treasury—yet any attempt to free the market for American commerce must begin with an attack on the tobacco monopoly. Jefferson made a persuasive case for its abolition. The Americans, he argued, are reluctant to enter a market where there is but one buyer, who sets the price, and that buyer one who does not engage in mercantile exchange but pays in coin, which is promptly remitted to Britain, thus supporting the industry of the common enemy. "By prohibiting all His Majesty's subjects from dealing in tobacco except with a single company," Jefferson said, "one third of the exports of the United States are rendered uncommerciable here. . . . A relief from these shackles will form a memorable epoch in the commerce of the two nations. It will establish at once a great basis of exchange, serving like a point of union to draw to it other members of our commerce. . . . Each nation has exactly to spare the articles which the other wants. . . . The governments have nothing to do but *not to hinder* their merchants from making the exchange."[40]

Actually, as Jefferson soon learned, the tobacco monopoly had not one but two heads; for the Farmers-General had awarded to Robert Morris an exclusive three-year contract for the supply of American tobacco. European monopoly had straddled the Atlantic, with predictable consequences for tobacco prices and ominous forebodings for American freedom. The combined efforts of Jefferson, Lafayette, and others led Vergennes to appoint the so-called American Committee to study and recommend measures for the promotion of Franco-American trade, starting with tobacco. As a result of the Committee's work, the Morris monopoly was broken, a highly beneficial measure even if it did not go to the root of monopoly in France; and some months later, in October, 1786, the government announced a host of concessions to American commerce and navigation, freeing exports as well as imports, lowering bars in France as well as in the Antilles. It was another fourteen months before this "ultimate settlement" obtained the force of law.[41] The delay, so vexatious to Jefferson and his friends, was

[40] Jefferson to Montmorin, July 23, 1787, *ibid.*, XI, 617.
[41] The concessions are set forth in a letter from Calonne, the Comptroller General, to Jefferson, October 22, 1786, *ibid.*, X, 474–478. The final decree of December 29, 1787, appears *ibid.*, XII, 468–470. The negotiations are covered in Gottschalk, Chaps. 15–17.

perhaps to be expected. For the decree, when it finally came, presaged a virtual revolution in the French commercial system.

As Jefferson said, the tobacco trade was to be the "point of union" for a flourishing commerce in many articles of American industry. The next most important of these were train oil and rice, one so vital to the New England economy, the other to South Carolina and Georgia. The whale fishery had not recovered from the damage wrecked by the Revolution. Britain levied prohibitive duties on American whale oil and under elaborate subsidy built up her own fishery. Between the two fisheries, France held the balance; but instead of freely admitting the American supply, France labored against enormous odds and at heavy fiscal sacrifice to revive her own fishery, succeeding only in further impoverishing the American and enriching the British. The intimate connection between fisheries and sea power gave the issue an importance that transcended economics. "Is it not better then," Jefferson pleaded, "by keeping her ports open to the U.S. to enable them to aid in maintaining the field against the common adversary . . . ? Otherwise her supplies must aliment that very force which is keeping her under."[42] All that was needed was an order excluding *European* oil from France. The decree of December, 1787, had gone some way toward this objective, only to be followed by a reaction against which Jefferson struggled for many months. He finally triumphed. In December, 1788, France gave the American, together with the French oil, a monopoly of the market.[43] How the arrangement advanced the "freedom of trade" he had started out to promote, Jefferson did not explain; but it was a great stride toward Franco-American partnership. Versailles threw itself into the scales of American power against Britain, and despite formidable political and mercantile opposition left French industry to the hazard of American competition.

The American Minister's campaign in behalf of American rice reveals still another side of his commercial diplomacy. Rice exports were less than one half the prewar figures. Britain continued to dominate the trade—a highly profitable re-export trade on her part—through the controls of debt and credit and the excellent

---

[42] *Observations on the Whale Fishery* (1788), Boyd, XIV, 249.
[43] The *Arrêt* of December 7, 1788, appears *ibid.*, XIV, 268–269.

facilities of the entrepôt at Cowes. The French, on the other hand, merely ate rice, some of it American, but the exacting requirements of the cuisine gave a preference to the Mediterranean variety. Having no desire to reform the cuisine, the American Minister tried rather to educate the Carolinians in the cultivation and preparation of rice suited to the French palate. The lengths he went, even smuggling Piedmont seed across the Appenines, proved the ardor of his commitment. In addition, and despite the disappointing returns from American voyages generally, Jefferson induced solid French houses to enter the Carolina rice trade. The venture was not entirely a happy one on either side; but the Carolinians were deeply grateful to him, and far more ships and casks of rice cleared the Charleston customshouse for France in 1789 than ever before.[44]

On the whole, however, Jefferson's labors to build a Franco-American commercial system were out of all proportion to the results obtained. After five years, the French Revolution intervened, disrupting further progress along the lines he had laid out. The available statistics on the trade between the two nations during this period point to several conclusions. First, the total volume of the trade, though there were ups and downs in key articles, fluctuated little and was about the same at the end of the period as it was at the beginning. Second, the trade with the West Indies greatly exceeded the direct trade with the mother country. And third, in both branches, the Americans had much the better of it. The balance of trade in the island commerce favored the United States on a ratio of nearly two to one, the direct trade on a ratio of perhaps five or six to one.[45] A bonanza for the Americans, the trade was a small disaster for the French.

What, then, becomes of Jefferson's constant plea for markets? Obviously, it did not go to the heart of the problem. Jefferson

44 The episode may be traced in Jefferson to Ralph Izard, August 1, 1787, Edward Rutledge to Jefferson, October 23, 1787, April 1, 1789, and Brailsford and Morris to Jefferson, October 31, 1787, March 10, 1789, *ibid.,* XI, 659; XII, 263–264, 298–301; XIV, 633; XV, 12–13.

45 Edmund Buron, "Statistics on Franco-American Trade, 1778–1806," *Journal of Economic and Business History,* IV (1931–1932), 571–580. An article based on these figures is John F. Stover, "French-American Trade during the Confederation, 1781–1789," *North Carolina Historical Review,* XXXV (1958), 399–414.

naturally fixed his attention on obstacles to American imports to
the neglect of France's difficulties in making exchanges for them.
He knew very well that an enduring commerce between the two
countries must be more or less equal in its benefits; and near the
end of his ministry especially, he was urging the French to look
beyond the luxury trade in wines and brandies, silks and linens,
and to adapt their industry more deliberately to the American
market.[46] But French industry was sluggish and inefficient; the
Anglo-French commercial accord of 1786 flooded the market with
English goods, in the process drowning many merchants and
manufacturers; and in the deepening depression of the following
years capital was simply not available for the improvements
Jefferson had in mind.[47] At any rate, though he did not fully
appreciate it, the difficulty of his system was less one of French
markets than of French supplies. By 1789 the markets were open
to an astonishing degree, largely due to Jefferson's efforts and the
influence of American commercial ideology at Versailles; and the
Americans exploited these markets, then transferred most of the
money balance in their favor to the support of British industry.
This was certainly not what Jefferson, or the French government,
intended. And even as liberal commercial policy gained in favor,
the country's merchants, manufacturers, *fabricants,* and shop-
keepers who were losing by it moved toward reaction and revolution. The American Minister had little contact with the bourgeoi-
sie. He moved in a restricted circle, the enlightened nobility for the
most part—friends of agriculture and free trade, of America and
republicanism—and so it is not surprising that some of the most
disturbing realities of the French economy eluded him. Some years
later, when these realities were more obvious, Gouverneur Morris,
who succeeded Jefferson at Versailles, passed the sophisticated
skeptic's slur, *visionary,* on the Jeffersonian plan of direct commerce between France and the United States.[48]

[46] See, for instance, *Observations on the Whale Fishery,* Boyd, XIV,
253.

[47] Taylor, "Problems of an Immature Economy."

[48] Gouverneur Morris to Robert Morris, March 7, 1791, in Beatrix Cary
Davenport, ed., *A Diary of the French Revolution, by Gouverneur Morris,
1752–1816* (Boston, 1939), II, 127–128.

The plan was, nevertheless, an important phase of Jefferson's, and America's, search for a sound commercial system. It was oriented to France primarily by virtue of its being against Britain. Britain was still the enemy in Jefferson's eyes, and so long as she dominated the American economy, national dignity and independence were more illusory than real. The advantages of direct trade with France and her dominions were self-evident from an economic standpoint. On moral and political grounds they appeared to be overwhelming, as a means of curbing British power and of multiplying ties of interest and affection with the only nation that deserved, or was likely to justify, American friendship. The true American policy toward foreign nations was one of perfect freedom and equality in trade and of strict political neutrality. Unfortunately, Jefferson reasoned from his own experience, the world was not ready for this policy. Young America must make the best commercial arrangements she could, and everything pointed to France, the proven friend and ally, as the best partner in a preferential system.

The French Revolution and the establishment of the new national government in the United States set the stage for the climactic phase of Jefferson's search. He returned home late in 1789 warmly attached to France and convinced that he had just witnessed in the momentous events there "the first chapter of the history of European liberty."[49] A free France was a more attractive partner than a despotic France. To the reasons the United States already had for alliance with France was now added union in the cause of freedom and self-government. And since monopolies and prohibitions would surely fall with the progress of European liberty, Jefferson expected the Revolution would clear the way for the promised new epoch of commercial freedom. In the United States the adoption of the Constitution made possible at last practical implementation of the national policy inaugurated in 1776. It was the responsibility of the new government to legislate the system that had heretofore floundered on the contingencies of treaties and could be but partially realized in diplomacy with a single foreign state. The commercial impotency of Congress had

49 Jefferson to Diodati, August 3, 1789, Boyd, XV, 326.

been a major factor producing the Constitutional Convention; now that Congress was well armed nearly everyone supposed it would act, indeed was obliged to act, in accordance with long-declared principles and aims. Alexander Hamilton stated the common sense of the matter in the eleventh paper of *The Federalist*. Under the new government an "active commerce" would replace a "passive commerce." "By prohibitory regulations, extending, at the same time, throughout the states, we may oblige foreign countries to bid against each other, for the privileges of our markets." Hamilton threatened the prospect of "excluding Great Britain . . . from all our ports," which could not fail to "produce a relaxation in her present system" and "would be likely to have a correspondent effect on the conduct of other nations."[50]

With these ideas and expectations, Jefferson entered upon his duties as Secretary of State in 1790. Next to the redemption and pacification of the West, the encouragement of foreign commerce was the leading object of his ministry. The two objects were not unrelated. In order to deal with the British in the Northwest and the Spanish in the Southwest, he needed a place to stand in European politics. The French alliance provided it.[51] The power to restrict or withhold American trade, especially in times of European war, was an instrument well-nigh indispensable to force Britain to honor American independence, commercial claims, and territorial integrity. Commerce was a minor consideration in negotiations with Spain, since it could be had only by abandonment of the American claim to free navigation of the Mississippi. After the controversy of 1786 on the abortive Jay-Gardoqui negotiation, Jefferson realized that the Western trade must flow, not eastward as he had earlier hoped and planned, but down the Mississippi, and to bargain away its navigation in exchange for privileges in Spanish ports was unthinkable.[52] Foreign commerce was a pri-

[50] *The Federalist* . . ., with an introduction by Edward Mead Earle (New York, [1941]), pp. 63–64.

[51] On the role of France in Jefferson's diplomacy, see especially Alexander de Conde, *Entangling Alliance: Politics & Diplomacy under George Washington* (Durham, 1958).

[52] See Jefferson's Report on Matters of Negotiation with Spain (March 7, 1792), *Writings of Thomas Jefferson* (Ford ed.), V, 441–449.

mary object only on condition that it served the interests of a growing Union.

The first attempt at commercial regulation, in the form of an American navigation act, had already been made when Jefferson took his post in New York. In the debate on the tonnage bill in the previous session, Madison had proposed a discrimination between the vessels of nations in and out of commercial treaty with the United States. But Congress had turned its back on this time-honored American principle and placed the trade of all foreign nations on the same footing.[53] Madison resumed the fight in 1790. Jefferson watched it closely, and from behind the scenes in the State Department worked to promote the discriminatory policy, which the Virginians always insisted was, in fact, one of reciprocity, since it only aimed to counter foreign restrictions, chiefly British, and would be altered as these restrictions fell. (Either term will do depending on the context: the policy called for discrimination on the just grounds of reciprocity.) A mixed majority in Congress—planters dependent on British ships and credit, importing merchants and shippers tied into the old channels of trade, Anglophiles, and Treasury men eying the abundant revenue collected on British tonnage and imports—defeated discrimination and renewed the original act.[54]

The French chargé d'affaires lodged a protest with the Secretary of State under threat of retaliation. Because the act placed the friendly commerce of France on the same basis as a commerce loaded with pains and penalties, it actually discriminated against France. Jefferson could not quarrel with the spirit of this protest, though he disagreed with Versailles's view that the law violated the letter, as well as the spirit, of the treaty of commerce. He faced a dilemma. If the United States conceded the tonnage exemption claimed by France under the treaty, it would be obliged to make the same concession to other countries with which it had "most favored nation" treaties. Yet the consequences of refusal, jeopar-

---

[53] The debate in the House is reported in 1st Congress, 1st session, *Annals of Congress*, I, 183–199, 294–302, *et passim*.

[54] The debate in the House is reported in 1st Congress, 2d session, *ibid.*, II, 1623–1635, 1712–1714.

dizing the position of American commerce in France, were equally
bad. He sought escape through an act of Congress that would
place French vessels on the footing of natives in consideration of
the favors granted by the royal decrees of 1787 and 1788. No
other nation would receive this remarkable privilege without similar concessions. Once again he was backing into a navigation
act.[55]

The Secretary of the Treasury opposed the recommendation. In
his opinion the proposed concession was too high a price to pay
for the favors France had granted, and it would excite unfriendly
feelings in Britain. Moreover, the fund from the tonnage law was
mortgaged to the payment of the public debt. "I feel a particular
reluctance," he said, "to hazard any thing in the present state of
our affairs which may lead to commercial warfare with any
power."[56] The Treasury coffers were filled with the revenue of
British trade. Until the United States could manufacture for itself,
Britain was its surest supplier, almost its only creditor, and its best
market. Hamilton was, therefore, despite earlier preachments to
the contrary, reconciled to the subordination implicit in the British
connection.

Jefferson had not expected to hear these opinions in the highest
quarters of the new government. He had clashed with Hamilton
before, but not on a major issue. This confrontation in the winter
of 1790–1791, a full month before the division of opinion on the
Bank, involved for Jefferson a fundamental question of national
policy. Should the United States push on toward the liberal
commercial goals of the American Revolution, or, trapped in the
web of debt, credit, and revenue, acquiesce in British maritime
dominion? Seeing the issue in this way, Jefferson also began to see
the larger implications of Hamilton's financial system. Indeed, for
the first time, Hamilton's different measures assumed in Jefferson's
mind the character of a system. It was permeated with fiscalism, of

[55] Report on Tonnage Law (January 18, 1791), *Writings of Thomas
Jefferson* (Ford ed.), V, 266–273.

[56] Hamilton to Jefferson, January 13, 1791, Harold Syrett and Jacob
Cooke, eds., *The Papers of Alexander Hamilton* (New York, 1961–   ),
VII, 426.

course; and from what he had seen of France and learned of Britain, fiscalism was the parent of monopoly and oppression. It was very partial in its distribution of benefits, enriching a few Eastern merchants and speculators, holding nothing material for Southern planters dependent on foreign markets, and, in general, checking the nation's agricultural expansion. In foreign affairs it tied the government into British politics. Despite new British attacks on American commerce, Jefferson wrote to James Monroe in April, 1791, the Treasury takes the line of "passive obedience and non-resistance, lest any misunderstanding with them should *affect our credit, or the prices of our public paper.*"[57] Jefferson was not indifferent to these fiscal considerations; but he believed that Hamilton, in making credit rather than commerce the engine of national power, drew the country into many evils.

Although the President backed Jefferson's recommendation on the tonnage law, it was defeated in the Senate, and he had to scramble with the French as best he could. As the year wore on, it became increasingly apparent that Franco-American commerce, instead of approaching a new epoch, was sliding back into an old one. The Revolution brought the merchants of the coastal cities to power in the National Assembly. They had never subscribed to liberal commercial ideas, and they considered the American trade a losing proposition, only made worse by the tonnage law. It was hard for Jefferson to believe that a liberal revolution could turn reactionary in commercial policy. The indisputable evidence came first on the article of tobacco. The Farmers-General was destroyed, but the Assembly imposed a discriminatory duty, nearly prohibitive, on tobacco carried in American bottoms. Jefferson was outraged. French nationalism seriously embarrassed his commercial diplomacy; yet he did not abandon it, and continued to press for the negotiation of a new and far-reaching commercial treaty which the National Assembly had earlier promised in the compassion evoked by Franklin's death.[58]

[57] Jefferson to James Monroe, April 17, 1791, *Writings of Thomas Jefferson* (Ford ed.), V, 319–320.
[58] See George F. Zook, "Proposals for a New Commercial Treaty Between France and the United States, 1778–1793," *South Atlantic Quarterly*, VIII (1909), 267–283.

The counterpart of the Secretary's advocacy of French commerce was his continued opposition to British commerce. Not long after the Report on the Tonnage Law, he sent to Congress his Report on the Cod and Whale Fisheries. The subject was familiar. He had become an expert on the whaling trade and whale oils, in particular, while in France. Now he marshaled the facts to show that the plight of the fisheries owed much to British bounties and restrictions. It could be overcome only by stiff counterregulations. The French, on the other hand, he praised as "cooperators against a common rival." "Nor is it the interest of the fisherman alone, which calls for the cultivation of friendly arrangements with that nation; besides five-eights of our whale oil, and two-thirds of our salted fish, they take from us one-fourth of our tobacco, three-fourths of our live stock . . . a considerable and growing portion of our rice, great supplies, occasionally, of other grain. . . ."[59] The contrast between British oppression and French liberality was unmistakable. The British consul in Philadelphia was not wrong in his estimate of Jefferson's Report: "designed," he said, "as the introduction of a series of proceedings calculated to promote measures very hostile to the commercial interests of Great Britain."[60] The cumulative impact of Jefferson's various reports on French and British affairs, together with a nudge by the President, led a committee of the House of Representatives to report a bill barring the importation of non-British goods in British vessels. Like previous essays at a navigation act, the bill was side-tracked. Congress, instead, referred the whole subject of commercial policy to the Secretary of State for study and recommendations.[61] It was this resolution of February 23, 1791, that finally produced Jefferson's Report on Commerce.

The threat of retaliatory legislation also contributed to the decision of the British government, at long last, to send a minister

[59] Report on the Cod and Whale Fisheries, February 1, 1791, *Writings of Thomas Jefferson* (Lipscomb and Bergh ed.), III, 140.
[60] Phineas Bond to the Duke of Leeds, March 14, 1791, J. Franklin Jameson, ed., "Letters of Phineas Bond . . . ," *Annual Report of the American Historical Association for the Year 1897*, I (Washington, 1898), 475.
[61] 1st Congress, 3d session, *Annals of Congress*, II, 2022.

plenipotentiary to the United States. George Hammond was apprised of the "extremely discordant" rift in the administration and instructed to make the most of it in order to combat the movement against British commerce.[62] With the assistance of the Secretary of the Treasury, he would do just that. Jefferson was under no illusions as to Hammond's intentions. He was in possession of a secret British report on commercial policy. This report, submitted in January, 1791, by the Committee of the Privy Council for Trade and Plantations, gave a very flattering picture of Anglo-American commerce since the Revolution. Britain's share of the shipping had increased; the tonnage and tariff duties of the United States were less by about one half than those levied by the states individually in 1787; British exports to the former colonies had fallen off about one third, but the loss was more than offset by expanded markets in the remaining North American colonies; and since imports from the United States had declined drastically, the balance of trade was actually more favorable to Britain than before the war. The report might have been subtitled, "How to Grow Rich by Losing an Empire." It was a thorough vindication of Josiah Tucker, Lord Sheffield, and the architects of British commercial policy in 1783–1784. "Government has indeed not been altogether deceived—," said the committee, "the new system [in the United States] is certainly more favorable to British navigation. And there can be no doubt from the proceedings of Congress, and from all that passed in their debate during the last two sessions, particularly in the *American Senate, that a party is already formed in favor of a connection with Great Britain,* which by moderation on her part, may perhaps be strengthened, as to bring about in a friendly way, the object in view."[63] The object: to detach the United States from France and to strengthen the connection with Britain. Commercial diplomacy was advised

---

[62] Bernard Mayo, ed., "Instructions to the British Ministers to the United States, 1791–1812," *Annual Report of the American Historical Association for the Year 1936,* III (Washington, 1941), 9–13.

[63] Report on the Committee of the Privy Council for Trade and Plantations, January 28, 1791, Jefferson Papers, Library of Congress, Washington, D.C. (underscoring in the manuscript).

chiefly as a check on retaliatory measures, for nothing was to be conceded or concluded. Such were Hammond's instructions, as Jefferson accurately surmised, with respect to commerce. As for the hint in a British state paper of collusion with a party in the government of the United States, many things combined in the early months of 1791 to convince Jefferson that such a party existed and that Hamilton was its leader. The British report helped to complete the picture. In Hamilton's subsequent course of conduct, Jefferson could discover only unlimited hostility to his commercial diplomacy.[64]

Jefferson's desire to pursue this diplomacy in 1793 was at the bottom of the controversy on American neutrality. Hamilton proposed at the outset to revoke, or suspend, the French treaties, an act as unwarranted as it was unnecessary, which must have the effect, Jefferson thought, of throwing the United States into the arms of Britain. Given the balance of forces in the transatlantic world, he considered the survival of the French republic necessary to the security of the American; and, though the risks were high in 1793, he proposed to make the European war serve his purposes with respect to both belligerents. Britain should not be offered American neutrality as a gift but be required to bid for it. He had a particular end in view: British recognition of the broadest neutral privileges, embracing the modern principle of "free bottoms make free goods," contained in American treaties of commerce.[65] He agreed, reluctantly, to the President's Proclamation of April 22 believing it still left him room for maneuver with Britain. The Secretary at once instructed Thomas Pinckney, the American Minister, to advise Whitehall of his government's desire for a fair neutrality, *"on condition* that the rights of neutral nations are

---

[64] Since this article was written, a thorough documentation of Hamilton's unofficial connections with agents of the British government has appeared in Julian P. Boyd's *Number 7, Alexander Hamilton's Secret Attempts to Control American Foreign Policy; With Supporting Documents* (Princeton, 1964).

[65] Opinion on Neutral Trade, December 20, 1793, *Writings of Thomas Jefferson* (Ford ed.), VI, 485–488. See also Opinion on French Treaties, April 28, 1793, *ibid.,* pp. 219–231.

respected in us, as they have been settled in *modern* times."[66] As it turned out, Jefferson had no room for maneuver at all. Events moved too fast; French precipitancy placed the government on the defensive against that nation; and the Proclamation, which Jefferson regarded as an announcement of the status quo in foreign relations, was construed as a definitive Proclamation of Neutrality. The gloss Hamilton put on it, as *Pacificus,* effectively obscured the motives and purposes of Jefferson's diplomacy.

With France Jefferson hoped the exigencies of war would revive the spirit of commercial liberality and concord. He was not disappointed. The West Indies ports were thrown entirely open, fulfilling a decade-long objective of American policy. The French Minister, Genêt, brought instructions to negotiate a new treaty of commerce on Jefferson's favorite plan of mutual naturalization. In this glittering emissary of the French republic, the Secretary of State saw a fresh embodiment of the dream of Franco-American partnership, though he also saw that it was crazily mixed up now with frenzies of war and revolution besetting the peace of the United States. The policy of neutrality, which he honorably supported, obtained an assured integrity during his tenure in the State Department. Yet on the baffling issues that arose from day to day in the divided cabinet, Jefferson's opinion as invariably squinted toward France as the opinions of his arch rival squinted toward Britain—neutrality was found, very imperfectly, somewhere in the field between these deviations. The conduct of both men was colored by policy commitments outside the straight and narrow path of neutrality. As an absolute concept, "neutrality" was a political fiction, exploited by both sides, but much more effectively by the British and their friends as the means of negating the French alliance. In this they were aided unwittingly by the French Minister. The little zealot played "the whole game . . . into their hands," as Jefferson said, discrediting the system pegged to friendship with France.[67] Genêt had to be abandoned, and with him

[66] Jefferson to Thomas Pinckney, April 20, 1793, *Writings of Thomas Jefferson* (Lipscomb and Bergh ed.), IX, 67.

[67] Jefferson to James Madison, July 14, 1793, Jefferson Papers, Library of Congress.

went the prospect of improved commercial collaboration. The
Jacobins now ruled in Paris. They repudiated Genêt, disowned the
dazzling ocean-girdling ambitions of the Girondins, revived mercantilism, and proclaimed total war—at home and abroad, commercial and military—directing against Great Albion the same
practices she had so successfully employed against her enemies.

These developments made a shambles of Jefferson's policy. To
be sure, the damage was offset in some limited degree by the
British Provision Order of June 8 authorizing the seizure of neutral
vessels ladened with flour and grain for France. Jefferson vigor-
ously protested this attack on American neutrality, and in other
ways sought to deflect the rising public anger from France to
Britain. But if these proceedings hurt one power, they did nothing
to close the breach with the other. The deterioration of Franco-
American relations was an unmitigated disaster from Jefferson's
standpoint. He was not responsible for it, and indeed managed to
prevent it from becoming total; but the damage to his system was
probably irreparable.

Viewed in this decade-long perspective, Jefferson's Report on
Commerce put the capstone on a system outmoded by events and
shaken to its foundations. It was, in a sense, Jefferson's "farewell
address," though he must have wondered if there was any future
for the policy it advocated. In its origins, it was not *his* system but
the system of the Continental Congress. It arose out of the
compelling need for new markets, and it expressed a revolutionary
new outlook on the "wealth of nations." It was carried forward in
the general European plan of 1784, of which Jefferson was a
principal architect and executor. As Minister to France, acting in
response to stubborn facts, Jefferson redirected the policy toward
Franco-American collaboration. This change of tactics had a
limited success, at least on the American side; but in practice
universal goals became increasingly bilateral, and the lengthening
chain of obligation to France would prove embarrassing in the
future. The policy entered still another phase when Jefferson
became Secretary of State. He began to see it as "my system," a
personal possession, but the possession, too, of the emerging
Republican party, which championed it against the British-

modeled fiscal system of Hamilton and the Federalists. While at first the French Revolution seemed to place Jeffersonian policy on a stronger footing, the effect proved to be altogether different. The crucial defeat came in 1793, and the Jay Treaty finished it. The record is one of failure. It is also, however, a record of persistent search for a national system of political economy capable of advancing the interests of the American republic upon the principles identified with its revolutionary birth. This was a reasonable, a progressive, even a necessary undertaking, conducted on Jefferson's part with admirable skill and intelligence. Quixotic he certainly was not; the odds were against him, and he knew it, but the stakes in the game were high and the very presence of the United States was changing the rules of the players. The venture failed finally not because it was wrong or visionary or insufficiently attuned to the national interest, but because forces and events, domestic and foreign, caused political preference to be given to another line of policy. It worked. But whether it worked better or worse than an ascendant Jeffersonian policy is a question admitting no satisfactory answer.

Jefferson himself, less inclined than most men to question the principles of his action, continued for years to insist upon the rightness of his policy. The government had chosen the wrong road in 1793–1794, inviting further British aggression, the humiliation of the Jay Treaty, the inevitable resentment of France, and "all the obliquities of the public mind" that fashioned the war hysteria in 1798. Had his own policy prevailed, he said, war with either of the great powers would have been avoided, commerce extended, and justice rendered. "War," he wrote in a memorable restatement of his position, "is not the best engine for us to resort to, nature has given us one *in our commerce,* which, if properly managed, will be a better instrument for obliging the interested nations of Europe to treat us with justice. If the commercial regulations had been adopted which our legislature were at one time proposing, we should at this moment have been standing on such an eminence of safety and respect as ages can never recover."[68] To get back on

---

[68] To Thomas Pinckney, May 29, 1797, to Doctor John Edwards, January 22, 1797, and to Archibald Hamilton Rowan, September 26, 1798, *Writings of Thomas Jefferson* (Ford ed.), VII, 129, 113, 280–281.

the track, having wandered so far from it, was full of difficulties. Jefferson never surmounted them, nor did he develop a satisfactory alternative to the system of policy that had been so emphatically rejected. Fragments of it remained after 1800—the protective instrument of "peaceable coercion," for instance—but they formed part of no coherent system.

And suppose that system could have been fairly and fully tried in the incipiency of the new government? Would it have forced a change in British policy and the direction of history to 1812? Would the United States have cemented bonds of trade and friendship with France and other European nations? Would the federal government have met its domestic responsibilities within a political fabric less threatening to the rights of states and individuals than the Hamiltonian one? Would the enlightened principles of free and pacific intercourse have gained an earlier and stronger foundation in the policies of nations? On such questions there is no end to speculation. Fruitless as it may be, it should not foreclose scrutiny and understanding of historical strivings and promises, like those contained in Jeffersonian commercial policy, to which the course of events proved untrue.

WILLIAM D. GRAMPP

✪

A Re-examination of Jeffersonian Economics[1]

> In so complicated a science as political economy, no one axiom can be laid down as wise and expedient for all times and circumstances, and for their contraries.
>
> —Jefferson, 1816

It is with some hesitancy and not a few misgivings that one must approach the economic writings of Thomas Jefferson. So much has been written about Jefferson in the past century and a half, so diverse are these expressions, and so overlaid has his thought become with the views of his interpreters, that any addition to this grand depository can be justified only as a departure from past efforts. The student of economic doctrine cannot but be a little bewildered upon comparing what Jefferson wrote on economic matters with what he is reputed to have believed. The purpose of this paper is mainly the negative one of demonstrating that the prevalent notions of Jeffersonian economics cannot be substantiated by reference to his works, and it would not be offered, at least in its present form, if these notions had not such general currency. To serve this end, I shall attempt (1) to show that there

[1] The writer wishes to express his indebtedness to Professors F. H. Knight, L. W. Mints, and H. C. Simons, of the University of Chicago, for their criticism, without, however, implying any responsibility on their part for errors of fact or interpretation.

was not one system of Jeffersonian economics, but three corresponding to three periods in his public life; (2) to set down the
sources of this thesis and to show its development in Jefferson's
hands; and (3) to show the relation between Jefferson's economic
doctrine and that prevailing concurrently in Europe, and the interrelations between his economic and political thought, the last
because of the intimacy of the connection and its importance for
understanding the man's doctrine. The method adopted in this
study is a genetic one. Because of the significant changes in his
thought, it can be examined most fruitfully by tracing its evolution
in some detail.

To the mystification of students in the economic field, Jefferson
has been fixed, variously, as a physiocrat, an advocate of agrarian
self-sufficiency, as an apologist for agrarian capitalism (a kind of
bucolic Hamilton), as a protectionist, single-taxer, disciple of
Adam Smith, forerunner of Marx, "democratic collectivist,"[2]—to

---

[2] One of the most celebrated of the many interpretations of Jefferson as a
physiocrat was made by V. L. Parrington, *The Colonial Mind,* Vol. I of
Main Currents in American Thought (New York: Harcourt, Brace, 1927),
pp. 346–348. Another is to be found in Francis W. Hirst, *Life and Letters of
Thomas Jefferson* (New York: Macmillan, 1926), p. 256. Here he is made a
disciple of both physiocracy and Adam Smith!

The agrarian emphasis is stressed to the exclusion of all else in the
collection of Jefferson's writings entitled *Democracy,* ed. S. K. Padover
(New York: D. Appleton-Century, 1939), Chap. IV on "Political Economy." The guide to the selection of this material, which purports to be
representative, is somewhat obscure, for the collection contains no evidence
whatever of Jefferson's change of doctrine in his later years omitting
completely all letters in which he accepted the protection of American
manufactures as a political necessity. The only reference to protection in the
entire collection is a letter in which Jefferson opposed the execution of the
tariff program; and it, appearing out of context, produces the impression that
he was opposed to protection, per se.

Jefferson's "pecuniary logic" is made the motif of his economic policy in
Joseph Dorfman's study of "The Economic Philosophy of Thomas Jefferson," *Political Science Quarterly,* LV, 98–121. In this study, one of the few
executed in any detail, Professor Dorfman maintains that Jefferson's ideal
economy was "commercial-agrarian" (p. 105), and states Jefferson's premises as follows:

"His was the planter's logic. Under it wealth meant landed possessions,
but specie, credit, markets and more lands were necessary for its maintenance and increase" (p. 99).

The differences between Professor Dorfman's conception of Jefferson's
doctrine and that presented in this paper will become evident below.

The portrait of Jefferson as the complete protectionist was made by say nothing of the more esoteric interpretations that have been laid upon his work.[3] It is obvious that he could not have been all of these, or even many of them, and it is equally true that, however valid some of these interpretations are for a particular period of Jefferson's life, each is in error to the extent that it purports to describe any doctrine as held throughout his entire career.

Neither the political nor economic principles of Jefferson's thought ranked as presuppositions, but were as sides of a coin minted from his conception of human nature. This conception was drawn from the systems of Helvétius and Holbach, who however much they may have antagonized Jefferson by their materialistic bias influenced him by their utilitarian doctrine. Human nature, to Jefferson, was not to be taken as given (as it was to Hamilton) but

---

Friedrich List, of the early German Historical School of Economics. See his *Outlines of American Political Economy* (Philadelphia: Samuel Parker, 1827), pp. 37–38, and *The National System of Political Economy* (London: Longmans, Green and Co., 1904), p. 83.

Henry George claimed Jefferson as an advocate of the single tax. See Henry George, "Jefferson and the Land Question," Andrew A. Lipscomb and Albert Ellery Bergh, eds., *The Writings of Thomas Jefferson*, XVI, i–xiv.

Charles Maurice Wiltse maintains that one facet of Jefferson's doctrine implied socialism, that he anticipated, "though did not clearly foresee," the concept of the class struggle as enunciated by Marx, and that he was similar to Lenin in being a "practical" theoretician whose great forte was an ability "to work out solutions demanded by the times." *The Jeffersonian Tradition in American Democracy* (Chapel Hill: University of North Carolina Press, 1935), pp. 5, 137, 214.

The elements of *laissez faire* in Jefferson's thought are stressed by Joseph Spengler, "The Political Economy of Jefferson, Madison, and Adams," David Kelly Jackson, ed., *American Studies in Honor of William Kenneth Boyd* (Durham: Duke University Press, 1940), pp. 3–59. This detailed study suffers from viewing Jefferson's doctrine as a set of static conceptions rather than as a system constantly changing to meet changing national problems. See, for example, Professor Spengler's summation of Jefferson's position on *laissez faire*, pp. 40–41; the three quotations here are extracted from declarations made in 1801, 1788, and 1808, respectively. Taken out of context they have a certain show of consistency, but when related to other statements of the respective periods they actually denote three very different points of view.

[3] As, for example, Ezra Pound, *Jefferson and/or Mussolini* (London: Stanley Nott, 1935), of which the following is suggestive: "Jefferson was one genius and Mussolini is another. I am not putting in *all* the steps of my argument but that don't mean to say they aren't there" (p. 19).

as subject to restraint and improvement at the hands of a government that would be subject to the same forces in the hands of the people. Neither governors nor governed could be trusted, nor could a system of checks and balances be relied upon to achieve an equilibrium of interests and thereby maintain peace and liberty. Elementary caution, he believed, demanded that governmental powers be few and extremely limited. He believed individuals should not be permitted to acquire wealth enough to give them great influence, and, that government should not be given significant powers to control economic behavior. Jefferson was at one with Hamilton's dictum, that power over a man's subsistence is power over his will,[4] but, unlike Hamilton, he did not believe that men were capable of looking after their own interests by creating a governmental structure in which an equilibrium between opposing interests would be established and departures from it would be largely self-correcting. Rather than give each individual and group the power to advance its own ends and to protect itself against incursions by others—which was the rationale of the tripartite structure of government—Jefferson believed that the sources of conflict had to be removed before "right" social relations could be established. The source of most evil was, he maintained, men's material interests. Hence the kind of economic behavior men engaged in was of fundamental importance to a government that wished to preserve order and liberty. If men were to be turned to the true path of social righteousness, they must be turned away from the mainsprings of corruption, and the great and leading principle of economic policy then became the cultivation of an economic environment that would be conducive to the realization of the ends of government.

Given these primary considerations, it is possible, I believe, to explain the great political and economic struggles of the years from the Constitution to the rise of Jacksonian democracy and to discover the essential differences that separated the first two parties and their successors to the year 1829. Though the convenient categories of "aristocrat and democrat," or "nationalist

4 Hamilton, *The Federalist,* No. 79.

and states' righter," "mercantilist and physiocrat" may serve for some purposes, they help but little in fixing clear-cut distinctions; and for purposes of discovering differences in economic doctrine they are of no help at all. Here it must be noted, that to speak of Jeffersonian *economics* is somewhat misleading, for neither Jefferson nor his followers pretended to develop a theoretical system embracing value, distribution, finance, and economic policy, as the British and French economists of the period were doing. No one in America attempted such a system until the third decade of the nineteenth century when Daniel Raymond wrote his *Thoughts on Political Economy*. "Jeffersonian economics" is really a set of ideas concerning the economic role of the state together with a few, and cursory, remarks concerning value and money. This is not to say that the early Americans were unaware of the totality of prevailing economic thought but that they were most concerned with those aspects relevant to the problem of government.

I

Jefferson's earliest expression of doctrinal importance was made in 1774 when he wrote in *The Summary View of the Rights of British America* that the exercise of free trade was "possessed by the American colonists, as of a natural right," and he described the act of George II forbidding Americans to make fur products as "an instance of despotism to which no parallel can be produced in the most arbitrary ages of British history."[5] He declared that freedom in the disposition of property was one aspect of the total endowment of freedom that man derived from the Creator.[6] Although the reference in this tract is to real property, or economic goods, Jefferson usually meant much more by the term "property" and most often used it as his spiritual forebear, John Locke, did, to comprehend man's "life, liberty and estates."[7]

[5] *Writings of Thomas Jefferson* I, 189. All references to Jefferson's works are to the Lipscomb and Bergh edition.
[6] *Ibid.*, I, 210–211.
[7] John Locke, *On Government, Two Treatises* (London: J. M. Dent, 1940), p. 180.

Jefferson believed with Locke that men form societies in order to protect their "property,"[8] and he meant by this, not that government exists to secure wealth and vested interests (as is so often claimed), but to guarantee each man's birthright to liberty.

Jefferson's next work of importance was the famous *Notes on Virginia* in which he described in encyclopedic fashion the most important agricultural state and one of the two or three most important economic regions in America, and appended sundry observations on man and the material with which he worked. These notes, from which Jefferson's reputation as a physiocrat is largely derived, were written before 1781 and hence before he left America to become Ambassador to France. They grew out of observations made over a number of years preceding his departure, and they were by no means intended to be exhaustive nor even to represent satisfactorily Jefferson's views on the limited subjects treated. They were published about 1785 with some hesitation, and then privately circulated. The original edition, published in French, was, in Jefferson's words, "interverted, abridged, mutilated, and often reversing the sense of the original." A partially corrected English edition was published later, but was not completely accurate.[9] Yet it is this admittedly tentative and not completely reliable publication that first gave Jefferson his reputation as a physiocrat.

In the English edition the *Notes* are still replete with panegyrics over the agriculturist. Agriculture begets self-sufficiency; it creates a stalwart yeomanry that is the bulwark of liberty and bearer of an elevated moral code. "Those who labor in the earth are the chosen people of God."[10] This agrarian strain runs throughout Jefferson's life. In 1804, he wrote to J. B. Say, the French classicist, that the agriculturist possessed a "moral and physical preference" over the laborer of the cities.[11] In 1816, after he had become a protectionist, he still clung to the supremacy of agriculture and maintained that it produced a value greater than an equal application of

[8] Jefferson to du Pont de Nemours, *Writings of Thomas Jefferson,* XIV, 490.
[9] Autobiography, *ibid.,* I, 90–92.
[10] *Writings of Thomas Jefferson,* II, 229.
[11] *Ibid.,* XI, 1–3.

labor and capital to manufacturing because of "the spontaneous energies of the earth."[12] Jefferson's agrarianism was infectious, and the superiority of farming became a byword among those who were opposed to the industrialization of America. The protectionists were forever confronted with a kind of moral superciliousness on the part of the agrarians. Matthew Carey, inveterate champion of a high tariff and prolific pamphleteer on its behalf, blamed this hauteur upon Jefferson and added querulously: "His Arcadia must have been sought, not in Virginia or Maryland, but in Virgil's or Pope's pastorals, or Thomson's seasons."[13]

Yet Jefferson's preference for agriculture does not necessarily make of him a physiocrat any more than a forerunner of the Congressional farm bloc. Even in the years before 1790 when his agrarianism was most pronounced, it was not a system of true physiocracy. Although Jefferson commended at various times throughout his life the work of *Les Économistes* and noted particularly du Pont de Nemours, Quesnay, Gournay, Le Trosne, Turgot, and Destutt de Tracy, he was also familiar with the doctrines of Say, Malthus, Sismondi, Hume, John Law, and Smith. Of the last, he declared: "In political economy, I think Smith's *Wealth of Nations* the best book extant."[14] Because he possessed an almost religious devotion to the soil, Jefferson usually has been called a physiocrat, the assumption apparently being that such devotion was the essence of physiocracy and the direct, tangible proof deriving from Jefferson's residence in France and his mention of the doctrine. Yet in his works there not only is no definitive exposition of physiocratic doctrine[15] but there is not even any

---

[12] Jefferson to Benjamin Austin, *ibid.,* XIV, 390.

[13] Matthew Carey, "The New Olive Branch," *The New Olive Branch* (Philadelphia: M. Carey, 1820–1831), p. 24.

[14] Matthew Carey to Thomas Mann Randolph, 1790, *Writings of Thomas Jefferson,* VIII, 31.

[15] *After* he had abandoned his early, and most intense, agrarianism, Jefferson wrote the following which contains one of the two most explicit references to physiocratic doctrine that I have been able to find: "A prosperity built on the basis of agriculture is that which is most desirable to us, because to the efforts of labor it adds the efforts of a greater proportion

evidence that he was more influenced by it than by British classicism. In point of formal respect paid to contemporary doctrine, Jefferson is much more of a British classicist than a follower of the French economists; even his rent theory is in no way inconsistent with that of Smith.[16]

The best statement of physiocratic doctrine came from an American opponent of the system, Alexander Hamilton, who set down its principles only in order to refute them. Hamilton evinced a thorough familiarity with the physiocratic concept of the *produit net,* the categories of productive and unproductive labor, and its capital and taxation theory.[17] Even in his most pronounced agrarian period, Jefferson did not express such notions. When Jefferson jotted down his *Notes,* he was, in common with many, extremely optimistic about the reaction which an independent America would receive from Europe. Like Paine, Hamilton,[18] and others, he expressed the belief that the nations of the world would spare no effort in bidding for the trade of the United States and in engaging it in a profitable commerce. This would enable the United States to specialize in agriculture, for which it was eminently fitted, and to draw manufactured products from Europe. The achievement would be twofold. It would enhance the wealth of America and would prevent the growth of manufacturing centers. He was frightened at the prospect of an urban proletariat dependent upon the "casualties and caprice of customers," for such "dependence

---

of soil." Circular to the American Consuls, May 31, 1792, *Writings of Thomas Jefferson,* VIII, 352.

It should be noted that the circular concludes with the very *un*physiocratic statement that the United States is not disposed to remove its restrictive commercial policy until Europe freely admits American goods.

[16] Cf. the above Circular and Jefferson's letter to Benjamin Austin, 1816, *ibid.,* XIV, 390, with Smith, *The Wealth of Nations,* ed. Cannan, p. 146.

[17] Alexander Hamilton, Report on Manufactures, A. H. Cole, ed., *Industrial and Commercial Correspondence* (Chicago: A. W. Shaw, 1928), pp. 248–250. This section may be compared with, e.g., Anne Robert Jacques Turgot, *Reflections on the Formation and Distribution of Riches* (New York: Macmillan, 1898), especially pp. 7, 83, 95–97.

[18] See Thomas Paine, "The American Crisis," *The Life and Works of Thomas Paine* (New Rochelle: Thomas Paine National Historical Association, 1925), III, 90–91; and Hamilton, *The Federalist,* XI.

begets subservience and venality."[19] He decried the depravity of the lower orders of Europe, which were held in bondage to a few "millionary merchants" and corrupted by their commercial morals.[20]

Jefferson was much more explicit in his opposition to manufactures than in his preference for agriculture; like many others of the period he was more vigorous in denial than affirmation. Throughout his life, he deplored industrialization even after he had come to accept its inevitability. Manufacturing centers were the mainspring of corruption, the prime source from which all evil flowed. Jefferson's reputation as a friend of man and a believer in the righteousness of the people is somewhat impaired when one considers his remarks on the proletariat of France and England;[21] these are no more charitable than the harshest strictures of Hamilton. Believing as he did that men should be removed from evil and confronted with good, Jefferson fought for many years against the development of an industrial environment in America and chose agriculture as an alternative. He was supported in his position by underlying economic conditions that were unfavorable to the natural development of manufacturing. He was hostile, needless to say, to any governmental action that would artificially alleviate the naturally unfavorable conditions and promote industrialization.

In 1788, while Ambassador to France, he was asked by a European who wished to establish a textile mill in the United States what assistance might be expected from the American government. Jefferson's reply is of interest for what it reveals of economic conditions in the United States and even of greater interest for what it tells of his own attitude. He noted very politely but nonetheless pointedly every conceivable reason why a textile mill would fail in the United States, and concluded that the manufacturer could not expect assistance of any kind from the government of the Confederation, adding:

It is not the policy of the government in that country [the United States] to give aid to works of any kind. They let things take their

[19] Notes on Virginia, *Writings of Thomas Jefferson*, II, 229.
[20] *Writings of Thomas Jefferson*, XV, 29.
[21] Jefferson to John Adams, *ibid.*, XIII, 401–402.

natural course without help or impediment, which is generally the best policy.[22]

He continued: "In general, it is impossible that manufactures should succeed in America," because of the scarcity of labor and the consequent high wages. To bring foreign artisans would be a wasteful expedient, according to Jefferson, for they would soon go into agriculture where opportunities were greater. But his opposition extended beyond manufacturing. He was really hostile to the main currents of economic behavior of the eighteenth century, because, quite consistently with his political premises, these forced men to a preoccupation with material endeavor, which he considered debasing. As will be seen from the following letter, written in 1785 to Hogendorp, he was opposed not only to manufacturing but to exchange as a method of economic organization:

You ask what I think on the expedience of encouraging our states to be commercial? Were I to indulge my own theory, I should wish them to practise neither commerce nor navigation, but to stand, with respect to Europe, precisely on the footing of China. We should thus avoid wars, and all our citizens would be husbandmen. Whenever, indeed, our numbers should so increase that our produce would overstock the markets of those nations who should come to seek it, the farmers must either employ the surplus of their time in manufactures or the surplus of our hands must be employed in manufactures or in navigation.[23]

However, such passive commerce was not to the taste of Yankee entrepreneurs, Jefferson noted, and added that in the circumstances the best policy was one which minimized the evil by keeping all manufactures in Europe.

Before 1790, Jefferson's conception of the ideal American economy was rather hazy, but it seems to have been one with a great deal of local agrarian self-sufficiency supported by household manufactures. This may be inferred from his aversion to the market,[24] which he believed was destructive to the independence of the mass of the people. Yet Jefferson was not at all consistent

[22] Jefferson to Mr. Thomas Digges, *ibid.*, VII, 49.
[23] *Writings of Thomas Jefferson*, V, 182.
[24] *Ibid.*, VII, 47–49.

on this point, for he advocated both self-sufficiency and international free trade—types of economic behavior that are mutually exclusive. If America were to become a nation of small agricultural units implemented by household manufactures, exchange as a form of economic organization would tend to become less and less important. On the other hand, if America were to specialize in agriculture and import manufactured products from Europe, self-sufficiency would vanish. In the latter case, the American farmer would become as dependent upon the market as the urban laborer of Europe. In either case the functions of the government would be much more meagre than if a policy were adopted of direct state intervention in economic life. If free international trade were the objective, the national government would have the obligation of enforcing the rules of the competitive game; if agriculture were combined with household manufacture, the national government would have virtually no economic functions and the functions of state and local governments would be negligible. The national government would not require the power which would be necessary in order to watch over a market economy, for the markets would be small, dispersed throughout the states, and would largely supervise themselves with the aid of state or local governments. If the objective of self-sufficient agrarian units were completely realized, markets would disappear.

Neither system of economic organization shows any affinity to physiocracy. The physiocrats believed in free trade, of course, but this was not their distinguishing characteristic. They also based their economy on the superiority of agriculture, but the justification did not run in vague terms of moral superiority but took the form of a very elaborate value theory. With the notion of self-sufficient agrarian units, physiocracy had nothing in common. As Smith has suggested, physiocracy may be considered a reaction against the special privileges obtained by manufacturing under the mercantilist regimes of France. Jefferson's preference for agriculture was hardly an aversion to manufacturing in this sense, for there was no manufacturing of any significance in America and it received no special attention until 1791, when Hamilton submitted his program of protection. This was some time after Jefferson's early agrarianism had been modified.

In the dual position which he held before 1790, the implications of agrarian self-sufficiency are fairly obvious. The meaning of free trade, however, is not always apparent, and the role of such doctrine is an elusive one, not only in Jefferson's system but in most of the writings of the years between the two wars with Great Britain. When Jefferson gave free trade the status of a natural right, as he did in *The Summary View,* and decried its interdiction by England, he wrote in an idiom common to the times. This has been interpreted in two ways: the Americans may have been insisting upon *laissez faire* in the conventional sense of a free and unrestricted international trade, or they may have used such doctrine as a rhetorical device to conceal economic motives.[25] Farther on in *The Summary View,* Jefferson indicated that the Americans simply wanted equality of treatment within the orbit of British mercantilism, that they were willing to grant all "reasonable" regulation of their trade by the mother country but insisted on disposing as they chose of those commodities which England could not use.[26] From the point of view of British mercantilism, such a concession was not at all reasonable, for the system of economic control had to be pervasive in order to be a system. To have permitted American manufactures, even of those commodities not directly in competition with British goods, would have increased the power of the colonies and eventually would have evoked direct competition.

To support the contention that free trade expressions were ephemeral rhetoric, the mercantilist practices of the states under the Confederation and Hamilton's economic policy are often adduced. Yet these were by no means universally approved. It is a common mistake to attribute the policy of one set of interests to the whole country. Writing a few years after the Peace of Paris, John Adams lamented the shackles that were imposed on com-

---

[25] This latter view is held by Vernon G. Setser, *The Commercial Reciprocity Policy of the United States, 1774–1829* (Philadelphia: University of Pennsylvania Press, 1937), p. 257.

[26] *Writings of Thomas Jefferson,* I, 189, 191, 210.

merce. The war, he said, had been fought for the "freedom of commerce," yet once it was won, commerce was treated with high disregard for its rights.[27] Doctrines of *laissez faire,* both in its French and British form, were frequently expressed in this period and later in the Constitutional Convention, either directly when the discussion turned on the scope of the economic powers of the government or obliquely when specific powers were considered.[28] It is true that certain mercantilist notions were also expressed, very often by the same people. The relationship cannot be examined here, but the real problem can be suggested.

More was involved than either free trade, mercantilism, or dissembling. The issue was the right and the power of one nation to determine its own economic policy. The question was whether the United States, Great Britain, or any other country could take the rest of the world as given. On this consideration, the cries of some "quasi-mercantilists" for the right of free trade do not appear absurd. They insisted that America could set any commercial policy that it pleased, that this was a natural right, even if it meant a policy that was hostile to free trade in the conventional sense. Hence, during the second war with Britain Hezekiah Niles, a staunch protectionist, could exclaim: "The gallant Decatur's toast, 'Free trade and no impressment,' unsophisticated and in itself, embraces the whole business of the war."[29] Actually one nation cannot take the world as a datum; such an assumption is both false to fact and to the natural right's doctrine of the period.[30] The simple act of levying an impost solely for revenue will eventually react on the restricting country. Nations cannot adopt an instrumental attitude, any more than individuals can.

Although he later became something of a parochial nationalist, Jefferson in the revolutionary and constitutional period gave to free trade the meaning it possessed in the works of Hume and Smith. His words and policy to the year 1805 reveal this.

[27] Charles Francis Adams, ed., *Works of John Adams,* IX (Boston: Little, Brown and Company, 1856), 560.
[28] This problem is the main subject of a larger work of the writer and can only be suggested here.
[29] *Niles Register,* March 5, 1814.
[30] Cf. Locke, p. 191.

II

When Jefferson returned from France and became Secretary of State in Washington's first cabinet in 1790, his economic policy began to change, and in the succeeding years, until 1805, the ideas which he expressed were markedly different from those of his early life. This period reveals two significant departures from his early position: the idea of self-sufficient economic units, in any *explicit* form, disappears, and his program of free trade is modified by a policy of reciprocity. In this period one can observe an intimate relation between Jefferson's political doctrine and his domestic economic policy. He pursued a policy that was largely in harmony with that of the British classicists; the elements of agrarianism were subsumed in the kind of synthesis made by Joseph Priestley between British classicism and physiocracy. Priestley, who is better known as the discoverer of oxygen, wrote considerably on political and economic matters, and was a close friend of Jefferson. (He fled to America in 1794, when the British government fell on sympathizers of the French Revolution and after Burke did him the honor of execration in his *Reflections*.) Priestley's *Lectures on History and General Policy* constitute an important liberal testament of the late eighteenth century and are especially relevant for the economic doctrine they expound. He adapted French notions of the supremacy of agriculture to a mixed—agricultural and manufacturing—economy, by declaring that the earth was the ultimate source of all wealth (suggestive of Ricardo's original and indestructible powers of the soil). Manufacturing, however, must be "excited," for it furnishes a market for agricultural products.[31] Where Turgot posited the labor of the husbandman as the only productive factor,[32] Priestley extended the labor theory of value to all productive activity (in the sense of labor as the source of all value).[33]

In his domestic economic policy Jefferson sought to implement

[31] Priestley, *Lectures* (Birmingham: Pearson and Rollason, 1788), pp. 365–369.
[32] Turgot, p. 9.
[33] Priestley, p. 369.

his political premises. Believing that society should be the impartial nurse of all of its members, he was opposed to any fiscal policy that benefited one group at the expense of another. He averred that Hamilton's fiscal policy injured the poor mechanics and the small farmers in order to aid the commercial classes and to build a political machine around the Secretary of the Treasury.[34] Although the nature of Jefferson's agrarianism changed after 1790, he did not change his opinion of merchants and manufactures. He continued to oppose any measures that would work to their advantage and assist in the development of an environment that bred "corruption and depravity." Believing that material interests were the principal source of discord in society, he opposed any economic policy that appealed to these interests and sought to make men's support of the government dependent upon the realization of their material objectives. He could never agree with Hamilton that the ideal government connected men's "interests with their virtue," and secured their loyalty by satisfying their material desires. Jefferson's fiscal policy in this period was much less formidable than his criticism of Federalist policy. He opposed the assumption of state debts until their exact amount was known,[35] and he proposed that funding be limited to the redemption of debt within the lifetime of the security holder.[36] Since no generation has a claim upon the future, no debt can be valid beyond the lifetime of the original holder, he declared. He denied that the debt certificates were a form of capital and cited Smith as his authority.[37] His criticism of funding anticipated John Taylor's elaborate critique of the Federalist "paper system." Jefferson declared

that all the capital employed in paper speculation is barren and useless, producing, like that on a gaming table, no accession to itself, and is

[34] The Anas, *Writings of Thomas Jefferson,* I, 271–274.
[35] *Ibid.*
[36] Jefferson to John Taylor, *ibid.,* XV, 18.
[37] Jefferson to John W. Eppes, *ibid.,* XIII, 423. In this letter, he also cites Smith to support his contention that the proper quantity of money for the United States is between eight million and thirty-five million dollars. Jefferson held the quantity theory of money. *Ibid.,* XIII, 410–411, 415.

withdrawn from commerce and agriculture, where it would have produced an addition to the common mass: that it [funding] nourishes in our citizens habits of vice and idleness, instead of industry and morality: that it has furnished effectual means of corrupting such a portion of the legislature as turns on the balance between the honest voters, whichever way it is directed: . . .[38]

Jefferson's criticism of the Bank of the United States was similar in moral tone to that made of the funding program. He considered the first Bank a nursery for "gamblers in corruption," and its specious legality a stain on the Constitution.[39] In his denial of its legality he insisted upon a strict construction of the Constitution. He was opposed to any broad interpretation of the welfare clauses in order to justify the power of incorporation and the granting of subsidies.[40] He saw in Hamilton's banking program a new design to foster despotism by appealing to men's material interests in order to acquire their unquestioning loyalty to the Federalist party.[41] Jefferson originally believed that the evils of banking could be eliminated if the monopoly of the Bank of the United States were broken, but by 1802, when the number of state banks had increased, he held that banking in any form was an unmitigated evil.[42] Just how the economic system was to operate without banks, or what would be established in their place, are matters upon which he did not enlarge.

Jefferson's most specific measures of domestic policy were proposed in relation to the land problem. They embraced two objectives, which again derive from his political principles: he sought for equality, or the elimination of gross inequality, of possession, and freedom in the use of land. In 1785, he proposed a

[38] Jefferson to the President of the United States, 1792, *ibid.*, VIII, 343–344. Cf. the *magnum opus* of John Taylor, of Caroline, whom many historians believe to have written the only satisfactory criticism of Federalist economic doctrine: *An Inquiry into the Principles and Policy of the Government of the United States* (Fredericksburg: Green and Cady, 1814), pp. 244 f., 249, 280.

[39] Jefferson to John Taylor, *Writings of Thomas Jefferson*, XV, 18.

[40] Against the Constitutionality of the Bank, *ibid.*, III, 149–150, and The Anas, *ibid.*, I, 291.

[41] The Anas, *ibid.*, I, 277.

[42] Jefferson to Albert Gallatin, *ibid.*, X, 323, 436.

redistribution through a progressive tax, with exemptions for small holdings.[43] He opposed all feudal fees and proposed free distribution to settlers as a means of populating the country and of increasing its wealth.[44] In an interesting letter to Madison, he related his land policy to his political objectives. Just as he believed that government should be dedicated to the living and not to the dead, he believed no generation should encumber those to come with its methods of holding and using property. He opposed, for example, any generation accumulating debts beyond its ability to pay them, thus preventing it from placing its aggregate property holdings in lien to creditors. (This held, he said, for society in the aggregate; an individual could not deny a creditor's claim against inherited property.) Such debt accumulation would restrict the freedom of each generation to use its property as it wished. "The earth belongs in usufruct to the living," he declared. "On similar grounds it may be proved, that no society can make a perpetual constitution, or even a perpetual law."[45]

The first modifications in Jefferson's free trade policy were made in 1791 in his report on fisheries in which he proposed that the national government protect the fishing industry by a remission of duties on raw materials, by levying retaliatory duties on whale oil,[46] and by opening foreign markets to American fishery products. Jefferson considered such a policy was essential to the safeguarding of the American fishing industry from the hostility of Great Britain and to the building of a merchant marine that would be of value in time of war.[47] The report obtained a generally

[43] *Writings of Thomas Jefferson*, XIX, 17–18.
[44] *Ibid.*, IV, 275–277.
[45] *Ibid.*, VII, 454, 459. The intent here is somewhat ambiguous. To prevent any generation from living beyond its means is to prevent it from consuming its capital. This of course restricts its freedom to use its property as it will, and imposes the obligation at least to keep its capital intact. Many Republicans held such an idea of progress. Cf. Paine's *Agrarian Justice*.
[46] Britain levied a duty on importations of American whale oil and exported the oil of its own fisheries to the United States to be re-exported in American vessels. This retaliatory measure is significant as marking the beginning of Jefferson's policy of reciprocity.
[47] On the Subjects of the Cod and Whale Fisheries, etc., *Writings of Thomas Jefferson*, III, 139, 141.

favorable response in the Senate, primarily because of its consequences for the maritime power of the nation.[48]

In 1793 Jefferson submitted his famous report on commercial policy to the House of Representatives. After reviewing the restrictions placed upon American exports by the different nations of Europe, he declared that two courses of action presented themselves. The United States could seek the removal of these restrictions by "friendly arrangement" with the various nations imposing them, or it could impose restrictions of its own in retaliation. He continued:

There can be no doubt but that of these two, friendly arrangement is the most eligible. Instead of embarrassing commerce under piles of regulating laws, duties and prohibitions, could it be relieved from all shackles in all parts of the world, could every country be employed in producing that which nature has best fitted it to produce, and each be free to exchange with others mutual surpluses for mutual wants, the greatest mass possible would then be produced of those things which contribute to human life and human happiness; the numbers of mankind would be increased, and their condition bettered.[49]

A perfectly free commerce with the rest of the world should be the objective of American commercial policy, he stated. This can be realized through the negotiation of reciprocal trade agreements with other nations. But the United States should not give free commerce and navigation "in exchange for restrictions and vexations."[50] He proposed five methods of retaliation, to be exercised against those nations that refused to adopt "friendly arrangements" with America.[51] All of these methods were inspired by the

---

[48] Edgar S. Maclay, ed., *Journal of William Maclay* (New York: D. Appleton & Co., 1890), p. 384.

[49] Report on the Privileges and Restrictions on the Commerce of the United States in Foreign Countries, *Writings of Thomas Jefferson*, III, 274–275.

[50] *Ibid.*, III, 276.

[51] *Ibid.*, III, 278–281. The retaliatory methods proposed were: extremely high duties tending to prohibition; exclusion of foreign merchants from the United States; limiting national goods to national bottoms; recognizing as national vessels only those constructed within the nation whose flag they fly; and a boycott of the ships of all nations that refuse to admit American goods in American ships.

mercantilist practices of European nations, particularly Great Britain, and they are as obviously mercantilistic in form as the practices that provoked them. The first, high duties, is of special interest, because Jefferson declared that they would have "the effect of indirect encouragement to domestic manufactures of the same kind [as the restricted imports]," and in time "may induce the manufacturer to come himself into these States, where cheaper subsistence, equal laws, and a vent of his wares, free of duty, may ensure him the highest profits from his skill and industry." He continued:

And here, it would be in the power of the State governments to co-operate essentially, by opening the resources of encouragement which are under their control, extending them liberally to artists in those particular branches of manufacture for which their soil, climate, population and other circumstances have matured them, and fostering the precious efforts and progress of *household* manufacture, by some patronage suited to the nature of its objects, guided by the local information they possess, and guarded against abuse by their presence and attentions.[52]

This expression of protectionism may ring strangely against the prevalent notion of Jefferson as an agrarian, but before hastening to identify him with Hamilton it will be well to examine the expression more closely.

Jefferson's advocacy of protection was really incidental to his policy of reciprocity. Hamilton's program of protection had as its principal and exclusive objective the development of domestic manufactures; it was not combined with a commercial policy of reciprocity, nor was it an outgrowth of such a policy. This was one important difference between the two men on this point. (It is to be wondered whether Hamilton's Report on Manufactures, submitted two years previously, had any effect on Jefferson, antagonistic as he was to Federalist economic policy. Although Hamilton's effort brought no immediate legislative action, it was obviously a state document of great importance and attracted immediate attention. Jefferson was curiously hesitant about submitting his

52 *Ibid.*, III, 279 (italics in original).

report, which was written in compliance with a request of the House that had been made some two years previously and about two months after Hamilton had submitted his work.)

A second difference between the two positions is to be found in Jefferson's insistence that the power of protection be exercised by the state governments. Neither the political nor economic effects of Jefferson's protectionist program of this period could have been as important as those of Hamilton's program. The exercise of economic power by the state governments could not have been of any significance as long as the Union was to be maintained. Had the states exercised broad powers of allocation and distribution, the United States as an economic and political entity would have ceased to exist, and the condition of the country would have reverted to the near-chaos of the Confederation. The very condition of union and the very reason for the calling of the Constitutional Convention was the subordination of state power and the creation of a national state. (This must be asserted despite the fact that the nominal form of the government was a federation.) Jefferson's program in this period was consistent with his doctrine of the political importance of the states and with his doctrine of a minimum government. It removed the protection of industry from the province of the national government and placed it where its exercise could not have important political or economic consequences.

A third feature which distinguished Jefferson's program from that of Hamilton was the emphasis on the encouragement of household manufacture. Compared to Hamilton's objective of widespread industrialization, Jefferson's purposes were extremely modest. Small economic units were consistent with his ideal political state: originally he advocated self-sufficient agrarian units supported by household manufacture, and after 1790 he proposed a system of small farms engaging in free trade with the rest of the world or, failing this, the development of agrarian self-sufficiency through household manufacture. Jefferson's commercial policy of reciprocity, it may be noted, shows very visibly the influence of his early agrarianism. Reciprocity was designed to cultivate free trade, but also to protect America should it fail to achieve this goal. The principal way in which the policy was to protect America was by encouraging the development of household manufactures which would assist in making the small agrarian units self-sufficient.

Jefferson nowhere in his report explicitly stated that agrarian self-sufficiency was the real objective of his commercial policy. However, it is a reasonable deduction both from the report itself and from other of his statements made at that time and previous to 1790. Jefferson had a deeply rooted aversion to commerce from the days of the Revolution to the beginning of the second crisis in British-American relations in 1807. This was really an opposition to the market and to exchange as a method of economic organization. Before 1790 he proposed agrarian self-sufficiency as an ideal form of organization, and after 1790 his greatest interest in addition to agriculture was household manufacture. Finally, it may be observed that the methods of retaliation which he proposed would have had the effect of diminishing American foreign commerce almost to a vanishing point. To obtain needed manufactured goods, the United States would then, by Jefferson's proposal, have turned to state protection and, more importantly, to household fabrication. It is conceivable, of course, that Jefferson's policy of retaliation might have forced Europe to open its markets to American goods. The more probable reaction of Europe would have been to adopt retaliatory measures against the United States. These would have been countered with more restrictions, and eventually commerce would have ceased. It may be noted that this is not sheer conjecture, for it actually happened after 1807 when Congress, acting on Jefferson's advice, adopted the Embargo and later the Nonintercourse Act which brought to a complete cessation all lawful foreign commerce. (Smuggling was engaged in to some extent.) Ironically, these acts operated to promote nationwide industrialization, which was just what Jefferson tried to avoid.

That Jefferson became aware of the diminishing reality of his ideal of agrarian self-sufficiency and came to accept the necessity of exchange is manifest in his writings after 1793. His commercial policy was not adopted by Congress, which accepted the Federalist position of equal treatment for all nations. Hamilton's fiscal and banking policy operated to unify the United States and to promote internal exchange, and it also pointed to greater interference by the government in national economic life. By 1801, Jefferson no longer dwelt upon the form of agrarianism explicit before 1790 and implicit in his report of 1793. In his first annual message to Congress, 1801, three important aspects of doctrine are discernible: Jefferson implied that agricultural specialization was most desirable (rather than agricultural self-sufficiency); he admitted the legitimacy of other forms of economic behavior, and he urged a policy of *laissez faire*. He declared at one point: "Agriculture, manufactures, commerce, and navigation, the four pillars of our prosperity, are the most thriving when left most free to individual enterprise."[53] Jefferson reiterated this position in 1804 in a letter which more explicitly states his new conception of the role of agriculture. He wrote that it would

be better that all our laborers should be employed in agriculture. In this case a double or treble portion of fertile lands would be brought into culture; a double or treble creation of food be produced, and its surplus go to nourish the now perishing births of Europe, who in return would manufacture and send us in exchange our clothes and other comforts.[54]

In this same letter Jefferson explained his ideas concerning the population problem, which was one of his many special interests. He was in agreement with the Malthusian doctrine that, in most nations, the population increased geometrically while the means of subsistence increased arithmetically.[55] He observed the statistical verification of Malthus' premises in the figures of the second American census.[56] He denied, however, the general applicability of the doctrine, for he believed that in the United States the means of subsistence were adequate not only to satisfy the American people but also to alleviate much of the misery of

[53] *Writings of Thomas Jefferson,* III, 337.
[54] Jefferson to J. B. Say, *ibid.,* XI, 2–3.
[55] Of Malthus' essay on population, Jefferson wrote: "It is one of the ablest that I have ever seen." Jefferson to Joseph Priestley, *ibid.,* X, 447.
[56] First Annual Message, 1801, *ibid.,* III, 330.

Europe.[57] Jefferson's proposals respecting population did not change as significantly as the other aspects of his policy. In his *Notes on Virginia,* he urged that the immigration of skilled workers be encouraged by offering them special inducements, but he was reluctant to admit large numbers of them, believing that they would unsettle American conditions by overwhelming the country with European manners and morals.[58] He did not believe immigration would promote manufacturing, as Hamilton did, for after a while, the immigrants would "go to the plough and the hoe, but, in the mean time, they will teach us something we do not know."

III

Beginning in 1805 there was a pronounced change in Jefferson's economic policy. Both the early objective of agrarianism and the free trade which supplanted it were given over for a system of protection. The continued hostility of England and the Continental System of Napoleon forced a new assertion of national power from the United States at a time when the Republicans were in office. In his Second Inaugural Address (1805) Jefferson revealed the progress that Federalist ideas had made within his own system and within the Republican party. Gone were the proclamations of a revolution in public polity that had ushered in the regime in 1801. In the first administration, Gallatin had attempted to execute a policy of strict economy in governmental expenditures, and Jefferson had attempted to relegate the state to the rank of a wise and tolerant overseer of economic behavior. Gallatin's policy of economy had effected a reduction in the size of the army and navy, instituted savings in the diplomatic and customs services, and reduced the national debt. The Jeffersonian administration between 1801 and 1804 was much more conducive to *laissez faire* than the preceding administrations, simply because the government

[57] Jefferson to J. B. Say, 1804, *ibid.,* XI, 2, and to David Williams, 1803, *ibid.,* X, 430.
[58] *Ibid.,* II, 119–124.

exercised so few economic powers. But such an administration was destined for a short life. Even had there been no opposition within the nation, the turmoil of Europe would have forced a change.

Jefferson began his second administration by looking forward to the time when the public revenue would be freed from debt service in order that it might be applied "to rivers, canals, roads, arts, manufactures, education, and other great objects within each state."[59] Such a policy would first have to be legitimated by a constitutional amendment and probably would have to be executed in cooperation with the governments of the states.[60] The promotion of American manufactures, however, did not wait for a constitutional amendment, any more than did the Louisiana Purchase. The Embargo and nonintercourse policy after 1807 furnished more assistance to American manufacturing than the entire Federalist policy had been able to offer. Although the intent was to preserve American neutrality in the Napoleonic Wars, the effect was not out of harmony with Jefferson's new economic position.

In these later days, Jefferson devised an economic policy which he thought would establish a "national equilibrium" between agriculture, manufactures, and commerce; such a policy would "simplify" the economic organization of the United States and restrict economic activity to meeting simple needs, and it would make the United States self-sufficient and removed from the turmoil which international economic relations engender. He declared that the Embargo and related policies had promoted domestic manufactures:

They will have hastened the day when an equilibrium between the occupations of agriculture, manufactures, and commerce, shall simplify our foreign concerns to the exchange only of that surplus which we cannot consume for those articles of reasonable comfort or convenience which we cannot produce.[61]

[59] Jefferson, Second Inaugural Address, *ibid.*, III, 377.
[60] *Ibid.* Three years before this address, Jefferson declared that the national government should "protect manufactures" but only those "adapted to our circumstances." This advocacy was purely rhetorical at the time (1802).
[61] To the Democratic Republican Delegates from the Township of Washington County, etc., 1809, *ibid.*, XVI, 355–356.

Jefferson also proposed that all raw materials produced in the United States be worked into manufactured commodities rather than be exported, in order to lessen the nation's dependence on the rest of the world. His opponents charged that this was a "Chinese" policy of commerce, which indeed it was.[62] To avoid the embarrassment of advocating that which he had once decried —a manufacturing system—Jefferson urged that Americans concentrate on household fabrications as a complement to their agricultural pursuits. Indicating that he was aware of the dilemma, his letters between 1810 and 1815 reiterate the virtues of household manufactures.[63] These, he said, would beget diligence and self-reliance among the citizenry and remove them from the caprices of the market, and would make the United States economically independent of the rest of the world. He repeatedly urged that all foreign (particularly British) goods imported into the United States be boycotted (with the exception of extreme necessities). Jefferson himself established an extensive spinning mill at Monticello.

Yet the course of American industrial growth during the years of conflict with Britain, from about 1807 to 1816, was not marked by such a development. Although many household manufactures were introduced these were insignificant beside the larger-scale industry that developed under the protection furnished by the war. And the rising class of manufacturing entrepreneurs viewed the development very differently from Jefferson. Eventually Jefferson abandoned his insistence on household manufactures and accepted the inevitability of the factory system. When the war with Britain finally closed in 1815, so many vested interests had developed that the protective tariff of 1816 was virtually a foregone conclusion. Substantial and very vocal opposition was voiced to it, but this was of no avail against the legacy of the war and the incessant clamors of the protectionists for still higher duties.[64]

[62] Many years earlier Jefferson advocated such a policy in the very same terms and its intent was not essentially different from his later program. See above, p. 144.

[63] *Writings of Thomas Jefferson,* VIII, 352; XII, 294; XIII, 122, 123, 170, 207.

[64] See the interminable tracts of Matthew Carey who was never satisfied with the level of duties regardless of their magnitude.

After he had retired to Monticello, Jefferson looked wistfully back upon the years between the Declaration of Independence and the peace of 1815. The free traders had taken up the pre-1790 Jefferson to advance their case. He wrote in 1816 to Benjamin Austin that he had once believed in free trade,

but who in 1785 could foresee the rapid depravity which was to render the close of that century the disgrace of the history of man?

. . . .

We have experienced what we did not then believe, that there exists both profligacy and power enough to exclude us from the field of interchange with other nations: that to be independent for the comforts of life we must fabricate them ourselves. We must now place the manufacturer by the side of the agriculturist . . . Shall we make our own comforts, or go without them, at the will of a foreign nation? He, therefore, who is now against domestic manufactures, must be for reducing us either to dependence on that foreign nation, or to be clothed in skins, and to live like wild beasts in dens and caverns. I am not one of these; experience has taught me that manufactures are now as necessary to our independence as to our comfort; . . .[65]

One may say he looked back wistfully, for in this same letter he again reiterated his faith in the superiority of agriculture, in its supremacy over manufacturing, and in the bounty of the earth.

It was not only in international economic policy that Jefferson adopted Federalist methods. His program of subsidizing domestic industry and of giving the national government the direction of internal improvements was similar to the policy of the Federalist party. It differed from it in theory in that Jefferson insisted upon a constitutional amendment as a prerequisite to the exercise of the latter power, which he was almost forced to do in view of his past strictures on the unconstitutionality of Hamilton's measures.

Over the years Jefferson gradually abandoned his categorical opposition to monopoly. He had written in 1785 that monopoly was "contrary to the spirit of trade, and to the dispositions of merchants,"[66] yet even then he recognized that governmental

[65] *Writings of Thomas Jefferson*, XIV, 390, 391–392.
[66] Jefferson to the Count de Vergennes, *ibid.*, V, 69–70.

grants of monopoly privileges could be of advantage. He remarked on the question again in 1787 in considering the problem of exclusive rights in patents. Government interposition in such matters was of great value, he wrote, but "in practice so inseparable from abuse that it is best to leave citizens free in their pursuits with neither aid nor hindrance."[67] A few years later he declared that the constitutional provision for exclusive patent rights had "given a spring to invention beyond my imagination."[68] Eventually Jefferson settled upon the compromise of giving the inventor an exclusive grant but prohibiting him from imposing any conditions upon the user of the invention.[69] What he wanted essentially was the increased incentive resulting from monopoly grants without the ill effects of monopoly.[70] In conditions where free enterprise was unable to function, Jefferson approved of exclusive grants of trade. An instance of this was his approval of John Jacob Astor's plan to open fur trade in the Columbia River territory. He wrote to Astor, the founder of the famous family, "Your name will be handed down with that of Columbus and Raleigh, as the father of the establishment and founder of such an empire" (which would arise from commerce). And while Astor was providing for future generations, Jefferson hoped that he might "find a present account in the just profits you are entitled to expect from the enterprise."[71] The generous tone of the letter is remarkable in view of Jefferson's ill-concealed dislike of "millionary merchants."

IV

In recapitulation, an examination of Jefferson's papers and their relation to the economic problems of the United States between 1774 and 1816 reveals not one Jeffersonian system of economic policy but three. Until about 1790 he was dominated by agrarian-

---

[67] Jefferson to Monsieur L'Hommande, *ibid.*, VI, 255.
[68] Jefferson to Benjamin Vaughan, 1790, *ibid.*, VIII, 50.
[69] Jefferson to Dr. Thomas Cooper, 1815, *ibid.*, XIV, 174.
[70] Cf. the letter to Oliver Evans, 1807, *ibid.*, XI, 200–202.
[71] Jefferson to John Jacob Astor, *ibid.*, XIII, 432 f.

ism, and his expressions of policy most often took the form of advocating self-sufficient agrarian units. From 1790 to 1805, Jefferson formally adopted *laissez faire* as an objective but his expressions were still tinged with the earlier form of agrarianism. After 1805, he proposed measures that were consistent with the objectives established by Hamilton, though his methods differed from those of Hamilton in revealing a greater concern with constitutional legitimacy. That these periods in Jefferson's policy have not been distinguished and that he is most often categorized as a physiocrat (for which, as we have seen, the evidence is unsatisfactory) is not difficult to understand. His stature as a statesman and political thinker makes him vulnerable to willful interpretations. No little violence has been done to his ideas in the past century or so. Even after his declaration of 1816 in favor of protection, the Southern free traders continued to claim him as their own. Nor could the protectionists agree on what he said or what he meant. Matthew Carey castigated him for romantic agrarianism while Friedrich List set him at one with Hamilton.

This threefold development in Jeffersonian economics might suggest fundamental inconsistencies in his system of thought, and in one important aspect it does. Before 1805 he could very easily harmonize his minimum state with his economic policy, for the policy required no great concentration of power. After 1805 serious difficulties arose, however, over the compatibility of state and individual power in relation to the avowed economic functions of government. Because the international economic policy of the state cannot be separated from its domestic policy, the problem of protection cannot be viewed differently from the question of internal improvements. Here Jefferson's logic was impaled. He was alarmed by federal power over internal improvements, even though he admitted the power of protection. In the constitutional controversy of the twenties, he submitted to Madison a "Solemn Declaration and Protest of the Commonwealth of Virginia, on the Principles of the Constitution of the United States of America, and on the Violations of Them," which condemned internal improvements under direct or indirect federal auspices but said not one word on protection. This artificial separation was forgotten in the resolutions actually passed by Virginia.[72] However anomalous this declaration is in a political sense, it is significant as Jefferson's last pronouncement on economic policy, revealing that he maintained his advocacy of protection to the end.

---

[72] Cf. Jefferson's draft, *Writings of Thomas Jefferson*, XVII, 442–448, with the resolution adopted by Virginia, Herman V. Ames, ed., *State Documents on Federal Relations: The States and the United States* (Philadelphia: University of Pennsylvania Press, 1900–1906), pp. 141–142.

Jefferson, Hamilton, and the Constitution

Jefferson and Hamilton had much to do with interpreting the Constitution, but little or nothing to do with its framing. Had Jefferson been available, he could hardly have failed to be a delegate from his state to the convention which met in Phila- delphia in 1787, but he was then Minister of the United States at the court of France; he did not return to his own country, in fact, until after the Constitution had been ratified and put into operation with George Washington as President. Hamilton was a delegate to the Convention from the state of New York, but, since they voted in the Convention by states and he was regularly outvoted by the other New York delegates, he soon withdrew, realizing that he was virtually without influence on the deliberations. From what he said, however, and from what he wrote out for incorporation in the record, we know that he favored a national government so strongly centralized, so consolidated, that it would have had no chance of adoption by the states of the Union if it had been submitted to them. He would have reduced these states to administrative prov- inces, the governors of which were appointed by the President, who would himself hold office for life; and he would have reduced popular control to a very low point, for he had no confidence in the wisdom of the people. No doubt he would have accepted something less, as of course he had to do, but these views could not command much favor. Since the deliberations of the Convention were secret, they did not need to be made public, which was fortunate for him.

One person who certainly knew about them and, in fact, knew more about these proceedings than anybody else was James Madison, the man who best deserves to be called the father of the Constitution. (Biological figures of speech do not really fit; there were too many fathers.) Not only was he there all the time; he also kept careful notes on the proceedings. These were not published in his own lifetime, but it is safe to say that no man of his generation knew as much about what actually went on in the closed meetings in Philadelphia and about what the framers had in mind. His intimate knowledge was fully available to Jefferson after that gentleman returned from France, for these two had no secrets from each other. It is my own guess, however, that Jefferson did not take time to study the written notes carefully, and that he got his impressions chiefly from what Madison told him personally. This must have included some reference to the extreme views which Hamilton had expressed with respect to national consolidation.

Hamilton settled for considerably less in the ratification fight and performed magnificent service in that fight. Madison's service in it was comparable, and these two men cooperated in writing *The Federalist* papers, a work which excited Jefferson's enthusiasm and which has been universally recognized as a classic interpretation of the American governmental system under the Constitution. Since the original purpose of this series of essays was to win votes for ratification, however, and it was written in great haste, both men said some things they afterward regretted. For this reason no doubt both of them were glad that the authorship of the individual essays was not revealed. Since we now know just who wrote what, we can perceive that the constitutional philosophies of the two men were not identical, but it is as indisputable that they stood shoulder to shoulder in this fight as that they afterward diverged.

The explanation of this later divergence most favored by Hamilton's partisans was that it was owing to the sinister influence on Madison of Jefferson, after he came back from France full of wild revolutionary ideas. One difficulty about that fanciful theory is that Madison began to diverge from Hamilton before Jefferson got back on the national scene. Furthermore, in constitutional matters at this stage and perhaps at most times, it is nearer the truth to say that Madison told Jefferson than that Jefferson told Madison. Finally, it may be seriously doubted whether Jefferson brought back from France any important ideas that he did not already have when he went there. A more plausible explanation, it seems to me, is that Madison concluded that Hamilton in office as Secretary of the Treasury was seeking a greater degree of consolidation than he had argued for in the ratification fight, that he was in fact moving toward the sort of government that, as his expressions in the Philadelphia convention showed, he really wanted. This is to oversimplify the matter, however. Economic considerations were involved, and political opinion in Virginia surely was. That is, this was not merely a matter of constitutional theory. Further explanation must be sought in the actualities of the political situation. This episode bears directly on the central theme of this volume, that is, the interrelations of the theoretical and the practical.

Let us now return to Jefferson, who had been relegated to the role of distant observer while he was in France. If the Constitution as framed was a less powerful instrument than Hamilton wanted, it was a more powerful one than Jefferson had expected or thought necessary, and at first glance he feared that it might be made into an instrument of oppression. Unlike Hamilton and Madison, he had seen despotism at first hand in Europe and had recoiled against it. One of his specific objections—of which there were really only two—was to the perpetual re-eligibility of the President, which seemed to leave the way open to the eventual establishment of a monarchy. He had a phobia about kings which now appears to have been unwarranted so far as his own country was concerned, but we must remember that he lived in a world in which kings were the rule and republics the very rare exception. He was determined that in America the clock should not be turned backward, that there should be no resort to the British example, no return to the political system from which the young American republic had so painfully emerged. In that context his talk about kings and monocrats in this period of history does not sound so unrealistic. He continued to be disturbed, throughout this period, by what he described as monocratic tendencies, but his immediate fear that there might be an American king was quieted by the reflection that George Washington would be the first President. Jefferson, who viewed the national hero with a respect bordering on reverence, never thought he would permit himself to be made king. (In passing we may remind ourselves that Washington started the two-term tradition, and that Jefferson confirmed it.)

The second specific objection was not, as some might suppose, that the Constitution went too far in curtailing the powers of the states. He was surprised that the states had yielded so much but was fully aware that their powers had been far too great, and as an official he had had abundant reason to recognize the imperative need of bolstering up the general government. No, his immediate fears were not of what might happen to states; they were of what might happen to individuals. This is a crucial point, I think. A good reason for not putting tags on people is that it is generally impossible to find a perfect fit, but if I had to designate this complicated man of diverse genius by a single term I would call him an individualist. We must remember also that, although in his own commonwealth of Virginia he had observed and been part of a mild government, he had seen nowhere a government which in a positive way could be truly called beneficent. There was nothing remotely suggesting the welfare state, which renders direct services and benefits to its individual citizens. He had insufficient reason to think of government as a positive good. He did not say that government is a necessary evil and I do not believe that his approach to it was as negative as has often been alleged, but unquestionably he believed that all sorts of governments tended to be repressive and that rulers tended to become tyrannical.

In other words, individuals needed to be protected against their rulers, against any rulers. Specifically, the American Constitution needed a bill of rights and he was shocked that it did not have one. His correspondence with Madison on that subject is most interesting and illuminating. It made an impress on Madison, who was himself a staunch friend of human rights but had been giving most of his thought lately to the creation of an effective federal government. It was Madison who introduced the Bill of Rights in the form of amendments to the Constitution in the First Congress. Indeed, the promise of some action of the sort was a virtual condition under which his state and other states ratified the Constitution, and we have always regarded the Bill of Rights as a part of the original document, though it was not actually quite that. (Incidentally, it should be noted that Madison was particularly aware of the criticisms of the Constitution in the ratification fight, and of the explanations and assurances that were then given by its advocates. These bore chiefly on the limitation of centralized authority, and he took them so seriously that perhaps it may be said that he was now prepared to settle for less central power than he had advocated in the Federal Convention.)

Since Jefferson's major objections to the Constitution were met, he accepted it. He would never have assumed the Secretaryship of State if he had not. The partisan charge of later years that he was against the Constitution meant nothing more than that in his interpretation of that document he did not agree with Hamilton. He was no anti-Federalist in the original meaning of the term, whatever his political enemies might say.

The two men did not disagree on all points, of course, and we must recognize the danger of exaggerating their differences and ignoring the very large area of agreement. They approached constitutional questions from opposite angles, however, and the gap between them widened in the actualities of successive political situations. Had situations been different it is certainly conceivable that the gap would never have become so wide. I regard it as exceedingly unfortunate that it became such a chasm. I am disposed to explain it on the ground of what appears to be virtually a law of history, namely, that excess tends to promote excess, that extremes on one side lead to extremes on the other. To be more specific, I do not believe that Jefferson would have gone as far as he did in interpreting the Constitution in this era if Hamilton had not pressed things so far and so hard, and in the duel with Jefferson which ensued, I regard Hamilton as the aggressor, even though he himself claimed just the opposite.

Some degree of conflict was probably inevitable, however, in view of their antithetical philosophies and incompatible personalities. The temptation to dwell on their personalities must be resisted, for this conflict went much deeper than that. But in this connection Hamilton's personality is of particular importance, because the reaction against his policies and the constitutional interpretation with which he supported them cannot be dissociated from the personal reaction against him. He had constructive talents of the first order and in the realm of government and finance may truly be described as creative. But he was an exceedingly aggressive man, inordinately ambitious, and undeniably arrogant. He was a hard man to like unless one agreed with him completely, and it was easy to believe that he was doing everything possible to increase his own power. He provoked resistance. That he wanted power for himself cannot be doubted, but he also wanted it for the nation. Indeed, that is the best way to describe his central purpose.

Hamilton's patriotism cannot be questioned, but one can ask what he wanted a powerful nation for. He himself gave one of the best answers in something he said later in this decade, at a time when he and his partisans would have liked to enter the international arena on the side of Great Britain and against France. He wrote Rufus King, then our Minister in London: "I anticipate with you that this country will, ere long, assume an attitude correspondent with its great destinies—majestic, efficient and operative of great things. A noble career lies before it."[1] He wanted it to play a great and active role in the world, and it is easy to see why Theodore Roosevelt admired him. In the perspective of history it seems that Hamilton's major service was in laying foundations of national power for the future, and for this we should be grateful,

[1] Hamilton to Rufus King, October 2, 1798, H. C. Lodge, ed., *Works of Alexander Hamilton* (1904), VIII, 511.

since we have had to enter the world arena. In his own time he seized every opportunity to extend the authority of the general government; indeed, he created opportunities. He wanted as much as possible to be done at the center; regarding the state governments as a good deal of a nuisance, he had no concern for state rights; and he was indifferent to, even contemptuous of, the ordinary individual.

His attitude toward ordinary individuals would not commend him to our democratic age, but in certain respects he was a notably prophetic figure. Indeed, he was far ahead of his time. The United States was not ready to play a great role in the world until the era of Theodore Roosevelt, and prior to our own century its major task was to open up its own land and develop its own resources. That sort of thing could not be well directed from the center. Jefferson correctly perceived that at this stage it was of the utmost importance to have local vitality, or, if you will, vitality at the grass roots; and he believed that men will do and dare most if they breathe the air of freedom. It can be argued, therefore, that after Hamilton's great financial measures, which served not only to make the nation solvent but also to widen the authority of the national government, centralization had gone far enough. He envisioned a more spacious governmental edifice than these times required. That was the way Jefferson and Madison felt about it anyway, and if they could not stop him one way they would try another.

They did not do too well when they sought to check him on constitutional grounds in the most important theoretical conflict (outside the field of foreign affairs) in Washington's administration, the one over the first Bank of the United States. In this, Hamilton had much the better of the argument. Here is an excellent example of the impingement of political considerations on constitutional interpretation. Madison and Jefferson opposed the creation of this bank for a good many reasons, including their own ignorance of banking. Their own state had benefited relatively little from Hamilton's financial system, of which he regarded the bank as the crown, and they saw this as another instance of federal encroachment. Madison opposed it in the House on its merits, but he was not at his best in the field of banking, and he fell back on the Constitution. He could find nothing in the Constitution which, in his opinion, empowered Congress to grant a charter to a corporation. The bill was passed nonetheless, but Washington hesitated to sign it, since he rightly had a very high opinion of Madison as an interpreter of the Constitution. He passed it on to the Attorney General, who agreed with Madison, and then to Jefferson. It is from the latter's argument that we generally date the doctrine of strict construction. We might date it from Madison's speech, which contained essentially the same arguments, though they sound stricter in Jefferson's paper.

The doctrine of strict construction is much easier to understand than the one with which Hamilton opposed it. It is simply that a document means just what it says—no more, no less. According to the Constitution the general, or federal, government possesses only specifically enumerated powers, all the others belonging to the states. In none of these enumerated powers is there any reference to granting charters of incorporation. Accordingly one must have recourse to the general expressions—the necessary and proper clause, for example. This Jefferson construed with complete rigidity, as meaning in effect "absolutely necessary." At this point I begin to be somewhat repelled by his argument; it is too rigid; he is imposing too severe a test. And I wonder if he would have taken so stiff and unyielding a position if he had not had so many grounds for wanting to stop Hamilton. As for the general welfare clause, his discussion of that, while somewhat pedantic, makes a lot of sense. If that clause were construed too liberally, Congress could do anything it liked, and there would be no need to have in the Constitution a list of the things it could do. Like Parliament, the legislature would be omnipotent.

The forbidding rigidity he displayed in this argument is not at all like Jefferson when he was discussing science or religion, and does not sound like the man who had said that constitutions should be revised every twenty years or so. But he would stand for no trifling with law while it was still on the books, least of all with a constitution; he regarded basic law as a shield or fence for the protection of human beings against wrong; he distrusted rulers who might interpret law in their own way for their own purposes; and by now he deeply distrusted Hamilton. So he prepared a paper which, though narrow, was utterly logical and which upon its face looked unanswerable.

Hamilton's answer to it is, in my opinion, the greatest paper he ever drew. He had to prove that the Constitution meant more than it explicitly said, that no government could be effective if rigidly confined within a narrow framework, that latitude must be permitted in the interpretation of basic law. He did this by starting with the premise that the federal government has sovereign power within the field allotted to it, and by concluding that in the exercise of this it may reasonably employ any means not specifically prohibited. There is more to his argument than this, but the important thing to remember is that the dominant trend of constitutional interpretation in our country was here anticipated. And whatever else this meant, it surely meant that our constitutional system would not be static but would be allowed to grow and might become dynamic. The essence of the matter Hamilton himself stated in a passage which ought to be quoted more often than it is: "The moment the literal meaning is departed from, there is a chance of error and abuse. And yet an adherence to the letter of its powers would at once arrest the motions of government." If Jefferson's observations of government and of his colleague had not rendered him so distrustful, he might have fitted these words into his own philosophy of progress, for certainly he did not believe in a static society. There is more sweet reasonableness in Hamilton's words, however, than those who differed with him in policy had detected in his public conduct; and they may be pardoned for believing that he was interpreting and would continue to interpret the Constitution to suit himself. They did not give up the fight, and it is well they did not, for he was a man who had to be kept in bounds. He was always likely to overreach himself.

This conflict had been waged behind the scenes, not in public; and there is no reason to suppose that Hamilton's opinion was shown to Jefferson and Madison. They undoubtedly knew his general line, but they did not see his full argument and had no occasion to rebut it. They did not abandon strict construction, though I do not believe that they again used it in a form which was quite this rigid. It was a natural, almost inevitable line for them to take afterward as leaders of the opposition to a government which was exercising powers which they thought unwarranted and regarded as dangerous to human liberty. This was after Washington had relinquished the first office but when Hamilton was more powerful than ever. It was the time of the Alien and Sedition Acts.

(Some extremely interesting constitutional questions, relating to the powers of the House of Representatives with respect to treaties, came up in the long fight over Jay's treaty. Jefferson was then in retirement and Republican policy was determined by Madison, Gallatin, and others in Congress. The episode is an unusually good illustration of the effect of party policy on constitutional positions. Jefferson expressed himself freely on the subject in private, showing himself a complete Republican in this matter and taking a different position from the one he probably would have as Secretary of State. Since this subject is relatively technical, however, I shall not enter into it here.)

The situation created by the notorious Alien and Sedition Acts was far more dangerous to Jefferson's dearest interests than the one in which Hamilton successfully defended the Bank of the United States. That proved to be an excellent institution even though it did relatively little for the agricultural districts. These measures were adopted at a time of hysterical patriotism and fantastic fear of subversive foreign influences (especially French) the like of which our country has rarely seen, though our own generation can perceive a certain similarity to it in the madness we had to live through shortly after World War II, when some excited people saw subversives behind every bush. There was no single public figure in this earlier period of hysteria who can be properly compared to the late Senator Joseph McCarthy, who played a unique role as an inciter of suspicion and hatred, but on the whole I believe that the situation then was considerably worse. There was a concerted campaign, in the name of patriotism, against every form of criticism of the federal government, and against the very existence of political opposition. In short, freedom of opinion and speech was at stake, and the party of which Jefferson was the undisputed leader was threatened with destruction. By silencing its newspapers the party in power sought to deprive it of a voice. This was the policy of the extreme section of the party commonly described as High Federalists. Their acknowledged leader was not John Adams but Hamilton, who was not in office but whose influence was at its height. If I seem to ignore him in discussing this particular matter you may safely assume that Jefferson and Madison were battling against him, more than against any other man, and that he opposed them on all points.

All I have space for here is the response to this challenge which Jefferson and Madison made in the Kentucky and Virginia Resolutions. These were conceived in no vacuum, and the direction they took, though not necessarily the details, was determined by the actualities of the situation. The three branches of the general government—executive, legislative, and judicial—were united with respect to these detested laws. Hence Jefferson turned to the states because he had nothing else to turn to. He had said very little about the rights of states before he became fearful of Hamiltonian consolidation. Now, under the pressure of circumstances he found intolerable, he took the most extreme position of his entire life with respect to states' rights.

The direct part he played in these events was not made public until long years afterward, by which time he had returned to a more moderate position and his own administration as President had been assailed on grounds of states' rights by his political opponents. Not until after his retirement was it known that he drafted the Kentucky Resolutions. But they and their companion Virginia Resolutions, which Madison drew, became part of the public record. In later years these documents were often cited by upholders of the states'-rights tradition—a tradition which our Southern forefathers naturally clung to as they passed into the minority, but in the name of which they took actions which proved disastrous. Many of these forefathers of ours misinterpreted Jefferson's position. Never again did he emphasize the theory of states' rights as he did here, and not even here were these the prime consideration. What he did was to invoke states' rights in defense of human rights, as a means and not an end. And it is as a champion of human rights that he should be best remembered.

This question has so many ramifications that I cannot possibly do justice to it in brief compass. For the purposes of the present discussion, I should remind you that the Alien and Sedition Acts have received virtually unanimous condemnation at the bar of history. Therefore, Jefferson was abundantly warranted in inducing the states of Kentucky and Virginia to protest against them. He sought to support his position, as the Republicans had already done in Congress, by arguing that these acts were unconstitutional. Without entering into these arguments I simply make the point that in a dangerous political situation he and his party resorted to the Constitution for defense. Naturally, they followed the line of strict construction and, against what they regarded as an unwarranted assumption of power by the federal government, they talked of the reserved rights of states. In the Kentucky Resolutions of 1798, Jefferson went to the dangerous extreme of asserting the right of a single state to declare unconstitutional an act of Congress which it judged to be in violation of the original compact, and in his draft he said that the nullification of such a law within a state's own borders was proper procedure. This proposal the Kentuckians left out of their first set of resolutions but they used it the next year in a second set which Jefferson did not write.

The South Carolinians resurrected the word "nullification" a generation later in a wholly different situation. They were then opposing a tariff which was obviously disadvantageous to them, but their protest, unlike Jefferson's, was not in the name of the universal human right to freedom. Madison in his resolutions did not claim the right of nullification by a single state. In the final document of this series, his magnificent Report of 1800, he refined away the original excesses and put the Republican party on defensible ground. Without implying that I now agree with everything he said, I can safely say that there is real validity in the doctrine of states' rights as presented in this report. With all this Jefferson went along, showing increased moderation as dangers lessened. But the highest wave at the peak of the storm left its mark on the shore.

This episode provides a striking illustration of the intimate connection between constitutional interpretation and political situations. Indeed, we would do well to think of these historic resolutions primarily as political documents. We should certainly remember that Jefferson never attempted to put into practice the extreme theory he advanced at a time when he almost despaired of human liberty and the survival of his party. This was a theoretical matter altogether. It is far more important to remember what he fought against and what he fought for than a particular weapon which he never regarded as anything but a threat and which in fact he afterward discarded.

In dealing briefly with so complicated a subject as this, it is easy to create a confused impression. I hope that one impression at least is clear: namely, that people ought to know more about history. We have no right to expect highly detailed and special knowledge of many people, but surely we can ask that anybody who draws on ancient documents or doctrines to support a position he himself is taking should inform himself of the major circumstances which caused that document or doctrine to come into being. The only thing that can be safely quoted out of context is something that bears upon itself the mark of timelessness and universality. Constitutional interpretations do not do that, even when they are reiterated often enough to become doctrines, even when they harden into dogma. They cannot be divorced from circumstances. It is fortunate that this is so, for no constitution which cannot be adjusted to changing conditions can be expected to survive. One of the major reasons for the long survival and recognized success of our Constitution is that it has proved flexible. Judges have to consider all that has gone before, and they should anticipate as best they can what the future effects of their judgment may be, but, after all, they are addressing themselves to particular cases in specific situations.

In constitutional matters, as in theological, I regard the absolutist spirit as unfortunate. It is presumptuous to think that God is on one side or the other in a constitutional debate. The truth need not lie precisely in the middle, but in major controversies there are generally important conflicting interests which must somehow be reconciled. One of the major tasks of government is to reconcile them. To me it is regrettable that the two eminent men we have been talking about diverged so far, and I dislike the excesses of both, though I do not say that I dislike them equally. I can forgive Jefferson more because I tend to value freedom more than power, to be more fearful of power than of liberty. But if we now had as feeble a national government as he advocated a century and a half ago, our liberties would surely perish. So I must recognize that somehow we must reconcile ourselves to Hamilton. Indeed, I suppose that we have been reconciling the conflicting philosophies of these two men from their day to this as we have found ourselves in a succession of particular situations.

JULIAN P. BOYD

✪

Thomas Jefferson's "Empire of Liberty"

On March 4, 1801, Chief Justice John Marshall administered the oath of the highest office in the land to Thomas Jefferson. Six decades were to elapse before History, with her exquisite if often perverted sense of drama, would again bring to the inaugural ceremony an equally ironic symbolism. Those six decades would witness the play and counterplay of two great conflicting ideas concerning the origin, nature, and ends of the American Union, ideas and conflicts symbolized almost perfectly in the persons of Marshall and Jefferson. Lincoln, drawing heavily upon Jefferson for his ideals and humane attitudes, entered upon the task of preserving the Union by taking his oath of office under a Chief Justice whose most conspicuous decision had speeded its disruption. But Taney's predecessor, as no one knew better than Jefferson, was composed of different mettle. On that dramatic morning in March, 1801, as the newly chosen President looked into the calm black eyes of the Chief Justice, each must have been conscious of the symbolism of their meeting, as they indubitably were of their opposing concepts of the Union.

Both were Virginians. Both had been born within the frontier, though far enough on the outskirts of settlement to feel the challenging winds from the vast wilderness to the westward. Both

---

Reprinted from *The Virginia Quarterly Review,* Vol. XXIV (1948), pp. 538–554, by permission. Copyright © 1948 by Julian P. Boyd.

stemmed from the same distant and progenitive Randolph, deriving from him a consanguinity that neither exhibited in outward expression. Both grew up in the same kind of sturdy, self-reliant home environment, each possessing at its head a stalwart, intelligent, respected leader of the county. Both had been bred to the law under that noble teacher, George Wythe, though his tutelage of Marshall was but a brief and tenuous relationship and that of Jefferson a profound and transforming influence. Both had eagerly embraced the principles of the Revolution and had served the American cause well, the one distinguishing himself in the field and the other in legislation. Yet out of this remarkable identity of background came one of the mighty opposites of American history. The explanation of this divergence arising from similarity is as baffling as the explanation of genius, but the fact of its existence and of its dynamic influence on this nation is indubitable. Sharing an indentity with the heroic conflict between Hamilton and Jefferson, it was both more dramatic in its steady unfolding to its climactic opposition and more incisive in its delineation of the issues.

Late in life Marshall, out of the fullness of his judicial power, set down a brief but penetrating account of his own political change and development. Applying to himself the same clear intellect that he applied to the principles of law, he remembered "the wild and enthusiastic democracy" with which his political opinions were colored at the opening of the Revolution. "I had grown up," he declared, "at a time when a love of union and resistance to the claims of Great Britain were the inseparable inmates of the same bosom;—when patriotism and a strong fellow feeling with our suffering fellow citizens of Boston were identical . . . and I had imbibed these sentiments so thoroughly that they constituted a part of my being. I carried them with me into the army . . . where I was confirmed in the habit of considering America as my country, and congress as my government." He had suffered with the army, returning to civil life with the viewpoint of the veteran soldier. A member of the Virginia legislature in the 1780's, he found what the postwar soldier had so recurrently found—that "everything was afloat," that principles he had regarded as unchallengeable were "brought annually into doubt," that in general "we had no safe anchorage ground." These things, Marshall remembered, "gave a high value in my estimation to *that article in the constitution which imposes restrictions on the states.*"

These precise recollections of the aged jurist are revealing. Here, in these reminiscent pages, we see the young zealot turned conservative. Here was the revolutionary at twenty seeking safe anchorages and undoubted principles at thirty. Here was the inflamed patriot, risking life in defense of his fellow-men in distant Boston, turned skeptic and fearful of betrayal by the elected representatives of his native Virginia. Here was the Virginian becoming a nationalist to help magnify the powers of the whole and so administer them as to restrict the parts. Fear of the turbulences of democracy, concern for the interests and safeguards of property, and distrust of the wisdom of the people in their political decisions combined with respect for the talents and virtues of the elite to produce in Marshall a pattern endlessly recurring in human society. It was a pattern that he shared with many of the most virtuous and patriotic of Americans, including George Washington, Alexander Hamilton, Rufus King, Fisher Ames, Gouverneur Morris, and others. It was, indeed, a pattern that Jefferson believed to be one of the two natural political divisions into which men fall in all countries: "those who fear and distrust the people, and wish to draw all powers from them into the hands of the higher classes." It was the pattern that led Marshall, at Washington's suggestion, to enter Congress to try to stem the subversive tide of Jacobinical principles. It was the pattern that impelled him to give to the Supreme Court an unrivaled prestige and to set the course of constitutional law for more than a century, exercising a jealous guardianship over contractual rights, curbing the legislative powers of the states, and enlarging the authority of the federal government. It was the pattern of government by a ruling group of the good, the rich, and the wellborn and under the federal Constitution, which had been shaped largely to their purposes, one of the most effective implements was Marshall's doctrine of inherent sovereignty against which the Tenth Amendment opposed a steadily crumbling barrier.

Opposite the pattern that Marshall embodied was the second of Jefferson's two natural political categories: "those who identify themselves with the people, have confidence in them, cherish and consider them the most honest and safe, although not the most wise depository of the public interests." This was not an attitude of protecting and buttressing what some men had achieved, but a faith in what all men might accomplish. It was an attitude designed not to insulate the good, the rich, and the wellborn, but to draw forth that natural aristocracy of virtue and talent which Jefferson regarded as "the most precious gift of nature for the instruction, the trusts, and government of society."

What, then, must Marshall have thought as he listened to the stirring sentences that Jefferson expressed a few moments after taking the oath of office? "I know indeed that some honest men have feared that a republican government cannot be strong; that this government is not strong enough," the President declared. ". . . I believe this, on the contrary, *the strongest government on earth.* I believe it the only one where every man, at the call of the law, would fly to the standard of the law; and would meet invasions of public order, as his own personal concern." Men, that is, could be led by a human ideal to give their last strength where distrustful rulers could not compel.

Was this mere rhetoric? What must Marshall and those who shared his view have thought of this resolute declaration coming from one who, since 1798, had been foremost amongst defenders of the rights of the states against the powers of the national government and who came into office with an overwhelming public approval of that constitutional principle? The words were at war with every tenet in the Hamilton-Marshall concept of national authority. Could any government long exist, to say nothing of becoming strong, if any or all of its constituent parts might exercise the right of veto? Had not the British Empire failed to preserve its strength in 1776 when local constituencies asserted their equality with what Blackstone called the supreme, absolute, uncontrolled authority of Parliament? Had not the government under the Articles of Confederation exhibited a fatal weakness because sovereign states linked in that compact could ignore or resist with impunity the resolutions and requisitions of Congress? Had not the Federal Convention of 1787 devised a more perfect union specifically to remedy this weakness? On this great issue, the correct principle was as clear to Marshall as it had been to Blackstone.

If Marshall wondered, doubted, and frowned in disagreement as he listened to the haunting phrases of the First Inaugural, he was not alone. History, too, has doubted. Less by historians, more by popular legend, and most of all by partisan claims, Jefferson has been regarded not as the staunch advocate of a strong, indissoluble union but as the zealous champion of states' rights. Opposing the ends for which Hamilton and Marshall sought to mobilize the national power, he has become for many the foe of national power itself. In 1788 Hector St. John de Crèvecoeur, writing to Jefferson, expressed the hope that "the destructive jealousy, the fatal influence of local prepossessions" would be at least partly extinguished by the adoption of the federal Constitution and that "one great national prevailing sentiment" would operate throughout the nation. De Crèvecoeur, knowing Jefferson's political principles and public acts, wrote with the confidence of one who felt that his hope was deeply shared. But he little dreamed that the great spokesman for national ideals to whom he addressed these remarks would become to many of his countrymen a spokesman also for these local jealousies and prepossessions and, even worse, would find the principles that he employed to protect human rights turned against them. Macaulay in 1857, in the first of four remarkable letters that he addressed to H. S. Randall, noted—and deplored—the fact that during the first half of the nineteenth century American institutions had been "constantly becoming more Jeffersonian and less Washingtonian. It is surely strange that, while this process has been going on, Washington should have been exalted into a god, and Jefferson degraded into a demon." A demon, that is, who advocated principles of human right that the mid-nineteenth century called glittering generalities and who advanced the doctrine of the rights of "sovereign" states. The process that Macaulay noted has been enormously accelerated since he wrote. Extension of the popular control of political institutions has proceeded inexorably. This much is admittedly Jeffersonian. But at the same time, parallel to this development, national power has grown in gigantic measure, reducing the doctrine of states' rights almost to the ignominious status of a shibboleth. This, according to the generally accepted view, is Hamiltonian and Marshallian.

Such a view, I venture to suggest, has done both Jefferson and his country a disservice. It has obscured the great end he labored to achieve and has magnified unduly the means he employed, means which the passage of time rather than the conditions of his day made irrelevant. His was a constructive achievement, grounded upon an enlarged view of man in relation to his potentialities and to the society in which he moves. His devotion to the Union, his belief in its strength and immense potentialities, his wholehearted and undeviating acceptance of the idea and meaning of nationhood were characterized by a faith, a vision, and an elevation of purpose that made him all but unique among the Founding Fathers. Only Franklin was his peer as an embodiment of the Enlightenment which provided the intellectual climate for this new and unprecedented nation and even Franklin was not his peer in grandeur of moral purpose.

Methods of arranging and distributing political power were not among Jefferson's absolutes. His advocacy of an agrarian commonwealth, its greatest concentrations of political power localized within the immediate purview of the citizen, its distant agencies of government restricted to foreign affairs and such domestic concerns as were specifically delegated to it, its executive, legislative, and judicial functions carefully compartmented, was a realistic, effective arrangement under the social and economic conditions of his day. He did not believe that those conditions would continue unchanged and unchangeable; still less did he expect succeeding generations to be bound by the contractual commitments of his generation. "Nothing, then," he declared in 1824, "is unchangeable but the inherent and inalienable rights of man" and to protect these, as he had expressed it half a century earlier, the people had the right to change their government, "laying its foundations on such principles, and organizing its powers in such form, as to them shall seem most likely to effect their Safety and Happiness." Believing the people to be the ultimate source of power and constitutions and laws merely their instruments, he believed unfalteringly in the destiny of a nation whose only immutable foundation was the rights of its citizens. Perhaps better than any other contemporary he sensed the fact that the people, too, believed in their own national destiny. This was the irresistible force, the abundant source of national strength and unity, that he understood and voiced.

Understanding history, he perceived that laws and constitutions merely codify and do not create the elements of nationhood. The monumental achievements of American constitutionalism—the Declaration of Independence, the Articles of Confederation, the Northwest Ordinance, the federal Constitution—were the written expressions of a people already unified in ideals, as Jefferson clearly perceived. History offered abundant evidence of the futility of attempting to reverse this process. John Locke's Fundamental Constitutions of Carolina, as Jefferson must have known, endeavored to establish centralized power in the hands of a ruling class far exceeding anything proposed by Hamilton or his contemporaries, but these were merely acts of intellectual virtuosity and not a crystallization of national aspirations. Lacking the cementing force of an ideal sprung from human hearts and minds, they were cast upon history's intellectual rubbish heap along with scores of written charters of the past century and a half that have tried to imitate the act of drafting a document without matching a people's act of faith. Funding acts, national bank charters, theories of inherent sovereignty, and doctrines of judicial review might organize the credit of the nation and enlarge its powers but these, important as they were, could not in themselves create enduring bonds of nationality. The great fiscal measures of Hamilton and the judicial statecraft of Marshall, universally regarded as achievements by advocates of a strong national government, rest at bottom upon an abstraction phrased by Jefferson in the opening paragraphs of the Declaration of Independence and upon its validity as an expression of the mind of the people. It was this exalted statement of the national ideal and Jefferson's undeviating pursuit of it that entitle him to rank not with those who employ an outworn doctrine to oppose the national will, but among the foremost advocates of "the strongest government on earth." Those who feared this ultimate force or sought to circumscribe it stood in uncomprehending resentment at their defeat by one whose political principles seemed to them to reveal more of inconsistency than of firm conviction. Historians and political scientists, no less than contemporary partisans, have mislabeled his adherence to the national ideals as political opportunism if not constitutional hypocrisy. But Jefferson's devotion to a nation based on the unchanging rights of men and his concept of a readily changeable distribution of national power were not conceived for the comfort of political opponents or for the accommodation of scholars' generalizations. They were intended for the support of a self-governing people in their pursuit of an ideal. Many of his contemporaries, of whom Hamilton and Marshall are conspicuous because of their stature, embraced this ideal in youth, faltered in midcourse, and came at last to oppose its implications if not its terms. Theirs was the ultimate opportunism, his the settled and unchanging course.

Jefferson's assertion of belief in the strength of republican government was, therefore, not a rhetorical gesture but an expression of a profound conviction. His daring to mention in the First Inaugural the possibility that some honest patriots might be induced to abandon the great experiment in the full tide of success was evidence that he knew quite well many had indeed considered its abandonment. He must have remembered how, in the debates of June, 1776, even before the Declaration of Independence was proclaimed to the world, the threat of disunion had been voiced, paradoxically making disunionism older than the Union itself. A year after his inauguration, during the thunderous debate over the repeal of the Judiciary Act of 1801, the threat of separation would again be made. In another decade and a half the men of the Essex Junto against whom he had declared implacable hostility would come near to the establishment of their New England Confederacy. These assertions of the right of secession, as historians have long since pointed out, were repeated in many forms and in many causes by different political parties from the earliest days of the republic. For, as the twentieth century would rediscover, this was the central problem of all politics—that of balancing and adjusting the rights and claims of conflicting sovereignties. If the solution to this problem were to be that of Calhoun, logic if not the dynamic of history would lead inevitably down the path to disunion or, as phrased by another great Southerner, to self-determination. If the solution were to be of the sort linked with the names of Hamilton and Marshall, the steady flow of centripetal forces would create an ever-growing vortex of power at the center and an ever-diminishing area of authority at the periphery. In our own pragmatic way we have disposed of the issue for ourselves without solving the problem at all. Perhaps it is one of those problems we refuse to recognize as insoluble. Certainly the Founding Fathers, as astute and as disinterested a group of men as ever faced the fundamental issues of government, could only dispose of the enigma by passing it on to a later generation, trusting to its wisdom, forbearance, and skill in adjustment to keep the greatest of experiments going.

But to Jefferson, upon whom fell the first great crisis calling for statesmanlike adjustment, the issue was one lying far deeper than those that might be arranged by harmonious political manipulations. It lay deeper even than an intellectual acceptance of the philosophy of self-government. It lay so deep as to reach the innermost loyalties. The salient fact that we have too long overlooked is that the cardinal principle of Jefferson's life was his uncompromising devotion to the Union because of its identity with human rights. It was a compact with the future of man, not with his past errors. Jefferson knew the world and its imperfections too well not to be aware of the immense obstacles that needed to be removed before a government based on reason and justice could realize its promise. In this respect we must except him from the generalization made in Carl Becker's profound work *The Heavenly City of the Eighteenth Century Philosophers* that the faith of the Enlightenment in man's capacity for rational and just behavior was a naïve faith, engaging and humane though it might be. Jefferson was too great a humanist, too much the embodiment of the universal man of the eighteenth century, to place his reliance solely upon the intellect. His devotion to liberty, to freedom of inquiry, to an educational system that would enlarge moral and intellectual capacities, to the idea of the destiny of the American people was a passionate loyalty. In this respect we must except him from the generalizations of those modern philosophers—Niebuhr, for example—whose reaction to eighteenth-century rationalism and secularism has led them to minimize its moral content and to attribute contemporary ills to the supposed "shallowness of a liberalism based on illusions of reason." Because this republican experiment held forth a promise for all men everywhere, Jefferson believed with overwhelming conviction that it would endure. "I own," he declared in 1801, "that the day which should convince me of the contrary doctrine would be the bitterest of my life." The second number of *The Federalist* declared that "politicians now appear, who insist that . . . instead of looking for safety and happiness in union, we ought to seek it in a division of the States into distinct confederacies or sovereignties." This was a doctrine of Patrick Henry, George Mason, and many other stalwart Americans in 1788, but it was never a doctrine of Thomas Jefferson. Its acceptance would have meant a denial of the ideal for which the nation had been founded.

The "Empire of Liberty" that Jefferson envisaged was one with that described in the same number of *The Federalist*—"a people descended from the same ancestors, speaking the same language, professing the same religion, attached to the same principles of government, very similar in their manners and customs, and who, by their joint counsels, arms, and efforts, fighting side by side throughout a long and bloody war, have nobly established general liberty and independence." But the Jeffersonian Empire of Liberty was also more than this. Language, religion, customs, and traditions shared in common indubitably provided the sense of commonalty essential to nationhood, but an insistence upon uniformity might also be equated with tyranny. Toward tyranny in any form Jefferson had vowed eternal hostility and in his Empire of Liberty, therefore, tolerance of diversity was implicit. His devotion to this nation was not the narrow patriotism of the Greeks nor the barbaric sense of fatherland that Goethe and Lessing abhorred. Though he called it an Empire of Liberty, it was to be neither an isolated political entity nor an imperialistic force for compulsory extension of ideals of liberty: its domain and compulsions would be in the realm of the mind and spirit of man, freely and inexorably transcending political boundaries, incapable of being restrained, and holding imperial sway not by arms or political power but by the sheer majesty of ideas and ideals. The great republican experiment would be an example and a beacon, unsheltered and unafraid of the light of truth. Its own people would be at once its greatest strength and its most searching critics.

To this task of remolding ancient institutions, stripping away the incongruous heritages of the past, and planning the route to the future, Jefferson dedicated himself with the urgent industry of a zealot. His great legal and political reforms in Virginia during the Revolution provide the first comprehensive index to his concept of the Empire of Liberty. Privilege was at war with the principles of this new nation and so he aimed a destructive blow at primogeniture and other pillars of what he considered an artificial and unnatural aristocracy. So great was the weight of custom that Rochefoucauld-Liancourt, two decades after the abolition of primogeniture in Virginia, found testators still favoring the eldest son with their inheritances, but the privilege was no longer protected legally and in time the force of an idea destroyed the inherited custom. An established religion was also an incongruity in a society dedicated to freedom of conscience and the protecting barriers surrounding it were removed. Education in such an Empire of Liberty was of the utmost importance if the people in general were to understand their rights and responsibilities, if the superior talents scattered by nature through all parts of society were to be improved, and if the geniuses so necessary to the development of man's potentialities were to be encouraged. Hence Jefferson envisaged a system of education not to accommodate an average mediocrity but to give every individual the privilege of unlimited opportunities for development—an aristocratic system of education equated with the natural aristocracy of virtue and talent. These and other enactments in Jefferson's political reforms in Virginia, which he hoped to see duplicated in all parts of the nation, he conceived "as forming a system by which every fibre would be eradicated of ancient or future aristocracy; and a foundation laid for a government truly republican." As a legislator, as Governor, as chief executive, and as private citizen, Jefferson guided his entire conduct by these concepts of his Empire of Liberty. His angry rejection of the theories of Buffon and Abbé Raynal concerning the degenerative quality of all life in America was not the chauvinism of a narrow patriot: it was a rejection made with passion because such a theory struck at the roots of his profound belief in the destiny of the American people and in the endurance of their nation.

Next to his role as spokesman for the national ideal, Jefferson perhaps made his greatest contribution to the number, strength, and duration of the bonds of union by his understanding of the relation of a people to its land. Brought up on the fringes of settlement in the Virginia piedmont, son of an explorer and cartographer, he early realized the vast potentialities awaiting the American nation in the West. The letter that he addressed to George Rogers Clark on December 25, 1779, was one of the earliest of his statesmanlike expressions concerning westward expansion. Its essence was that military conquest should be so conducted, and conquered people so treated in respect to their enjoyment of religion and customs, that there should be added "to the empire of liberty an extensive and fertile country, thereby converting dangerous enemies into valuable friends." During the years immediately following the Revolution when leaders along the Western frontier, drawing their arguments from the Declaration of Independence itself, began organizing movements for separate, independent states, Jefferson deplored this "Vermont doctrine" as an abrogation of the compact of the states. "I wish to see," he wrote in 1788, "the Western Country in the hands of people well disposed, who know the value of the connection between that and the maritime states and who wish to cultivate it. I consider their happiness as bound up together, and that every measure should be taken which may draw the bands of union tighter."

Both in his public duty and in his private capacity, Jefferson acted consistently upon this policy. He was one of the first and

most zealous advocates of a surrender of claims to Western territory by Virginia and other states, moving resolutely against this
great obstacle to the consolidation of the Union. He was assiduous
in his efforts to persuade legislators that it was individual pioneers
and settlers, not great Eastern land capitalists, who would develop
the West and cause it to add strength to the Union. While Robert
Morris, George Washington, James Wilson, Benjamin Franklin,
and many other founders of the republic were heavily engaged in
this favorite form of investment in eighteenth-century America and
saw no necessary conflict between their private acts and public
policy, Jefferson refrained. Just as he refused to become involved
in the engrossment of vast tracts of land for private gain, so he
stood fast against state rivalries and claims that jeopardized the
Union in its most critical years. He advocated, moreover, such a
system of sale and tenure of land—low costs and allodial titles—
as would protect the "great bulk of his countrymen" who were not
always in a position to protect themselves. But these were attitudes
toward the extension of the Empire of Liberty westward that
Jefferson could not always implement as legislator or executive.
Jealousies among states because of conflicting territorial claims
came all too close to disrupting the Union and land speculators
commanded a voice in the Continental Congress that sometimes
drowned the voice of statesmanship.

Yet on two great occasions Jefferson's constructive acts leading
to the expansion and solidarity of the Union were unparalleled in
their importance. The first was the enactment of the Northwest
Ordinance of 1784 and the second was the Purchase of Louisiana
of 1803. Both, be it noted, were based upon the doctrine of implied
powers of the national government, a doctrine usually more closely
linked to the names of Hamilton, Wilson, and Marshall than to
that of Jefferson.

Scarcely had the final act of separation from the British Empire
been completed before the Continental Congress was obliged to
face this central problem of balancing the sovereign rights of the
whole against those of the parts—the same problem that had
troubled the statesmen of Whitehall for a generation. Were the
new sovereignties proposed by leaders in the West to be tolerated

and encouraged to set up such forms of government as would "seem most likely to effect their Safety and Happiness"? The arguments concerning the natural rights of the conquerors of a wilderness that Jefferson had stated in his "Summary View" and in the Declaration of Independence were as valid here as they had been in 1776. Or, since these Western areas lay within the territory ceded to the United States by the Treaty of Paris—territory won by the joint efforts of the states in their bid for nationhood—were they to be regarded as colonial dependencies of the older Confederation? Neither extreme was acceptable. Though American constitutional lawyers in the early days of the Revolution had argued that there was no "Middle Doctrine" for this perennial problem, Jefferson and his colleagues in Congress now proceeded to act upon such a middle doctrine and to lay the foundations for an indefinite expansion of the Empire of Liberty. The new governments in the West would be neither colonial dependencies nor independent sovereignties: they would be admitted to the Union on a plane of equality with the original states. Their governments would be republican in form, they would share in the public debt, they would participate as equals in the authority exercised by the general government. This much the Continental Congress would accept. But two other propositions advocated by Jefferson were so far-seeing, so wise, so statesmanlike in their implications that he stood almost alone in advancing them. One would have riveted the bonds of union so firmly as to make national dissolution impossible, since it provided that the new governments should "forever remain a part of the United States of America." The other provided that slavery should cease to exist in the new governments established in all territory ceded or to be ceded. The tragic events of the succeeding century would reveal, too late, the wisdom of Jefferson's attempt to strengthen the bonds of union by disallowing the right of secession and by prohibiting the extension of the institution that helped to bring separatism to its final stage. It was with complete truth that Jefferson, in closing his legislative career in Congress in 1784, could report to the Virginia legislature: "I have made the just rights of my country and the cement of that union in which her happiness and security is bound up, the leading objects of my conduct."

The Louisiana Purchase of 1803, fortuitous as it was, unconstitutional as Jefferson thought it to be, was another vast extension of the Empire of Liberty. By this one stroke, Jefferson added to the Union a domain whose influence upon the solidarity, the achievements, the cultural and material richness of this nation is incalculable. The Constitution made no specific authorization of the acquisition of new territory by purchase, nor did the principle established in the Northwest Ordinance apply. Though Jefferson seriously considered the idea of proposing an amendment to the Constitution that would remove all doubt as to the legitimacy of the purchase, he allowed his executive act to stand by itself even though, as he unquestionably knew, he would thereby expose himself to the charge of inconsistency in his constitutional principles. But inconsistency, if it were such, was in this instance only another name for statesmanship.

Yet there were other voices whose inconsistency at this juncture in American history has not been so closely noticed. "Adopt this Western World into the Union," warned one Federalist Senator, "and you destroy at once the weight and importance of the Eastern States and compel them to establish a separate and independent empire." "Our country," mourned Fisher Ames, "is too big for union, too sordid for patriotism, too democratic for liberty." Uriah Tracy, in grammar that matched the faultiness of his vision, solemnly proclaimed: "I am convinced that the accession of Louisiana will accelerate a division of these States: whose whenabouts is uncertain, but somewhen is inevitable." And Timothy Pickering, dour and querulous even when in office, declared: "I do not believe in the practicability of a long-continued union." These were the voices of believers in the theory of a strong, centralized government, the voices of a party whose leaders feared that the republican principles advocated by Jefferson would produce a weak, decentralized government and would ultimately "add the name of America to the melancholy catalogue of fallen Republics."

Nowhere in the entire legislative and executive career of the man who believed a government of republican principles the strongest on earth can one find comparable doubts, threats, and prophecies of disunion. Even in the disillusioning postwar period, when many stouthearted Americans yielded to doubt and despair and replaced the high hopes of the Revolutionary cause with the promotion of local interests, Jefferson never wavered. To have consented to the proposition that the country was too large for union and too sordid for patriotism would have been to deny the possibility and the hope of establishing a free society of free men. This he could never do. "I hope," he wrote to John Dickinson two days after his inauguration in 1801, "to see shortly a perfect consolidation, to effect which nothing shall be spared on my part, short of the abandonment of the principles of our revolution. A just & solid republican government maintained here will be a standing monument & example for the aim & imitation of the people of other countries; and I join with you in the hope and belief that they will see from our example that a free government is of all others the most energetic, that the enquiry which has been excited among the mass of mankind by our revolution & it's consequences will ameliorate the condition of man over a great portion of the globe. What a satisfaction have we in the contemplation of the benevolent effects of our efforts, compared with those of the leaders of the other side, who have discountenanced all advances in science as dangerous innovations, have endeavored to render philosophy & republicanism terms of reproach, to persuade us that man cannot be governed but by the rod &c. I shall have the happiness of living & dying in the contrary hope."

Such was the Empire of Liberty to which, unceasingly and unselfishly, he devoted his life. If the Heavenly City of this eighteenth-century philosopher was founded on a belief that we, in our superior enlightenment and in our skepticism of the power of reason and justice, begin to consider naïve, what of the promises and prophecies of those in Jefferson's day who thought with Gouverneur Morris that "To save the people from their most dangerous enemy: to save them from themselves" was the purpose and end of the national government? If the bright promise of his Heavenly City has become tarnished in the eyes of some, what of theirs? They spoke for the past, not of a Heavenly City to come.

"Jefferson aspired," wrote Henry Adams, "beyond the ambition of a nationality and embraced in his view the whole future of man." That future still stretches before us and we have the privilege of facing it under the guidance of his ennobling example. But, lest we become complacent, we also have before us those who yet repeat the cynical distrust voiced by the Gouverneur Morrises of an earlier day.

LOUIS B. WRIGHT

✪

Thomas Jefferson and the Classics

In the history of learning in America, Thomas Jefferson is a transitional figure. He marks the culmination of a great tradition of classical culture, a culture rediscovered in the Renaissance and transmitted with its Renaissance interpretations to fresh soil in colonial Virginia and New England. He also saw the beginning of a new era in which scientific and "practical" subjects would displace the classics and gain the ascendancy in the schools. Indeed, as everyone knows, Jefferson himself was a pioneer in this new era of education, though he would have sat in sackcloth and ashes had he dreamed that one day his beloved Latin and Greek would almost disappear, not only from the university that he created, but from the very consciousness of men throughout the land.[1] Necessary as were the practical subjects which he advo-

[1] Anyone who attempts an appraisal of Jefferson's literary interests finds himself indebted to Professor Gilbert Chinard, whose brilliant and penetrating studies have left little new ground to be explored. Particularly useful for the present purpose are: *The Literary Bible of Thomas Jefferson: His Commonplace Book of Philosophers and Poets* (Baltimore and Paris, 1928), *The Commonplace Book of Thomas Jefferson: A Repertory of His Ideas on Government* (Baltimore and Paris, 1926), *Thomas Jefferson, The Apostle of Americanism* (Boston, 1929), and "Thomas Jefferson as a Classical Scholar," *The American Scholar*, I (1932), 133–143. For a collection of material on Jefferson's ideas on education, see Roy J. Honeywell, *The Educational Work of Thomas Jefferson* (Cambridge, 1931).

Reprinted from *Proceedings of the American Philosophical Society*, Vol. LXXXVII, No. 3 (1944), pp. 223–233, by permission of the American Philosophical Society.

cated, he would have regarded the elimination of the classics as an irreparable loss to a republic that depended for survival upon the intelligence of its electorate and the wisdom and integrity of its leaders. The fact was that Jefferson, like the men of the Renaissance, considered the study of Greek and Roman literature as eminently practical preparation for intelligent living. The classics provided, not merely ornament and delight, but useful guidance in the affairs of daily life. The accumulated wisdom of the ancients was particularly valuable in the training of the *aristoi*, the aristocracy of intelligence, to whom Jefferson looked for democratic leadership.

The classical tradition which Jefferson inherited had long exerted a profound influence upon Virginia civilization.[2] From that day in the 1620's when George Sandys, on the banks of the James River, completed his translation of Ovid's *Metamorphoses*, until Jefferson's own time, the literature of Greece and Rome had helped to shape the thinking of Virginia leaders. In the little libraries which seventeenth-century settlers brought with them, works by Greek and Roman writers occupied a prominent place. These books, we can be certain, were not chosen for ostentation; they were considered essential to the reproduction of the kind of civil society that English settlers dreamed of establishing in the wilderness. That society in its main outlines still preserved cultural patterns developed in the sixteenth century when the belief in the civilizing and humanizing value of the classics reached its zenith in England. This Renaissance belief in the wisdom of the ancients became a vital element in the literary interests of the Virginia ruling class.

For example, the second Richard Lee (d. 1714)—ancestor of a famous line—showed such devotion to ancient languages and literature that he kept his notes in Hebrew, Greek, or Latin, and spent every spare hour in his library reading Homer, Virgil,

[2] For a more detailed consideration of this topic see Louis B. Wright, "The Classical Tradition in Colonial Virginia," *Papers of the Bibliographical Society of America* (1939), 85–97; *The First Gentlemen of Virginia* (San Marino, California, 1939), *passim;* and *The Secret Diary of William Byrd of Westover, 1709–1712,* edited in collaboration with Marion Tinling (Richmond, 1941), introduction.

Plutarch, Tacitus, or another of his favorite authors. But Lee was no recluse scholar, or even exceptional in his class. A busy planter who assumed the usual responsibilities of office, he performed his public and private duties conscientiously and still found time for the writers of antiquity. Indeed, in common with others of his generation, he looked upon these authors as sources of moral and political guidance.

Robert Carter (d. 1732)—known because of his pride and wealth as "King" Carter—was as calculating an architect of fortune as colonial Virginia produced and certainly not one to cultivate notions of pedantry; yet he was proud of being a Latinist and was eager to see that his sons were brought up to read and understand the best of Greek and Latin authors. Not content with mere lip service to learning, he wanted his sons to be grounded thoroughly in the ancient languages, after the methods of the great Czech teacher Comenius, for, as Carter observed, "it is not reading a few scraps from the poets and the other classics that makes boys understand the scope and design of authors."

Throughout a long and busy life as a planter and public official William Byrd of Westover (d. 1744) followed a rigid schedule of reading Greek and Latin writers, with some Hebrew thrown in for discipline. His taste was varied, and his choice of classical authors ranged from Homer to Terence. Byrd's library—the best in America at that time—contained a remarkable collection of Greek and Roman authors in the finest editions then available. In this library, which remained intact at Westover for many years after Byrd's death, Jefferson himself may have read when he was a student at the College of William and Mary.

Other members of the ruling planter class shared the interest in the classics displayed by Richard Lee, Robert Carter, and William Byrd. Although no realistic historian would pretend that these colonials were a race of notable scholars—or even that many were exceptional linguists—it is highly significant that they clung to the old Renaissance belief in the practical value of classical literature and endeavored to provide adequate opportunities for their own edification and the instruction of their children by the collection of books and the employment of classically trained tutors. Even if colonial Virginians sometimes lacked the ability to read Greek and Latin with ease, their libraries were not lacking in translations which revealed the meaning of the philosophers, poets, and historians of antiquity. Colonial libraries, in fact, are noteworthy for the number of their translations, and many a planter who had scantily learned or forgotten his languages could still profit from the morals of Epictetus or the historical parallels in Plutarch.

The accepted belief in the value of Greek and Roman literature determined the course of Thomas Jefferson's education. His father, Peter Jefferson—a man of greater cultivation than some historians have implied—left dying instructions that his son should be given the best classical training available.[3] Already, at the age of nine, the child had begun the study of Latin, Greek, and French under the tutelage of William Douglass, a Scotch clergyman. After his father's death, he spent two years at the school of the Reverend James Maury, "a correct classical scholar," and a little later entered the College of William and Mary where his natural tendency toward classical literature received further stimulation from a learned Scotchman, Dr. William Small, professor of mathematics, who also lectured on ethics, rhetoric, and belles-lettres. Not least of the influences on Jefferson was his close association with the great teacher of law, George Wythe, also noted in the colony as a Greek and Latin scholar. Under such circumstances, a youth with Jefferson's keen and impressionable mind could not have escaped a sound classical training.

In later life, Jefferson frequently expressed his gratitude for the early opportunities of learning the fundamentals of Greek and Latin. Writing to Joseph Priestley in 1800, he remarks:

To read the Latin and Greek authors in their original is a sublime luxury; and I deem luxury in science to be at least as justifiable as in architecture, painting, gardening, or the other arts. I enjoy Homer in his own language infinitely beyond Pope's translation of him, and both beyond the dull narrative of the same events by Dares Phrygius; and it is an innocent enjoyment. I thank on my knees him who directed my early education for having put into my possession this rich source

[3] Henry S. Randall, *The Life of Thomas Jefferson* (New York, 1858), I, 18.

of delight; and I would not exchange it for anything which I could then have acquired, and have not since acquired.[4]

The literature of antiquity, Jefferson learned as a student, was the ultimate source of both delight and instruction—a precept which George Wythe would have given him if he had not already gleaned it from Horace. But it would be a mistake to assume that the Albemarle youth, like an eighteenth-century type of Browning's grammarian, devoted himself to the past with the zeal of a specialist. The tradition which he had inherited, a tradition developed in the sixteenth century, emphasized a well-rounded education and an amateur standing in a number of useful and ornamental arts. Balance and symmetry were important, and Jefferson, consciously or unconsciously, followed the Renaissance theory of education, which gave him an enormous curiosity about a variety of things and contributed to the development of his many-sided personality. He read Shakespeare, Jonson, Milton, Dryden, and other more recent authors; he gained an easy acquaintance with French which later led him to read Montesquieu and his contemporaries; he found a particular interest in mathematics and natural science; but the literature of Greece and Rome was the core around which all other studies were grouped. From the classics Jefferson believed that he obtained the basis of an ethical and philosophical system as well as the means of satisfying his aesthetic longings.

The respect for the classics acquired in his youth Jefferson retained throughout his life, but this interest was never merely academic or pedantic. For him the literature of the ancient world had a utilitarian value of the highest importance, a value which he constantly emphasized later in his plans for public schools in Virginia and the foundation of a university. Unlike some scholars who reverence antiquity, Jefferson displayed a common-sense attitude toward classical learning. The battle of the books, which aroused the biased excitement of eighteenth-century protagonists of ancient or modern learning, had no interest for Jefferson. All

[4] *The Writings of Thomas Jefferson,* Memorial edition (Washington, 1903), X, 146–147, January 27, 1800. Unless otherwise stated, citations are to this edition.

learning had its proper place, and he was not concerned to elevate one school over another. Both the ancients and the moderns were essential in their particular spheres.

The classics should not always be chosen in preference to modern writings, Jefferson clearly stated on several occasions, pointing out that more recent literature, even imaginative works, might have an equal or superior value. In a letter to Robert Skipwith recommending a certain course of reading, he observes that "the entertainments of fiction are useful as well as pleasant." And he adds a query certain to be made by classical purists: "But wherein is its utility, asks the reverend sage, big with the notion that nothing can be useful but the learned lumber of Greek and Roman reading with which his head is stored?" In answer, he shows that imaginative works like *Macbeth* and *King Lear* teach lessons as profound as those in factual history.[5] In another letter of advice, to J. W. Eppes, he remarks that up to the age of sixteen, one's principal study ought to be languages—Latin, Greek, French, and Spanish—and of these, "I think Greek the least useful."[6] Yet he himself regarded the ability to read Greek as one of his most valuable accomplishments. But he was too wise to believe that Greek was for everyone more necessary than a modern language, or some other subject of immediate utility.

The ideas in Jefferson's letters advising his nephew Peter Carr on the choice of studies sound like those of Vittorino da Feltre or another of the humanist educators of the early Renaissance. One finds the same insistence upon the development of the complete man, the necessity of exercise and physical development, the advantages of literary learning—not as an excuse for hermitlike retirement from the world, but as a means of service to the state—and lastly, the practical utility of classical authors as guides and counselors. To young Carr, Jefferson wrote from Paris on August 19, 1785:

I have long ago digested a plan for you, suited to the circumstances in which you will be placed. This I will detail to you, from time to

5 August 3, 1771, *ibid.,* IV, 237.
6 July 28, 1787, *ibid.,* VI, 189–190.

time, as you advance. For the present, I advise you to begin a course of ancient history, reading everything in the original and not in translations. First read Goldsmith's history of Greece. This will give you a digested view of that field. Then take up ancient history in the detail, reading the following books in the following order: Herodotus, Thucydides, Xenophontis Anabasis, Arrian, Quintus Curtius, Diodorus Siculus, Justin. This shall form the first stage of your historical reading, and is all I need mention to you now. The next will be of Roman history. [Note: "Livy, Sallust, Caesar, Cicero's epistles, Suetonius, Tacitus, Gibbon."] From that we will come down to modern history. In Greek and Latin poetry, you have read or will read at school, Virgil, Terence, Horace, Anacreon, Theocritus, Homer, Euripides, Sophocles. Read also Milton's *Paradise Lost,* Shakespeare, Ossian, Pope's and Swift's works, in order to form your style in your own language. In morality, read Epictetus, Xenophontis Memorabilia, Plato's Socratic dialogues, Cicero's philosophies, Antoninus, and Seneca. In order to assure a certain progress in this reading, consider what hours you have free from the school and the exercises of the school. Give about two of them, every day, to exercise; for health must not be sacrificed to learning. A strong body makes a mind strong. As to the species of exercise, I advise the gun. While this gives a moderate exercise to the body, it gives boldness, enterprise, and independence to the mind. Games played with the ball, and others of that nature, are too violent for the body and stamp no character on the mind. . . . Walking is the best possible exercise.[7]

Advice like this would have been understood and approved by Vittorino, or Battista Guarino, or the Elizabethan humanist, Roger Ascham.

In this and in other letters to Carr, Jefferson outlines the training necessary to a man destined for public life. The backbone of his study must be classical literature, with emphasis upon history, but other subjects are also necessary: the French language, for instance, because the advanced literature of mathematics and science is in that tongue; and Spanish, because the future destiny of the United States lies with the Latin nations to the south.[8]

Jefferson's formal proposals for educational reform in Virginia expressed a similar view of the importance of classical learning,

[7] *Ibid.,* V, 84–85.
[8] August 10, 1787, *ibid.,* VI, 256–262; May 28, 1788, VII, 43–44.

though he repeatedly emphasized the necessity of a balanced program of studies, in both the elementary schools and the university.[9] Every citizen ought to know something about antiquity, even if all could not learn the languages, Jefferson believed. Hence, in his *Bill for the More General Diffusion of Knowledge,* submitted to the House of Delegates in 1779, he suggested reading books based on Greek, Roman, English, and American history. The ancient world was a part of the universal heritage which young Virginians of all classes must be taught to appreciate. From the Greeks and Romans the people would learn lessons of history valuable to the preservation of republican liberty.

Jefferson's goal in the various schemes of education which he devised was always practical. His aim was to provide the type of education most useful in raising the general level of intelligence, assuring adequate leadership, and promoting the public welfare. In planning the University of Virginia he constantly emphasized the practical aspects of higher education, showing little sympathy for the pursuit of abstract learning merely for its own sake. But Jefferson's concept of the practical was broad. He would have been appalled at the ignorant shortsightedness of present-day theories which assert the same intentions. For Jefferson did not confuse education with a smattering of miscellaneous information, or with learning a trade or profession. The university should provide the broad base of knowledge needed by an intelligent leader in the state. It is significant, therefore, that although Jefferson vastly extended the scope of university education, he insisted upon the retention of adequate instruction in the classical languages and literature.[10] These studies, he believed, were useful in the development of wise leadership. Naturally he insisted that a purely philological interest in language was of far less importance than an understanding of the substance of classical literature. In a letter to Priestley about the proposed University of Virginia, he declared that he did not consider a knowledge of classical languages absolutely essential for eminence in all sciences, "but I

[9] Details of Jefferson's educational theories, with relevant documents, are given in Honeywell, *passim.*
[10] *Ibid.,* 10, 113, 123, 284.

think them very useful towards it"; and he added the opinion that
the Greeks and Romans had left the best "models which exist of
fine composition, whether we examine them as works of reason, or
of style and fancy; and to them we probably owe these character-
istics of modern composition."[11] No man could be educated
without a thorough knowledge of history, especially the works of
the Greek and Roman historians. These authors should be read
preferably in the original tongues, but if that was impossible, they
must be studied anyway in translation. The founder of the University of Virginia intended every citizen trained therein to see his
world from the long perspective of the past.

Jefferson summarized his views on the place of the classical
languages in American education in a letter written to thank John
Brazier for a copy of his review of John Pickering's essay on
modern Greek pronunciation:

You ask my opinion on the extent to which classical learning should
be carried in our country. . . . The utilities we derive from the
remains of the Greek and Latin languages are, first, as models of pure
taste in writing. To these we are certainly indebted for the rational and
chaste style of modern composition which so much distinguishes the
nations to whom these languages are familiar. . . . Second. Among
the values of classical learning I estimate the luxury of reading the
Greek and Roman authors in all the beauties of their originals. . . . I
think myself more indebted to my father for this than for all the other
luxuries his cares and affections have placed within my reach; and
more now than when younger and more susceptible of delights from
other sources. . . . Third. A third value is in the stores of real science
deposited and transmitted [to] us in these languages, to wit: in history,
ethics, arithmetic, geometry, astronomy, natural history, etc.

But to whom are these things useful? Certainly not to all men. There
are conditions of life to which they must be forever estranged, and
there are epochs of life too, after which the endeavor to attain them
would be a great misemployment of time. Their acquisition should be
the occupation of our early years only, when the memory is susceptible
of deep and lasting impressions, and reason and judgment not yet
strong enough for abstract speculations. To the moralist they are
valuable, because they furnish ethical writings highly and justly

[11] January 27, 1800, *Writings of Thomas Jefferson*, X, 146–147.

esteemed. . . . The lawyer finds in the Latin language the system of
civil law most conformable with the principles of justice of any which has
ever yet been established among men, and from which much has been
incorporated into our own. The physician as good a code of his art as
has been given us to this day. . . . The statesman will find in these
languages history, politics, mathematics, ethics, eloquence, love of
country, to which he must add the sciences of his own day, for which
of them should be unknown to him? And all the sciences must recur to
the classical languages for the etymon, and sound understanding of
their fundamental terms. For the merchant I should not say that the
languages are necessary. Ethics, mathematics, geography, political
economy, history, seem to constitute the immediate foundation of his
calling. The agriculturist needs ethics, mathematics, chemistry, and
natural philosophy. The mechanic the same. To them the languages are
but ornament and comfort. I know it is often said there have been
shining examples of men of great abilities in all the businesses of life,
without any other science than what they had gathered from conversations and intercourse with the world. But who can say what these men
would not have been, had they started in the science on the shoulders
of a Demosthenes or Cicero, of a Locke or Bacon, or a Newton? To
sum the whole, therefore, it may truly be said that the classical
languages are a solid basis for most, and an ornament to all the
sciences.[12]

If Jefferson had merely followed his personal taste, he undoubtedly would have given an even larger place in his educational
program to classical studies, for early in life he had come to look
upon Greek and Roman literature as an unfailing repository of
wisdom, as well as a fountain of delight. The clues to his favorite
authors and their influence upon him are revealed in the commonplace book, where, as a young man, he wrote down his favorite
passages. Since Professor Gilbert Chinard's edition of this notebook, every student of Jefferson is aware of the preponderance of
classical authors in his reading during the formative period of his
life. Long passages from Homer, Herodotus, Euripides, Anacreon,
Virgil, Cicero, Horace, and Terence, chosen because of the preg-
nancy of their meaning, he painstakingly copied, against the time

[12] August 24, 1819, *ibid.*, XV, 207–211.

when he might wish to refresh his memory. These authors and many others from the ancient world continued throughout the rest of his life to provide enjoyment and food for reflection. His letters, even in the busy years while he was President, reflect his constant reading of classical authors from whom he received refreshment and support.

Although Jefferson read widely and knew the French and English philosophers and historians of his own age, his thinking was chiefly influenced by the writers of antiquity. From the Greek stoics, he gathered the elements of his personal philosophy, and in Latin historians he found confirmation of much of his political theory. Not Montesquieu, not Voltaire, not Bolingbroke, but Homer, Epictetus, Cicero, Tacitus, and other Greeks and Romans supplied him with inspiration and ideas. "By a strange anomaly," Professor Chinard remarks, "the son of the pioneer, the young man supposedly brought up under frontier influence, felt more kinship with Greece and republican Rome than with the philosophers of London, Paris, or Geneva."[13]

Like others educated in the classical tradition of the eighteenth century, Jefferson thought of himself as a Roman in the days of the republic's purity—a sort of Virginian Cincinnatus. Indeed, he often implies the parallel. When he is busiest with affairs of state, his letters express a yearning to return to the simplicity of his farm. When he is at Monticello, he writes in Horatian phrases of the pleasures of country life and the freedom from cares of office. Although he is the last person to be accused of living in the past, he adapted the ideas of antiquity to his own day. Significantly he copied in his notebook a rural idyl from Horace, the Second Epode, leaving out the passages that were inapplicable to a Virginia plantation.[14] In his "edited" version Horace reads like an American pastoral poet writing from an Albemarle hilltop. Long after he copied this passage, Jefferson continued to describe to his friends the pleasures of his simple existence at Monticello, and his

[13] Chinard, *Thomas Jefferson*, p. 26.
[14] Chinard, *The Literary Bible*, pp. 32–33, 184–187.

own reluctance to take time from Horace and Tacitus, even to read the newspapers.[15]

Great as was his admiration of the Greeks, Jefferson clearly felt more at home with the Roman historians and moralists. In fact, he placed Tacitus first among the world's writers. In a letter to his granddaughter, Anne Cary Bankhead, December 8, 1808, he commends her program of reading:

> I like much your choice of books for your winter's reading. Middleton's *Life of Cicero* is among the most valuable accounts we have of the period of which he writes; and Tacitus I consider the first writer in the world without a single exception. His book is a compound of history and morality of which we have no other example.[16]

Many years later, hearing of the discovery of a great collection of Greek manuscripts in a vault at Athens, he wrote to Joseph Coolidge, Jr.: "If true, we may recover what had been lost of Diodorus Siculus, Polybius, and Dion Cassius: I would rather, however, it should have been of Livy, Tacitus, and Cicero."[17] That Tacitus with his sententious moralizations on the virtues of republican government should have become Jefferson's favorite author is easy to understand. Parallels of political wisdom evident in other Latin historians gave them also a preferred place in his reading.

Cicero he respected and read for moral wisdom, but he disliked his style. No orator himself, Jefferson had a contempt for the windy speeches of politicians, and he particularly disliked the rolling periods of Ciceronian oratory, much affected on the public platform in his time. If Congressmen would read Livy, Tacitus, and Sallust, he declared, they would find models and material more suitable for their purposes than in Cicero's orations. In fact, he believed that Ciceronian speeches in Congress would create

[15] Jefferson to David Howell, December 15, 1810, *Writings of Thomas Jefferson,* XII, 437. The same idea is repeated in a letter to Charles Pinckney, February 2, 1812, *Jefferson Papers* (Massachusetts Historical Society Collections, 7th series), I (1900), 169. In a letter to John Adams, January 21, 1812, Jefferson says he has given up newspapers in exchange for Tacitus and Thucydides, *Writings of Thomas Jefferson,* XIII, 124.

[16] *Jefferson Papers,* pp. 128–129.

[17] January 15, 1825, *Writings of Thomas Jefferson,* XVIII, 336–337.

such public disgust that the governmental power would shift to the executive branch—which apparently was untainted by Cicero. "I observe," he wrote J. W. Eppes in 1810,

that the H[ouse] of R[epresentatives] are sensible of the ill effects of the long speeches in their house on their proceedings. But they have a worse effect in the disgust they excite among the people, and the disposition they are producing to transfer their confidence from the legislature to the executive branch, which would soon sap our Constitution. These speeches therefore, are less and less read, and if continued will cease to be read at all. The models for that oratory which is to produce the greatest effect by securing the attention of hearers and readers, are to be found in Livy, Tacitus, Sallust, and most assuredly not in Cicero. I doubt if there is a man in the world who can now read one of his orations through but as a piece of task-work.[18]

Fourteen years later, writing to David Harding, of Hingham, to express his pleasure at having a debating society named after him, Jefferson took occasion once more to commend short and logical speeches:

Antiquity has left us the finest models for imitation; and he who studies and imitates them most nearly will nearest approach the perfection of the art. Among these I should consider the speeches of Livy, Sallust, and Tacitus, as pre-eminent specimens of logic, taste, and that sententious brevity which, using not a word to spare, leaves not a moment for inattention to the hearer. Amplification is the vice of modern oratory. It is an insult to an assembly of reasonable men, disgusting and revolting instead of persuading. Speeches measured by the hour, die with the hour.[19]

These statements are revealing as evidence of the qualities that Jefferson prized in writers as well as in public orators. Substance, not ornaments and tricks of style, pleased him most.

Jefferson's ethical views were a fusion of classical and Christian ideals, a synthesis of the best that he could extract from Epictetus, Epicurus, and Jesus. Concerning his religion he was usually reticent, but in letters to a few friends—notably Joseph Priestley,

[18] January 17, 1810, *ibid.,* XII, 343.
[19] April 20, 1824, *ibid.,* XVI, 30–31.

Benjamin Rush, William Short, and John Adams—he expounded his opinions in considerable detail. One letter to Short, written in 1819, should be read in full for the insight it gives of Jefferson's ethics and the sources of his ideas. A few sentences will suggest the writer's point of view:

> As you say of yourself, I too am an Epicurean. I consider the genuine (not the imputed) doctrines of Epicurus as containing everything rational in moral philosophy which Greece and Rome have left us. Epictetus, indeed, has given us what was good of the Stoics; all beyond, of their dogmas, being hypocrisy and grimace. Their great crime was in their calumnies of Epicurus and misrepresentations of his doctrines; in which we lament to see the candid character of Cicero engaging as an accomplice. Diffuse, vapid, rhetorical, but enchanting. His prototype Plato, eloquent as himself, dealing out mysticisms incomprehensible to the human mind, has been deified by certain sects usurping the name of Christians; because, in his foggy conceptions, they found a basis of impenetrable darkness whereon to rear fabrications as delirious, of their own invention. . . . Of Socrates we have nothing genuine but in the Memorabilia of Xenophon; for Plato makes him one of his collocutors merely to cover his own whimsies under the mantle of his name; a liberty of which we are told Socrates himself complained. Seneca is indeed a fine moralist, disfiguring his work at times with some Stoicisms, and affecting too much of antithesis and point, yet giving us on the whole a great deal of sound and practical morality. But the greatest of all reformers of the depraved religion of His own country was Jesus of Nazareth. . . . Epictetus and Epicurus give laws for governing ourselves, Jesus a supplement of the duties and charities we owe to others.[20]

Appended to this letter is a syllabus of the doctrines of Epicurus. An outline of the philosophy of Jesus was omitted because it was "too long to be copied." Ten years before, in a letter to Benjamin Rush,[21] Jefferson had included a syllabus of Jesus' teachings. That outline, and his anthology from the New Testament, which he called "The Life and Morals of Jesus," indicate the way in which he harmonized the rationalism of Epicurus and the rational portions of Christian doctrine.

[20] October 19, 1819, *ibid.*, XV, 219–220.
[21] April 21, 1803, *ibid.*, X, 379–385.

Being a practical rationalist, Jefferson never comprehended the mystical concepts of Plato, and he usually spoke of the philosopher with contempt. Indeed, in another letter to Short, he declared that "no writer, ancient or modern, has bewildered the world with more *ignis fatui* than this renowned philosopher, in ethics, in politics, and physics." Upon Plato Jefferson blamed the contradictions in the character of Socrates. Since all antiquity testified to the wisdom of Socrates, Jefferson excused his apparent sophisms and puerilities as "the whimsies of Plato's own foggy brain."[22] Likewise, he attributed to "Platonizing Christians" the confusion and misinterpretation of the simple teachings of Jesus.[23]

If Jefferson was blind to the metaphor and mysticism of Plato, it must not be assumed that he was devoid of literary appreciation. Although purely ethical and utilitarian values largely determined his choice of authors, he read both prose and poetry with delight. Writing in his late fifties, he confessed to a lessening interest in poetry—as an excuse for failing to apprehend the beauties of Joel Barlow's *Columbiad*—and he had observed in his *Thoughts on English Prosody* (written shortly after 1789) that "as we advance in life . . . I suspect we are left at last with only Homer and Virgil, perhaps with Homer alone."[24] Actually, however, Jefferson continued to read both Greek and Latin poetry until the end of his life, as his letters prove, especially the remarkable correspondence with John Adams in which the two old men discussed everything from a theory of the Trojan origin of the Indians to the relative merits of the pastorals of Theocritus and David.[25] In his youth, he had found particular pleasure in Homer, Euripides, Anacreon, and Horace. His taste for these poets endured. When, bowed down with grief, he sought an appropriate epitaph for his wife, he chose two lines from the *Iliad,* and when he came to write the final directions for his own burial, he began the note with a quotation from Anacreon on the evanescence of man.

Although classical poetry made a deep impression upon Jeffer-

[22] August 4, 1820, *ibid.,* XV, 258.
[23] Jefferson to Benjamin Waterhouse, June 26, 1822, *ibid.,* XV, 383.
[24] Chinard, *The Literary Bible,* pp. 27–28.
[25] *Writings of Thomas Jefferson,* XIII, 246–249, 279–284, 387–394.

son, he continued to find his most satisfying reading in the prose of the historians and moralists. Some of them, notably Tacitus, he constantly reread. In these writers he could not help seeing parallels to contemporary affairs. A letter to John Adams in 1819 begins with a paragraph on the ominous threat of the Missouri agitation and continues with a long discussion of the Romans: "I have been amusing myself latterly with reading the voluminous letters of Cicero," he reports.

They certainly breathe the purest effusions of an exalted patriot, while the parricide Caesar is lost in odious contrast. . . . Your intimacy with their history, ancient, middle, and modern, your familiarity with the improvements in the science of government at this time, will enable you, if anybody, to go back with your principles and opinions to the times of Cicero, Cato, and Brutus, and tell us by what process these great and virtuous men could have led so unenlightened and vitiated a people into freedom and good government, *et eris mihi magnus Apollo. Cura ut valeas et tibi persuadeas carissimum te mihi esse.*[26]

Scores of similar observations in his letters indicate Jefferson's pleasure in reading classical history and his persistent belief in the value of its lessons.

We should not assume, however, that Jefferson had any sentimental illusions about the infallibility of the ancients. Concerning the practical utility of Aristotle's *Politics,* for example, he wrote some sound advice to Isaac H. Tiffany:

So different was the style of society then, and with those people, from what it is now and with us, that I think little edification can be obtained from their writings on the subject of government. They had just ideas of the value of personal liberty, but none at all of the structure of government best calculated to preserve it. . . . The introduction of this new principle of representative democracy has rendered useless almost everything written before on the structure of government; and, in a great measure, relieves our regret, if the political writings of Aristotle, or of any other ancient, have been lost, or are unfaithfully rendered or explained to us.[27]

[26] December 10, 1819, *ibid.,* XV, 232–235.
[27] August 26, 1816, *ibid.,* XV, 65–66.

Jefferson was opposed to the literal acceptance and application of political axioms on the authority of Aristotle or any other writer of antiquity; on the other hand, he advised making use of the experience, observations, suggestions, and general wisdom to be gleaned from the sages of earlier periods.

Too utilitarian in purpose ever to become a pedant, Jefferson nevertheless understood the pleasures of philological inquiry. One suspects that he sometimes had to reason with himself to restrain purely philological and antiquarian impulses. A man with sufficient interest in language to compile a usable Anglo-Saxon grammar would naturally not be blind to classical philology. A long letter to Edward Everett in 1823 thanks him for a copy of Buttman's *Greek Grammar* and remarks that the author "goes with the herd of grammarians in denying an ablative case to the Greek language. I cannot concur with him in that."[28] And Jefferson proceeds to argue for an ablative in Greek. After a discussion with Adams about the soundness of the Latin word *gloriola*, he observes: "Your doubt of the legitimacy of the word *gloriola* is resolved by Cicero, who, in his letter to Lucceius expresses a wish *'ut nos metipsi vivi gloriola nostra perfruamur.'* "[29]

But of all problems in classical philology, Jefferson was most interested in the recovery of the original pronunciation of the Greek and Latin tongues. Writing to Ezra Stiles from Paris in 1785 concerning the war in Europe, he observes: "We should wish success to the object of the two empires if they meant to leave the country in possession of the Greek inhabitants. We might then expect, once more, to see the language of Homer and Demosthenes a living language. For I am persuaded the modern Greek would easily get back to its classical models."[30] Two years later, in a letter to George Wythe, he remarks: "I cannot help looking forward to the re-establishing of the Greeks as a people, and the language of Homer becoming again a living language, as among

[28] February 24, 1823, *ibid.,* XV, 410–415. See another letter to Everett, March 27, 1824, *ibid.,* XVI, 20–22.
[29] September 12, 1821, *ibid.,* XV, 333–335.
[30] July 17, 1785, *ibid.,* V, 35–39. Cf. also pp. 89–90.

possible events."[31] Interest in Greek liberty—with Jefferson as with many another intellectual of the nineteenth century—was prompted to a considerable degree by love of Homer's language. Jefferson retained an interest in the re-establishment of classical Greek as a living language and was greatly interested in the comparison between modern and classical Greek pronunciation.

Likewise he was eager for American schoolmasters to adopt the Continental pronunciation of Latin because it was nearer to the original sound. The English style of Latin pronunciation, customary in New England, was an offense to his ears. In a letter to William B. Giles in 1825 he laments the low state of Latin scholarship at the University of Virginia and describes the horrors of a pronunciation imported from Connecticut:

> We were obliged last year to receive shameful Latinists into the classical school of the University, such as we will certainly refuse as soon as we can get from better schools a sufficiency of those properly instructed to form a class. We must get rid of this Connecticut Latin, of this barbarous confusion of long and short syllables, which renders doubtful whether we are listening to a reader of Cherokee, Shawnee, Iroquois, or what.[32]

Jefferson had a genuine interest in language and could appreciate subtle variations of idiom and style in Greek and Latin authors. From the classics he drew arguments to combat the authority of grammatical purists, particularly misguided sticklers for rules who insisted that the American language must remain in bondage to the vocabulary and pronunciation of the British Isles. A grammarian of a more liberal view received his commendation: "I concur entirely with you in opposition to purists who would destroy all strength and beauty of style by subjecting it to a rigorous compliance with their rules. Fill up all the ellipses and syllepses of Tacitus, Sallust, Livy, etc., and the elegance and force of their sentelious brevity are extinguished."[33] He points out that the Athenians did not consider the Greek language disfigured by

31 September 16, 1787, *ibid.*, XV, 296–301.
32 December 26, 1825, *ibid.*, XVI, 146–151.
33 Jefferson to John Waldo, August 16, 1813, XIII, 338–347.

Doric, Ionian, and other dialects, but on the contrary were aware that the language was enriched by them. In a similar way, the English language will receive enrichment from American dialects. Problems of textual scholarship excited Jefferson's interest in his later years, and, through the youthful George Ticknor, he learned to admire the scientific school of textual criticism developing in Germany in the early nineteenth century.[34] In February, 1815, about two months before Ticknor sailed for Germany, he visited Jefferson at Monticello. For three days the aging statesman and the enthusiastic student discussed literature and learning, and when Ticknor left he was commissioned by Jefferson to purchase a collection of the best European editions of Greek and Roman authors, needed at Monticello to replace books sold to the Library of Congress. In addition to critical editions, Jefferson wanted scholarly translations for the light they threw on the meaning of obscure passages. In a letter of instructions to Ticknor, after remarking on the corrupt text of Cicero's philosophical works, he adds: "Translations aid us with the conjectures of those who have made it a particular business to study its text." In another letter, after urging Ticknor to avoid unwieldy folios and quartos in favor of convenient octavos, he mentions the kind of texts most desired: "I value explanatory notes; but verbal criticisms and various readings not much. I am attracted to the scholia of the Greek classics because they give us the language of another age; and with the Greek classics prefer translations as convenient aids to the understanding of the author."[35] In the summer of 1815, Ticknor shipped some of the best editions available in Göttingen: Homer and Virgil by Christian Gottlob Heyne, Aeschylus by Christian Gottfried Schütz, Juvenal by Georg Alexander Ruperti, and Tacitus by Jérémie Jacques Oberlin. Jefferson was delighted with the quality of the textual scholarship and wrote enthusiastically to his friend and agent:

[34] For a discussion of this episode in Jefferson's career, see O. W. Long, *Thomas Jefferson and George Ticknor: A Chapter in American Scholarship* (Williamstown, Mass., 1933).

[35] *Ibid.*, p. 16.

The editions of Heyne, Ruperti, Oberlin, are indeed of the first order; but especially Heyne's of the *Iliad*. It exceeds anything I had ever conceived in editorial merit. How much it makes us wish he had done the same with the Odyssey. . . . This style of editing has all the superiority your former letters have ascribed to it, and urges us to read again the authors we have formerly read to obtain a new and higher understanding of them.[36]

In an outburst of renewed zeal for classical studies the sage of Monticello wrote Ticknor's father that if he were twenty years younger he would join the youth upon a journey to Rome and Athens.

When the British burned the Library of Congress in 1814, Jefferson sold to the nation his own magnificent collection of books for half their cost. Immediately he set about gathering a new library for himself. Thanks in part to Ticknor's help, the library at Monticello soon contained some of the best critical texts of the classics then available in Europe.[37] Not even the straitened state of Jefferson's finances prevented the buying of fine editions of his favorite authors.

The most obvious proof of Jefferson's debt to the classical world is to be seen, of course, in the architectural monuments which he left as memorials to the diversity of his talents. Architecture was something more than a hobby with him, and he applied himself to the art with singular devotion. During his travels in France he was fascinated with the remains of Roman architecture, particularly the Maison Carrée at Nîmes, which he chose as the principal model for the state capitol at Richmond. In a letter of September 20, 1785, to James Madison, he described the Maison Carrée as "one of the most beautiful, if not the most beautiful and precious morsel of architecture left us by antiquity," and he implored

---

[36] *Ibid.*, p. 30.

[37] Books in the second library collected at Monticello are listed in a *Catalogue: President Jefferson's Library . . . by Nathaniel P. Poor,* published by Gales and Seaton in Washington for the sale on February 27, 1829. The books in Jefferson's earlier and larger collection, sold to the nation after the Library of Congress burned in 1814, are listed in a *Catalogue of the Library of the United States* (Washington, 1815). Both catalogues show excellent collections of the classics.

Madison to try to delay work on the capitol until the model being prepared in France could reach Richmond. Already he dreamed of setting up a standard of aesthetic judgment based on classical examples. "How," he asked Madison, "is a taste in this beautiful art to be formed in our countrymen unless we avail ourselves of every occasion when public buildings are to be erected, of presenting to them models for their study and imitation?"[38] During the next thirty years, Jefferson labored unceasingly over his drawing board to provide the plans and diagrams of both public buildings and private residences, chastely classical in conception, to be examples for his countrymen's "study and imitation." The Virginia capitol, the Rotunda and the pavilions of the University of Virginia, Monticello, and many other structures demonstrate his ability to translate a belief in the superiority of the Roman style into tangible illustrations of his theory.

Jefferson learned architectural design chiefly in his library, where he had a collection of the best books on the subject, though his travels in Europe also strengthened his aesthetic judgment and sharpened his perceptions. In his study he pored over the designs of Vitruvius and the Roman's great Renaissance disciple Palladio. For the English imitations of Palladio, he had scant respect, but from French eighteenth-century interpretations of classical design he gained a certain inspiration.[39] From Palladio directly, however, came most of his own basic designs, which he adapted with remarkable ingenuity to the practical requirements of Virginia buildings, public and private. In architecture, as in history and literature, he took from the classics everything that was useful and adapted it to his own ends without becoming a slave to convention. Such skill of adaptation and creation could not have been shown by even an inspired dilettante; it was proof of painstaking and studious application to his art, an art which the best critic of Jefferson's architectural ability describes as the fusion "of retrospection and of science," and "above all, a critical historic spirit."[40]

[38] *Writings of Thomas Jefferson,* V, 134–137. Cf. also the letter to the Comtesse de Tessé, March 20, 1787, *ibid.,* VI, 102–106.

[39] Fiske Kimball, *Thomas Jefferson, Architect* (Boston, 1916), pp. 37, 81, 82.

[40] *Ibid.,* p. 83.

To American architecture he brought mathematical precision of line and correctness of detail based on the finest examples of Roman building. In the words of Fiske Kimball, "directly or indirectly, American classicism traces its ancestry to Jefferson, who may truly be called the father of our national architecture."[41] The modernistic critics who complained recently about the "outmoded classical style" of the Jefferson Memorial in Washington surely knew nothing of architectural history. To have erected in Jefferson's honor a structure in other than the Roman style would have been a supreme irony.

Thoroughly saturated in the literature and history of antiquity, Jefferson thought of the Greeks and Romans not as abstractions in books but as part of the organic stream of life. The personalities of Greece and Rome were almost as familiar as those of his own country. When Patrick Henry addressed the House of Delegates, Jefferson observed that the orator spoke "as old Homer wrote." When Jefferson's mind dwelled on ambitious dictators, he recalled Julius Caesar before he remembered Napoleon. When traitors were mentioned, he cited Catiline instead of Benedict Arnold. Speaking in admiration of his old friend George Wythe, he described him as "a Cato without the avarice of the Roman." Such references, of course, were conventional among educated men in this period, but Jefferson was remarkable for the way in which he assimilated the classical past into his own idiom. His language and his thought were singularly free from academic taint and bookishness. Only in a few instances—a very few—did his learning betray him into pedantry, as when he invented Grecian names for new states and territories—Cherronesus, Assenisipia, Illinoia, Polypotamia, Metropotamia, and Pelisipia.[42] Happily, this suggestion, more reminiscent of Shakespeare's Holofernes than the Virginian, was overruled, and it stands as the rare exception to the usual ease with which Jefferson wore his classical learning.

The most significant quality of Jefferson's classicism, in its various manifestations, was its vitality, the fact that it was a living

[41] *Ibid.,* p. 89.
[42] Paul L. Ford, ed., *The Writings of Thomas Jefferson* (New York, 1899), III, 410.

thing, a part of everyday life. He himself wisely advised against "the Gothic idea that we are to look backwards instead of forward for the improvement of the human mind,"[43] but he was conscious of being the heir of all the past. Systematically and intelligently, he investigated the true worth of that heritage and pointed out its utility to his own age and generation. His interpretation of classical culture carried with it no smell of the lamp, no atmosphere of musty books. Classical studies in America died only when they passed into the exclusive guardianship of the schoolmasters—when shibboleths and tags of language were substituted for the substance of the ancient civilizations. In the early years of the republic, the classics had not yet foundered on the arid shores of pedantry.

Jefferson and the men of learning contemporary with him still drew on classical sources for inspiration and instruction. They still believed that leaders in a democratic state had an obligation to be informed—and if possible, to be wise. Education meant something more than the cachet of an academic degree or technical training for a vocation. Special fields of human relations—the "social sciences," for example—had not yet invented a jargon unintelligible to ordinary mortals. Clarity of thought and expression and breadth of vision were still ideals to be sought; and in the attainment of these ideals, the literature of antiquity had a value unsurpassed. In his own person Thomas Jefferson exemplified the universal worth of classical cultivation—a cultivation which helps to explain the wisdom and the vision, not only of Jefferson, but of many others among that remarkable group of leaders who had the intelligence and the character which could create a nation.

[43] Jefferson to Joseph Priestley, January 27, 1800, *Writings of Thomas Jefferson* (Memorial ed.), X, 148.

HORACE M. KALLEN

✪

The Arts and Thomas Jefferson[1]

I

The Virginia in which Thomas Jefferson grew up was a province with a dual, still ununified culture. That which stands out in the tradition is signalized by the textbooks as "Cavalier." It grew by the tidewater and reproduced a version of the aristocracy of the homeland in its tastes and ways. It took from England its learning,

[1] Of the Founding Fathers, none has left us so unambiguous and precise a testament of his fighting faith, of his vision of man and nature, as Thomas Jefferson. The generations are not free, except out of malice, to mistake the source or the intent of his philosophy of life and art. He has named them by the remembrances that would be to his "manes most gratifying": author of the Declaration of Independence, of the Statute of Virginia for Religious Freedom, father of the University of Virginia. He has embodied them in the thousands upon thousands of letters "all preserved," written on equal terms with equal care and courtesy to all sorts and conditions of men upon all the themes that troubled mankind and "written . . . . in the moment . . . . in the warmth and freshness of fact and feeling" (to Judge William Johnson, Monticello, May 14, 1823, *The Writings of Thomas Jefferson,* Monticello edition [Washington, 1904], XV, 420–421) and with a sense that "the letters of a person . . . . form the only and genuine journal of his life" (to Robert Walsh, Monticello, April 5, 1823, manuscript, University of Virginia, cited by Bernard Mayo in *Jefferson Himself* [Boston, 1942]). But all the evidence as to how Jefferson felt and thought about the arts and sciences and their role in the shaping of human destiny is not yet in. Though thousands of his papers and letters have been studied and published, many thousands remain unexplored and unrevealed; and, until all those, too, have been reviewed and printed, any discussion of his philosophy of art must remain tentative and subject to continuous revision.

Reprinted from *Ethics,* Vol. LIII (1943), pp. 269–283, by permission of The University of Chicago Press. Copyright © 1943 by Horace M. Kallen.

its fashions, its art, and its fun. When it could, it sent its sons to be educated there, its daughters to be outfitted there. When it could not, it recalled in Jamestown or Williamsburg that in Oxford or London which it could not reach. The ground plan of its mores was the immemorial one established by the ancients and confirmed in each generation anew by the classical education of the schools and colleges. According to this ground plan, mankind falls broadly into three groups or castes: swordsmen, wordmen, and workmen. Wordmen and swordsmen are privileged. They are freemen, gentlemen of property, under no necessity to work for a living, therefore with leisure to enjoy their lives and thus classically capable of those employments that alone are worthy a freeman. The art of the word, which is oratory and poetry, and the art of the sword, which is war, and the two joined together, which is statecraft, are such employments. The free exercise of these arts distinguished the noble or the gentleman from the mere subject or citizen; excellence in them is the stuff of honor in the eyes of men, and workmen are not capable of this excellence or ever worthy of such honor. Their labor exists but to feed the others' leisure; they produce what the others consume. Their task is menial, their role servile; they are means to the consumer's ends. Their entire justification can be found only in the user's enjoyment and delight. As Aristotle had advised, he who dwells in the house is a better man than he who builds it; he who eats the meal than he who cooks it; he who plays the flute than he who makes it; he who contemplates the statue is nobler than its sculptor; he who looks upon the picture than its painter. Architects and builders, poets, painters, sculptors, and musicians are also but workmen. They exist only to serve the connoisseur, to bring him, by the contemplation of their works, rest, recreation, and amusement.

II

Through his classical education Jefferson received in his turn the impress of this doctrine and discipline. By propensity and discipline a wordman, with interest in the sword, his tasks as lawyer, as legislator, as Governor and Ambassador, as statesman and party

leader, and as President imposed on him a consideration of the art
of war, its causes and conditions, which brought him to hate war
yet made him fully aware that only those can honorably have
peace who are ready to fight for it. "When wrongs are pressed," he
wrote in 1807, "because it is believed they will be borne, resistance becomes morality." Although he wanted to be remembered
as the author of the Statute of Virginia for Religious Liberty and
as the father of the University of Virginia, as well as the author
of the Declaration of Independence, it is for the last that the world
most deeply remembers him, and not a little because in this his
skill and power as a wordman are at their optimal. Yet the verbi-
form distinction of the Declaration is the distinction of Thomas
Jefferson whenever he expresses himself and on whatever subject.
"Style," he wrote, "in writing or speaking, is formed very early in
life, while the imagination is warm and impressions are permanent." No speaker himself, but a master of the orator's art, he goes
directly to his theme, without images, tropes, or apostrophes, in a
diction fundamentally abstract and matter of fact and with a noble
and moving rhythm. Although the maxims of Aristotle, Horace,
and Quintilian define his wordman's habit, he yet imparts to them
a technical significance uniquely his own. Language is to him a
living instrument of communication that the grammarian cannot
cripple or the dictionary imprison. It undergoes a continual meta-
morphosis, in which old words die and new ones are born as
circumstance requires; and knowing the history of these changes
enriches our understanding and heightens our pleasure in the use
of words. But it is the classics which are most fundamental in
forming style. They provide "the purest models which now exist of
fine composition"; they deflate "the inflated style of our northern
ancestors and the hyperbolical vague one of the East." "Models of
pure taste and writing," they constitute "a solid base for most and
an ornament for all the sciences." In old age they "fill up the
vacuums of ennui and become sweet composers to that rest of the
grave into which we all sooner or later descend." To be able to
read these classics in the original is a "sublime luxury; and I hold,"
Jefferson wrote Dr. Priestley in 1800, "luxury in science to be at
least as justifiable as in architecture, painting, gardening or the

other arts." He deprecated the barbarous style of the law, with its tautologies, redundancies, and circumlocutions, and sought to put in their place accuracy, brevity, simplicity. These three words do express the quality of the man and, with its spacious music, the impact of his deliverance.

But at the same time this classicist shared with Goethe and Napoleon an enthusiasm for MacPherson's *Poems of Ossian,* for its vague, gigantesque scenery, its mighty and simple heroes whom no convention binds. But, then, are not Ossian and Ilion brothers under the skin? Also Homer can be savored romantically for its primitive passions, grandiose and grotesque, as well as for its hard, elemental wisdom of life. Ossian may have been synthetic, but he had his appeal to the mighty of brawn and brain. Chastellux tells how he and Jefferson capped quotations from this synthetic grandiose. In 1773 Jefferson, indeed, wrote to Charles MacPherson to find out if he could secure copies of the Gaelic *Ossian* so that he might enjoy in the poet's own tongue this "daily and exalted pleasure" of his, "the tender and sublime emotion of the greatest poet that has ever existed." If, while President, he translated twenty chapters of Volney's *Les Ruines, ou méditations sur les révolutions des empires,* it was as much for its Ossianic style as for its geopolitical ideas. Jefferson's taste for Ossian had its extension in his taste for Sterne.

However, the propensity which this evinces faded with the years. The Sage of Monticello seems always to have preferred blank verse to rhyme and quantity to accent. Yet he did not permit his preference to affect his judgment. He followed his argument with Chastellux over the nature of English verse by an analysis of its prosody, which ended in his abandoning his own position and adopting his opponent's. His feeling, nevertheless, stayed with his first love, and as he grew older he held to his Homer but dropped most English verse. Fundamentally, Jefferson's concern was with the function of language, not its sonorities; and the art of composition was first and last the communication of ideas, and only incidentally the expression of feelings. He burned up feeling in idea: when this was not possible, he resorted to one of his rare images. I cite the note found in his pocketbook after he died:

"There is a time in human suffering when exceeding sorrows are but like snow falling on an iceberg."

III

Wordman as he was, Jefferson's attention fell far less on the reader's or listener's reaction than on words as signs and on the technique of their use. He gives first place to workmanship, not effect; and he gives workmanship the same primacy in the other arts. The impulsions of this passion for workmanship belong with the second of the dual cultures of his Virginia. That lived on the Western frontier and was a growth of the frontier soil. Largely unverbalized, a way of doing rather than talking, it elaborated no tradition comparable to the Cavalier's. Its avatar was the pioneer who had to work if he wanted to live, to watch and to fight if he meant to survive. "It is part of the American character," Jefferson once wrote his daughter Patsy, "to consider nothing as desperate, to surmount every difficulty by resolution and contrivance." The tidewater culture was a culture which others had already made and which the users remembered and repeated. The culture of the frontier was a culture which the users were making, which they invented and repeated in order to consume for themselves. Their livings and their lives were confluent and one, not separate as means and ends. If their preoccupation was work and workmanship, that preoccupation was consummatory.

Travelers in America saw this preoccupation with techniques, this versatility and workmanlike readiness, in all walks of life, in the towns as well as on the countryside. "The American," wrote De Crèvecœur, who for many years had himself been a successful farmer in the new society, "is a new man who goes upon new principles. . . . Most of them entertain new ideas and develop new opinions. . . . From involuntary idleness, penury, useless labor, he has passed to toil of a very different nature, developed by ample returns." The Comte de Beaujour noted that, while Americans show a marked inclination for science and the mechanical arts, they show less for literature and the fine arts. Both De Chastellux and Beaujour were impressed with the American's curiosity and inventiveness. The number and variety of religious sects (Beaujour counted sixty-three, and the Abbé Robin counted nineteen in Boston alone) were regarded as expressions of the same versatility; and their equal liberty, if not their mutual tolerance, was admired. The Frenchmen were aware of an abundance in the American economy which Jefferson was particular to signalize after his return from Europe in 1789. De Chastellux observed none very poor and all hopeful; he noted that "those things which would be elsewhere regarded as luxuries are here considered necessities"; and Beaujour remarked on the anonymity of dress and the equality of luxury. Bayard attributed luxury also to the Quakers. Gérard wrote that a "European army of 60,000 men would be well kept on what 15,000 men cost in the United States." It was thus observation which time sustained, and not a patriot's prejudice, that led Jefferson himself to retort to Buffon in *Notes on Virginia* that Americans had given hopeful proof of genius in "government, in oratory, in painting, in the plastic art, as well as of the nobler kinds which arouse the best feelings of man, which call him into action, which substantiate his freedom and conduct him to happiness, as of the subordinate which serve to amuse him only."

The distinction between arts which substantiate freedom and conduct to happiness and arts which amuse recurs in various expressions throughout Jefferson's career. His disposition to assimilate the latter into the former does not frequently receive expression. But it remains operative so long as he lives. Observers and friends testify to it. The Marquis de Chastellux, who in 1782 spent four days with Jefferson, described him as

a sage and man of taste. . . . . He calls his home Monticello . . . . it shows the owner's fondness for the language of Italy and even more for the fine arts. . . . . The house in nowise resembles the others to be seen in this country; in fact it may be said that Mr. Jefferson is the first American to consult the fine arts in regard to his dwelling-place. . . . . I should portray a man not yet forty, with a tall figure and a kind agreeable face, but whose wit and information could sufficiently replace all external claims . . . . an American who, though never yet out of his country, is musician, draftsman, geometrician, astronomer,

physicist, jurisconsult, statesman. . . . . Lastly a philosopher, withdrawn from the world and affairs, because he loves the world only so
far as he believes he can be useful to it, and because his fellow-citizens
are not yet in a state to bear the light or to suffer criticism. . . . . It
seems as if, from his youth up, he had set his mind like his house, on
heights from which he could contemplate the entire universe.[2]

But, had the noble wordman and swordsman of France observed more closely, he would have found a strange thing. He
would have found that Jefferson's contemplation was hardly distinguishable from manipulation. Philosophy, of which Jefferson
said he "was always fond even in its drier forms," and the tranquil
pursuits of science, for which, Jefferson wrote Dupont de Nemours, nature had always intended him by rendering them his
supreme delight, embraced the scientific agriculture and gardening
of the dirt farmer, viticulture and wine making, the gourmet's arts
of the kitchen and wine cellar, the bettering of old farm implements, and the invention of new ones. The philosopher analyzed
the steam engine and its possible uses; he welcomed phosphoric
matches, and himself made improvements in household illumina-
tion by tinkering with the Argand lamp; he facilitated correspondence by changing the copying press and inventing a portable
writing desk; he concerned himself with the construction of musical instruments and the uses of the newly invented metronome. He
likewise described the activity of "putting up and pulling down" as
his favorite amusement and architecture as his delight. A violinist
from boyhood, he also designated music as his "supreme delight"
and the "favorite passion" of his soul. Nevertheless, contemporary
though he was of Gluck and Mozart and Beethoven, friend and
correspondent though he was of the operatic composer Piccinni
and of the English musicologist, Fanny Burney's father, Dr.
Charles Burney, no letter of his yet brought to light says anything
of musical composers and their compositions; many discuss the
working of musical instruments and musical performance. His
letters to Francis Hopkinson, who claimed the credit of being the
first native of the United States to produce a musical composition,

[2] *Voyages de M. le Marquis de Chastellux dans l'Ameriqué septentrionale*
(2 vols.; Paris, 1784).

deal with the latter's "improved method of quilling the harpsichord" but not the tunes played on it. From Europe Jefferson writes circumstantially about musical instruments—the violin, the footbass, the harpsichord, the pianoforte, the harmonica—and their construction, but nothing of the music produced with them. In 1778 he wrote that, fortune having cast his lot in a country where music is in a state of deplorable barbarism, he envies the French their opportunity to enjoy it; in 1818 that music "furnishes a delightful recreation for the hours of respite from the cares of the day and lasts us through life."[3] Unable to afford a "domestic band of musicians" as such, he inquired in 1778 of an unidentified French correspondent whether the latter might not procure for him seven domestics of as many different crafts who could also play different wind and string instruments and thus double as a household band. But he was the "Father" of the United States Marine Band, which was organized during his term as President with only nine instruments: a drum, two clarinets, two bassoons, two oboes, and two French horns. As a youth, he himself had played fiddle in a quartet organized by Governor Fauquier.

So far as the present available evidence goes, musician Thomas Jefferson was much more articulate about the processes of musical production than about the enjoyment of the musical product; his delight was more in the how than in the what of music. It is a maker's, a workman's, delight—the delight of the technician, the man of his hands, the idealist working in matter whose skill reshapes the original forms of nature to human uses, substantiating freedom and conducting to happiness. In Jefferson, the gentleman wordman is taken up and digested in the workman. Returning after ten years' absence to a run-down estate, he took to nail making for money income until he could again render his farms profitable. "My new trade of nailmaking," he wrote in 1795 to M. de Meunier, "is to me in this country what an additional title of nobility or the ensigns of a new order are in Europe."[4]

[3] Jefferson to Nathaniel Burwell, Monticello, March 14, 1818, *The Writings of Thomas Jefferson*, Memorial edition (Washington, 1903), XV, 167.
[4] Paul L. Ford, ed., *The Writings of Thomas Jefferson* (New York, 1892–1899), VII, 14.

IV

Jefferson's aesthetic intent, as evinced in the posture of his mind toward music, stands out even more clearly when we turn to architecture. Victor Hugo wrote somewhere that, until displaced by painting, architecture had been the spiritual record of mankind. For Jefferson it was never displaced. He had from the beginning a sense of symbolic significance which architecture takes on when what we today call "streamlining" refines use to beauty. And his perceptions and preferences initiated the tradition that still largely determines the configuration of public buildings in America. It is the figure we see at Monticello, at Charlottesville, in the capital of the nation at Washington and of the state of Virginia at Richmond, where, for the first time in America, Greek orders and Roman constructions were made the design of a public building. "The Capitol of Virginia," writes M. Louis Réau, "is in effect the first monument of the classical renaissance in the United States, and one might add, in the world."[5]

Into the selection of this style there entered, of course, the influence of Jefferson's youthful attraction to Palladio; his delight in the Maison Carrée at Nîmes[6] in the Hôtel de Salm in Paris; his wide readings in the literature of architecture; his consultations with French and American architects. But there were also two other forces. One was the temperament of the man himself, his emotional matter-of-factness and logic, his scientific sense of form. He disliked triviality and ineptitude; and building in America, also to the traveler's eye, was trivial and inept.[7] Jefferson wrote in *Notes on Virginia* that "the genius of architecture seems to have shed its maledictions on the land." Alike for inexpensive and for costly buildings

[5] *L'Art français aux Etats-Unis* (Paris, 1927), pp. 79–80.

[6] "The Maison Quarrée is very simple, but noble beyond expression and would have done honor to our country as presenting to travellers a specimen of taste in our infancy, promising much for our maturer age."

[7] "Except for certain edifices used for public banks, nothing could be more trivial than their architecture. It is much wedded to Chinese, if you can apply such names to this grotesque style." Felix de Beaujour, *A perçus des Etats-Unis* (Paris, 1814), II, 211–215.

it was impossible to devise things more ugly, uncomfortable and happily perishable. . . . . To give these symmetry and taste would not increase the cost. It would only change the arrangement of the materials, the form and the combination of the members. This would cost less than the burden of barbarous ornaments with which the buildings are sometimes charged. But the first principles of the art are unknown, and there exists scarcely a model among us sufficiently chaste to give an idea of them.

He had the workman's feeling for materials; at Bordeaux he measured the bricks of the old Roman Circus and studied their composition and texture—"fine," he wrote, "compact, and solid as that of porcelain." And always he had the craftsman's feeling for workmanship. The Vermont editor, Daniel Pierce Thompson, who visited at Charlottesville in 1822, tells of seeing the seventy-nine-year-old father of the University of Virginia take a chisel from the hand of an Italian stonecutter and show him how to turn the volute of a capital.

Jefferson's preferences in architectural form were like his preferences in verbal form, directed by functional good and channeled by his knowledge of the ancients. His concept of structure called for a space, order, and logic which to him the antique exemplified. That had, as he wrote to Major L'Enfant regarding the plans for the Capital in Washington, "the approbation of thousands of years." His desire for these qualities in buildings seems to have sprung from the same need that led him to build his house upon a hill: the need, shall we say, of great open spaces combining order with freedom.

The other influence was the new spirit which was spreading among the swordsmen and the wordmen of England, France, and America. It had come to prevail with Locke and Newton; Pope and Voltaire had made themselves its literary avatars. This spirit took the "Gothic" for its symbol of ignorance, of confusion, of weakness, superstition, and cruelty. It took the "classic" for its symbol of knowledge and order, of power, science, and loving-kindness. Its classicism obviously was no repetition of that of the Renaissance humanists. It was a new classicism, consonant with the Newtonian world-machine. Palladio's architectural patterns expressed it well and suited rightly enough the winds of its doctrines and the temperature of its disciplines.

For the architecture of his open spaces themselves, Jefferson seems to have preferred a contrasting figure. His taste as a landscape architect rated the neoclassic of rococo naturalism above Le Notre's geometric magnificences. He wanted wavy and wandering lines and masses: George Ticknor complained of the winding road up "the steep savage hill" of Monticello, the ascent "as pensive and slow as Satan's to Paradise." The dweller on that height disapproved of the straight roads and paths that cut the English gardens he had inspected. For gardens he preferred the serpentine, whether in walks or walls.

V

In such arts as architecture and gardening, use can rarely be a secondary consideration. Even the most exhibitionistic plans postulate form on function, tend to make the onlooker's interest secondary to the user's, and aspire only to crown practical efficacy with visual pleasure. If and when the two conflict and the ornament quarrels with structure and impedes functional economy, the causes of the conflict are not in the knowledge and skill of the workman but in the exhibitionism of the swordsman or wordman, whose land and whose house are like his dress and his hairdo, not achievements of his power but displays of his superfluity. Jefferson was disposed to regard painting and sculpture as such displays. He had learned of their cost directly from his efforts to gather a collection of pictures and statues for Monticello and from his negotiations for a pedestrian statue of George Washington for Richmond and of an equestrian one for the national capital. In 1788 he advised a couple of young Americans traveling in Europe that sculpture and painting were, for Americans, worth seeing but not studying. Too expensive for the state of wealth in the home country, these nonproductive arts did not call for the same connoisseurship as architecture and gardening.

At best, painting and sculpture could contribute but two things toward the freedom and happiness of mankind. One, Jefferson signalized in 1812 in his reply to Thomas Sully's notice that the American Society of Artists had elected him a member. That was "to give a pleasing and innocent direction to accumulations of wealth which would otherwise be employed in the nourishing of coarse and vicious habits." The other—to Jefferson far more important than "embellishing with taste a country already over-flowing with useful production"—was to keep present to posterity, by means of their representative and symbolic creations, the great men and the great events in the history of the race. Jefferson was fully aware that mankind are by nature symbol makers and symbol users. He noted concerning the writing box on which he had drafted the Declaration of Independence that its imaginative value would increase with the years: ". . . . another half century may see it carried in processions on the Fourth of July like a saint's relics. . . . if things acquire a superstitious value." He sur-rounded himself with busts and portraits of the mighty among men. In a letter of 1785, in which he tells Abigail Adams of the statues he had bought on her order—he had found only three she had wanted: a Minerva, a Diana, and an Apollo, and had had to use his own judgment about a fourth—he says he rejected a Venus and a Paris and Helen in favor of

a fine Mars . . . . bold, his falchion not drawn but ready to be drawn. This will do, thinks I, for the table of the American minister in London, where those whom it may concern may look and learn that though Wisdom is our guide, and Song and Chase our supreme delight, yet we offer adoration to that tutelar God also who rocked the cradle of our birth, who has accepted our infant offerings, and has shown himself the patron of our rights and avenger of our wrongs.

Baron de Montlezun, who visited Monticello in 1817, noted portraits of Locke and Bacon and Newton, of Columbus, Vespuc-cius, and Sir Walter Raleigh, of Washington and Lafayette and Franklin. There were busts also of the three latter, as well as of Turgot, Voltaire, Alexander I, John Paul Jones, and Cleopatra. The other paintings were mostly copies and on religious themes. They were probably those that had been selected for Jefferson when he was Ambassador in Paris, by the young, one-eyed American painter, John Trumbull, to whom he attributed "the most promising talents." The painter had practically carte blanche for his selections, Jefferson having specified only adequate portraits of Bacon, Newton, and Locke—"the trinity of the three greatest men in the world." A similar intent directed Jefferson's concern that the pedestrian statue of Washington which Houdon was to be commissioned to make for the state of Virginia should be life-size and in modern dress.[8] He felt that posterity should have a true figure of the original to copy from, a model such as only "the first Artist of France and even of the world" could produce, modeling from life. In making the arrangement with Houdon, he examined the setup of the latter's workshop in Paris with his usual thoroughness and speaks with sympathy and understanding of both tasks and tools.

But, although the painter, Maria Cosway, was his dear friend, although John Trumbull was an intimate, and although he sat to many painters for portraits, Jefferson seems to have been indifferent to the materials, the tools, and skills of the painter. True, he referred to the gallery of Düsseldorf as "sublime," but he wrote of drawing as a desirable feminine accomplishment and seems to have preferred the sculptor's monuments to the painter's. The painting he did prefer was also statuesque and commemorative. Writing to Mme de Brehan in 1789, he called the art "a subject in which I am ignorant," qualified it as "charming," and declared he did "not feel an interest in any pencil but that of David's."

At the time of writing, David had been back from Rome in Paris four years. He was doing in the "charming art" what Palladio generations before had initiated in architecture, only more spaciously, logically, and clearly and distinctly. His work had the "chastity" which Jefferson liked in buildings. In the painter's "Oath of the Horatii" the philosophes and the *précieuses* read in 1785 a Roman fable of republican virtue addressed to the French; and in his "Brutus Returning to Rome," all France read, in 1789, the call to the ultimate sacrifice for liberty. A master of portraiture, David somehow ennobled the contemporary countenance

[8] See Jefferson to Governor Harrison of Virginia, Paris, 1785, and to George Washington, Paris, 1787.

with the classical quality of ancient republican virtue. His figures and forms changed the fashion and furniture of the daily life. Like the Publicolas, Brutuses, Philodemuses, and Agricolas who debated over liberty and government, they signalized the time's aspiration to republican liberty. John Trumbull, indeed, emulated David; and his canvasses of the "Signing of the Declaration of Independence" and other momentous events in the epic of the Republic exemplify in the American theme what David later came to utter in that of Napoleon, who, incidentally, awarded the Yankee painter a gold medal for his "Marius on the Ruins of Carthage." Significantly, Jefferson was disposed to deprecate Trumbull's exercise of his *licentia pictoris* in his rendering of American history.[9]

The inference is reasonable that Jefferson appreciated painting and sculpture for what they communicated more than for what they were in themselves. When they combine verisimilitude with symbolism, they provide not only remembrance of times past but models for the new generations to emulate as well as to reverence. They work by a sort of empathy, like the right fictions of the literary artist and therein, he wrote to in-law Robert Skipwith in 1771, "are useful as well as pleasant." The good and evil which plays and novels portray call out in us appropriate emotions. The fictions are useful because "they exercise the moral feelings," they arouse in us desire to imitate the good and revolt against the evil. Be they fiction or fact, if they have verisimilitude we react to what they present without further ado. We are "framed to be as warmly interested for a fictitious as for a real personage" and hence able by their means to form "the habit of thinking and acting virtuously." Well-written romance, tragedy, comedy, and epic poetry cannot but facilitate such habituation. Of course, they may also have unwelcome consequences. Jefferson wrote to N. Burwell in 1818, deploring "the inordinate passion prevalent for novels." Where novels become distractions from the world of virtue, "they are poisons," wastes of time, foes to reason and fact, resulting in "a bloated imagination, sickly judgment and disgust toward all the real businesses of life."

9 See Jefferson to S. A. Wells, 1819.

VI

So much then for the record, as we have it at present, of Jefferson's actual disposition toward the various arts called "fine." It was not that of his gentlemanly contemporaries, to whose well-fed leisure those arts gave content and meaning, and it was a world away from our own more radical conception of art for art's sake. By and large, the arts which both we and he call "fine," as distinguished from literature, architecture, and gardening, Jefferson looked on as "subordinate"; their task was "to amuse." Those both he and we call "practical" he looked on as "nobler," capable of arousing the best feelings of man, of calling him into action, of substantiating his freedom and conducting him to happiness. All makers are artists to Jefferson; and he thinks of the balloonist Pilatre de Rozière and the astronomer David Rittenhouse, who made a model of the solar system, as artists. Fundamentally, Jefferson's aesthetic involved a dissolution of classical attitudes in spontaneously pioneer sentiments and practices. It is a philosophy entirely of a piece with his vision of the order of the world and of the nature and destiny of man.

This vision seems to have come to Jefferson early in his long life—certainly before he wrote the Declaration of Independence—and to have been consistently nourished by his observation and experience as well as his reading. In terms of books and authors it draws upon the whole intellectual tradition of the Western world, from Homer and Epicurus to Sterne and Voltaire. One could say of it what Jefferson had said of the Declaration of Independence: "Neither aiming at originality of principle or sentiment, nor yet copied from any particular and previous writing, it [the Declaration] was intended to be an expression of the American mind and to give that expression the proper tone and spirit called for by the occasion."[10]

Jefferson wanted to make his entire philosophy also such an expression, and believers in liberty can only wish that he had succeeded. He held it as a faith to live by, to fight for, his whole

[10] Jefferson to Henry Lee, Monticello, 1825.

life long. Like the tone and spirit of the Declaration, this philosophic faith enfolds something unique, personal to its author and, from the standpoint of a professorial philosopher, original indeed—original in so combining apparently contradictory ideas as to have caused a slightly patronizing professorial sneer.[11] The central article of Jefferson's faith, that to which all others are confirmation, was Freedom. All that he wanted to be remembered by—the Declaration of Independence, the Statute of Religious Liberty, the University of Virginia—are instruments of Freedom. The order of nature, the institutions of society, the conduct of the individual, have but one end and one means: Freedom. For Jefferson, Freedom is the going and the goal. Even happiness is not so elemental. For happiness is not an unalienable right; only the *pursuit* of happiness is. Happiness can be separated from existence as freedom cannot: "The God who gave us life gave us liberty at the same time; the hand of force may destroy but cannot disjoin them."[12] Freedom is at once the initiation and the consummation of reason; it is, in one connection, "the great parent of science and of virtue, alone able to make a nation great in both,"[13] and in another, "the first born daughter of science."[14] Freedom, again, is the *sine qua non* of toleration when error opposes truth on its merits and not by "the assistance of power or force." In the *Notes on Virginia* Jefferson asked: "What has been the effect of coercion?" And he answered: "To make one half the world fools, the other half hypocrites. To support roguery and error all over the earth. . . . . Reason and free enquiry are the only effectual agents against error." "If the magistracy," he wrote in his *Notes on Religion,* "had vouchsafed to interpose in the other sciences, we should have as bad logic, mathematics and philosophy as we have divinity, in countries where the law settles orthodoxy." And so Jefferson dedicated the University of Virginia to the "illimitable freedom of the human mind to explore and expose every

[11] See Woodbridge Riley, *American Thought* (New York, 1915), Chap. III.
[12] *The Rights of the British in America* (1774).
[13] Jefferson to Dr. Willard, Paris, 1789.
[14] Jefferson to M. d'Invernois, 1795.

subject susceptible of its contemplation." He declared that his one oath "upon the altar of God" was "hostility against every form of tyranny over the mind of man."

Regarding the nature of this mind and its relation to its body Jefferson speculated little. He thought that such speculations were futile insofar as they were metaphysical rather than empirical inquiries, such as those of Cabanis and Flourens into "the *modus operandi* of nature."[15] Plato, consequently, was to him not only a foe of freedom but also a "sophist, full of whimsies, puerilities, unintelligible jargon," whose nonsense has been incorporated in the body of Christian doctrine by its priests. Jefferson's own view was that of an enlightened yet disillusioned common sense. The world of thoughts and things, the world of our action and our passion, is the world which we see and hear and taste and smell and touch and feel—the world of space and matter and motion. It is the world whose dynamic Newton had precisely discerned and measured, whose laws he had precisely stated. It is the world that Bacon had taught us how to investigate, as Locke has taught us how we understand what we have found out. All of it, mind and matter alike, comes to us in sensation. Sensation, matter, and motion are "the basic fabric of all the certainties we can have or need. When once we quit the basis of sensation, all is in the terms."[16] All our knowledge, then, is a function of the impact of sense upon the thinking body. The arts and sciences are the conscious responses of that body to sense, and they are classifiable according to the character of that response. When Jefferson was preparing to part with his library to Congress, he made such a classification. His immediate precedent was Diderot's classification in the great *Encyclopédie;* Diderot's had been Francis Bacon's, and Jefferson had found a parallel for Bacon's in Pierre Charron's *La Sagesse.* Jefferson arranged his books, then, according to the powers of the mind involved in producing them. These are memory, reason, and imagination. Memory is the prime faculty in producing history, civil and moral; reason, in producing philosophy, moral and mathematical; imagination, in producing the fine arts, which include architecture, gardening, painting, sculpture,

---

[15] Jefferson to Cabanis, 1803; to Lafayette, 1815.
[16] Jefferson to John Adams, 1820.

music, poetry, and criticism. Those books which involved all three powers of mind Jefferson classified as "polygraphical."

The arts and sciences so signalized may be said to give us a world with articulations like those of a machine designed according to reason, by a mind whose providence thinks mechanically and whose causality is determinist. This seems to be what Jefferson for the most part means by "God eternal." And, while he does not say so, it is difficult not to infer that he holds the material universe to be somehow the body to which that divine mind belongs. He calls Locke to witness that there is nothing implausible or impious in the idea that lesser bodies can have minds. On the contrary, it is the bodiless soul which comes into conflict with the deliverances of both experience and reason regarding the laws of nature and nature's God, for these laws point to a material world of which thinking bodies are a natural part.

This world, moreover, comes to us as a manifold of matters and motions. In our sensory experience it flows and diversifies in measurable ways. "Nature," Jefferson wrote to Dr. Manners in 1814, "has not arranged her productions on a direct line. They branch at every step, in every direction, and he who attempts to reduce them into departments, is left to do it by the lines of his own fancy." Whatever comes to existence in nature is individual. No two things are exactly alike, or any two particles of matter. To remember, we group by resemblances and so make classes, orders, genera, and species. Which item shall be our measure or rule is arbitrary—a matter of choice.

The libertarian and deistic materialist was thus also a nominalist and a pluralist. Nor, in the logic of liberty, could it be otherwise. The implication that we do not remain alive after we are dead is likewise accepted, not without regret. Though Jefferson wrote nostalgic letters about reunion with his beloved after death, they expressed a present yearning rather than a future certainty. His convictions were in keeping with his remarks to Lafayette about Flourens' proof that animals deprived of the cerebrum remain alive and well, although without sense, intellect, and memory;[17] and with his letter to John Adams in 1820: "For if either the

[17] Jefferson to Lafayette, January 16, 1825, *Writings of Thomas Jefferson* (Memorial ed.), XIX, 280.

heart, the blood or the brains is the soul, then certainly, the soul being corporeal, must perish with the rest of the body; if it is air, it will perhaps be dissolved; if it is fire, it will be extinguished." However it perish, it will be without rights in this world. The dead, Jefferson wrote to Samuel Kercheval, are nothing, and nothing cannot own something. The earth, he advised Major John Cartwright, the earth and its usufruct belong to the living. The dead have neither right nor power in it, "nor a wisdom more than human . . . . beyond amendment." Manners and opinions change; new discoveries, new truths, new circumstances require new institutions. Let the generations make their own, putting them on and off like the garments of freedom they are. "Nothing is unchangeable, but the inherent and unalienable rights of man."

It would, of course, have been more in keeping with Jefferson's intent if he had written "men." He held uniformity whether mental or physical, to be unnatural. "Millions of innocent men, women and children, since the introduction of Christianity," he wrote, "have been burnt, tortured, fined, imprisoned; yet we have not advanced one inch toward uniformity."[18]

"The varieties in the structure and action of the human mind, as in those of the body," he added seventeen years later, "are the work of our Creator, against which it cannot be a religious duty to erect the standard of uniformity."[19] He told Charles Thomson in 1817:

If no varieties existed in the animal, vegetable or mineral creation, but all moved strictly uniform, catholic and orthodox, what a world of physical and moral monotony would it be. . . . . It is a singular anxiety which some people have that we should all think alike. Would the world be more beautiful were all our faces alike? Were our tempers and talents, our tastes, our forms, our wishes, aversions and pursuits cast exactly in the same mold?

Thus the affirmation of inherent and unalienable liberty was to Jefferson the affirmation of the inherent and unalienable right to be different. His pluralism extended to all things, tastes, and cultures, as well as to persons and beliefs.

[18] *Notes on Virginia, ibid.,* VII, 401.
[19] Jefferson to James Fishback, 1809.

And this is one among the reasons why he could see in the teachings of Epicurus and in "the pure gospel of Jesus" a harmonious intent and declare without self-contradiction: "I am an Epicurean"; "I am a Christian." True, even the Jesus of the "pure and unsophisticated doctrine" which Jefferson had distilled from the confused distortions of the New Testament took the side of "spiritualism," whereas Jefferson was a materialist,[20] who held that pure doctrine to be a "sublime philanthropism and deism."[21] And he felt it, if not confirmed, at least supplemented, by Epicurus' physical and moral philosophy, which he described as "the most rational system remaining of the philosophy of the ancients," with its rejection of desire and fear, its pursuit of the tranquillity which is happiness or pleasure based upon virtue and tested by utility, its recognition of freedom, and its emphasis upon the fortitude "that teaches us to meet and surmount difficulties; not fly from them like cowards, and to fly, too, in vain, for they will meet and arrest us at every turn of the road."[22] Our Christian-Epicurean spoke from experience. He had fled. But pain and pleasure are commingled, he wrote to Mrs. Cosway:

it is the law of our existence. The most effectual means of being secure against pain is to retire within ourselves and to suffice for our own happiness. Those which depend on ourselves are the only pleasures a wise man will count on, for nothing is ours which another may deprive us of. Hence the inestimable value of intellectual pleasures. Ever in our power, always leading us to something new, never cloying, we ride serene and sublime above the concerns of this mortal world, contemplating truth and nature, matter and motion, the laws which bind up their existence, and that Eternal Being who made and bound them up by these laws.[23]

But sixteen years later he wrote Mary Eppes[24] that "withdrawing from the world led to anti-social and misanthropic state of mind

[20] Jefferson to William Short, April 13, 1820.
[21] Jefferson to John Adams, May 5, 1817.
[22] Jefferson to William Short, October 11, 1819, *Writings of Thomas Jefferson* (Lipscomb and Bergh ed.), XV, 219–222.
[23] "Dialogue Between My Head and My Heart" in letter to Mrs. Cosway, October 12, 1786.
[24] Jefferson to Mary Jefferson Eppes, 1802.

which severely punishes him who goes in to it." Free communication, he concluded, is a condition of our happiness which "requires that we should continue to mix with the world and to keep pace with it as it goes."

Men were destined for society, Jefferson had written to his nephew, Peter Carr, in 1787, and were "endowed with a sense of right and wrong, merely relative to this. This sense is as much a part of his [a man's] nature as the sense of hearing, seeing, feeling; it is the true foundation of morality. . . . ." And by the same token it calls for the same moral duties between society and society.[25] How the moral sense works must vary, of course, with time and place and circumstances. These might make the same act "useful and consequently virtuous in one country which is injurious and vicious in another differently circumscribed." "Utility then, is the standard and test of virtue."[26]

VII

And if of virtue, can utility fail, when all is said and done, to be the test of beauty, too? If mind is an organization of innate sensibilities—its sensibility to self or egoism, to other selves or morality, and to the visual, auditory, tactile stuffs of things and events—then a sense of beauty is equally such an innate datum and equally relational.

We have indeed the innate sense of what we call *the beautiful,* but that is exercised chiefly on subjects addressed to the fancy, whether through the eye in visible forms as landscape, animal figure, dress, drapery, architecture, the composition of colours, etc., or to the imagination directly, as imagery, style, or measure in prose or poetry or whatever constitutes the domain of criticism or taste, a faculty entirely distinct from the moral one.[27]

Tastes, Jefferson remarked in his *Notes on a Money Unit,* cannot be controlled by law. Rules cannot inclose them; they have an autonomous spring. Jefferson wrote to William Wirt in 1816:

25 Opinion on the French Treaties.
26 Jefferson to Thomas Law, 1814.
27 *Ibid.* The omission of music from the list of subjects suggests a contagion from Lord Kames, who limited the field of beauty to the field of vision.

I have always very much despised the artificial canons of criticism. When I have read a work in prose or poetry or seen a painting, etc., I have only asked myself whether it gives me pleasure, whether it is animating, interesting, attracting? If it is, it is good for these reasons.

So he could defend the literary quality of Tacitus against "the hyperesthetics [who] call him barbarous" and could see aesthetic uses in Anglo-Saxon and Ossian and enjoy neologies.

But, as has already been noted, such impacts are but the beginnings of aesthetic goodness. Jefferson wanted beauty to come to some use, and aesthetic experiences to work out in moral consequences. Otherwise they are "a luxury." He recommended the novels of Laurence Sterne as "the best course of morality that was ever written."[28] He deprecated the comic spirit, ridicule, and wit. Molière's effect on medicine in France, he wrote, "furnished the most striking proof I have ever seen in my life of the injury which ridicule is capable of doing." In Paris in 1789 he found the laughter which greeted the Assembly of Notables a sign of weakness and desperation. "The people at large," he wrote to Abigail Adams, "view every object only as it may furnish puns and *bons mots,* and I pronounce that a good punster would disarm the whole nation were they ever seriously disposed to revolt." Jefferson's ultimate canon of taste called for a confirmation of beauty by use.

That taste cannot, any less than morality, fail to be a function of its conditions, therefore relational, goes without saying. The artist, the man of science, the genius, must cleave to his freedom even more than other men, especially in republics where "science is more important than in any other government." Society owes such a man—according to his quality—education, support, and encouragement. "I am. . . . satisfied that there is an order of geniuses above that obligation [of public service] and therefore exempted from it. Nobody can conceive that nature ever intended to throw away a Newton upon the occupations of a crown."[29] For the good of all mankind, neither the duties of the citizen nor the meddlings of the censor should have the power to limit this liberty of genius.

[28] Jefferson to Peter Carr, Paris, 1787.
[29] Jefferson to David Rittenhouse, 1778.

VIII

So we end with what we began—Liberty, inseparable from life. Even Jefferson's least scrupulous foes, considering the man and his works, concede Liberty's primacy in his faith and deeds. It is for this, in fact, that they hate him, because he made the other goods of life, which for them were the highest, Liberty's tools and sustainers. He was well aware of the dangers which beset the establishment and maintenance of Liberty, but not ever in his long life could they hold him back. Always making his first appeal to reason, which he regarded as both Freedom's peer and most precious handmaiden, he did not flinch from the appeal to force should that be imposed. "It is an eternal truth," he wrote, "that acquiescence under insult is not a way to escape war."[30] "Where wrongs are pressed, because it is believed they will be borne, resistance becomes morality."[31] Be the means reason or be it force unavoidable, he knew that the effort must never cease to convert the freedom and happiness of mankind from a dream and a faith into a continuing fact of experience. He knew the hazards; but he knew also, as he once wrote Gallatin, that "doubts and jealousies often beget the facts they fear." And fourteen years' correspondence with the rival of his middle years and friend of his late ones, John Adams, shows the latter learned, nimble, gracious, a doubter and skeptic who, like David Hume, lived a conservative because he doubted radically; while it shows Jefferson, no less aware of the alternatives than Adams and no less ready to take them into account, saying "Yea" to Liberty where Adams said "Nay." Jefferson willed to believe at his own risk. "My theory has always been," he wrote Marbois in 1817, "if we are to dream, the flatteries of hope are as cheap, and pleasanter than the gloom of despair." "I steer my bark," he advised John Adams, "with Hope in the Head, leaving Fear behind. My hopes, indeed, sometimes fail, but not oftener than the forebodings of the gloomy."

[30] Jefferson to H. Tazewell, 1795.
[31] Jefferson to Mme de Staël, 1807.

In 1821 he wrote to John Adams:

I will not believe our labors are lost. I shall not die without a hope
that light and liberty are on a steady advance. We have seen, indeed,
once within the record of history, the complete eclipse of the human
mind continuing for centuries. . . . . Even should the cloud of barbarism and despotism again obscure the science and liberties of
Europe, this country remains to preserve and restore light and liberty
to them. In short, the flames kindled on the 4th of July, have spread
over too much of the globe to be extinguished by the feeble engines of
despotism; on the contrary, they will consume these engines and all
who work for them.

True, pain and sorrow and uncertainty do beset the course of
the safest life, and danger attends our choices whatever they be. In
choosing, then, we must, of course, take thought, but bravely, with
a high heart. As against all traditionalists, he wanted the spirit of
man to trust its own vision, unafraid. For reason, by itself, would
overrule generosity in favor of prudence and courage in favor of
certainty. Reason disposes us to cling to the ills we have rather
than risk others we know not of. It votes for safety, against
freedom. In the "Dialogue Between My Head and My Heart,"
which sublimated into the restrained passion of a philosophy the
deep emotional conflict which his dear Maria Cosway's departure
from France brought to a crisis, Jefferson made his summing-up:
"As far as my recollection serves me," Heart told off Head, "I do
not know that I ever did a good thing on your suggestion, or a dirty
one without it."

Freedom and courage are first and last things in human nature,
and they are of the Heart.

If our country when pressed with wrongs at the point of the bayonet
had been governed by its heads instead of its hearts, where should we
be now? Hanging on a gallows as high as Haman's. You began to
calculate and to compare wealth and numbers; we threw up a few
pulsations of our blood, we supplied enthusiasm against wealth and
numbers, we put our existence to the hazard when the hazard seemed
against us, and we saved our country, justifying, at the same time, the

ways of Providence whose precept is, to do always what is right and
leave the issue to Him.

This holds, if I am not mistaken in my reading of Jefferson,
certainly no less, perhaps even more, for the enterprises of science
and the arts. It is the inward spring of all Jefferson's philosophy,
the life and meaning of his workman's philosophy of art.

GEORGE HARMON KNOLES

✪

The Religious Ideas of Thomas Jefferson[1]

Thomas Jefferson requested to have inscribed upon his grave marker the words: "Author of the Declaration of American Independence, Of the Statute of Virginia for Religious Freedom, And Father of the University of Virginia." Each of these achievements was concerned with liberty and reveals a passion for freeing men from political and intellectual dependence upon others, for Jefferson cared as much for freedom of the mind as for freedom of the state. He labored equally without stint to secure and safeguard the citizen from what he regarded as the oppression of priests as well as from the despotism of kings and entrenched social classes. His declaration that he had "sworn upon the altar of God, eternal hostility against every form of tyranny over the mind of man" provides an excellent key to an understanding of Jefferson's religious views, for in everything he wrote on the subject there is either explicit or implicit evidence of his determination to preserve his own and others' freedom and independence of judgment in matters of religion.[2]

[1] This paper represents a survey of the views held by Thomas Jefferson on the subject of religion. Its particular function is to present, insofar as possible, these views in the words of Jefferson as found in his published papers and correspondence.

[2] Jefferson to Dr. Benjamin Rush, September 23, 1800, *The Writings of Thomas Jefferson*, Monticello edition (20 vols., Washington, 1904), X, 175. (Hereafter, where *The Writings of Thomas Jefferson* are cited, reference will be to the Monticello edition.) To Edward Dowse on April 19, 1803,

Reprinted from *Mississippi Valley Historical Review*, Vol. XXX (September 1943), pp. 187–204, by permission. Copyright © 1943 by The Journal of American History.

The task of examining the religious ideas of Thomas Jefferson is not an easy one. For one thing, he was extremely reticent on the subject of religion, a reticence that extended from his conversation and discussion with others to his writings and correspondence.[3] Moreover, he seemed determined to avoid at all costs influencing others in their thinking. The testimony of members of his household, with whom he lived on the most intimate terms, is unanimous in emphasizing the total lack of any evident intent to indoctrinate them with his convictions.[4] Then, too, the task is complicated because, except for a few instances, Jefferson's practice of religious exercises appears out of harmony with what one would be led to expect from a knowledge of his religious views. For example, we usually associate the freethinker with nonconformity in such matters as church attendance, use of church ceremonials, and financial support of a church organization; but Jefferson was regular in his attendance at church, taking his own prayerbook and reading the prayers and responses with the congregation. He was baptized into the Anglican Church; married by one of its clergymen; his children were baptized into it and were married according to its ceremonies; its burial services were read for those of his family who preceded him to the grave and when he

---

Jefferson wrote: "I never will, by any word or act, bow to the shrine of intolerance, or admit a right of inquiry into the religious opinions of others. On the contrary, we are bound, you, I, and every one, to make common cause, even with error itself, to maintain the common right of freedom of conscience." *Ibid.,* 378.

[3] See, for example, Jefferson to Dr. Benjamin Rush, April 21, 1803: "I am . . . averse to the communication of my religious tenets to the public; because it would countenance the presumption of those who have endeavored to draw them before that tribunal, and to seduce public opinion to erect itself into that inquisition over the rights of conscience, which the laws have so justly proscribed." *Writings of Thomas Jefferson,* X, 380, 381.

[4] Thomas Jefferson Randolph, writing to Henry S. Randall and quoted in the latter's *The Life of Thomas Jefferson* (3 vols., New York, 1858), III, 672, reported that if a member of his family asked his opinion on any religious subject, Jefferson uniformly replied that "it was a subject each was bound to study assiduously for himself, unbiased by the opinions of others— it was a matter solely of conscience; after thorough investigation, they were responsible for the righteousness, but not the rightfulness of their opinions; that the expression of his opinion might influence theirs, and he would not give it!"

was buried, its rites were said over his body. He contributed freely to the support of churches, some of them not his own, and he continued to be a liberal contributor to the support of the clergy.[5] The student, therefore, is constantly confronted with contradictions presented by practice and belief.

Jefferson did not admit the possibility of revelation as a source of religious knowledge. Denying revelation, however, did not imply a denial of the possibility of achieving truth in religion, or in any other realm of human endeavor. "Reason and free inquiry," he believed, were "the only effectual agents" for discovering truth; they would "support the true religion by bringing every false one to their tribunal, to the test of their investigation."[6] If truth was not relative, certainly man's knowledge of it at any given moment was not complete; hence, no one had a right to impose his own opinions upon anyone else, since "every one must act according to the dictates of his own reason. . . ."[7]

Finally, it should be noted that Jefferson was not a systematic philosopher. He believed that everyday life presented problems sufficient to challenge one's attention and he rejected all "organs of information" save his senses, thus ridding himself of "the pyrrhonisms with which an indulgence in speculations hyperphysical and antiphysical, so uselessly occupy and disquiet the mind." The senses evidence enough realities "for all the purposes of life, without plunging into the fathomless abyss of dreams and phantasms. I am satisfied, and sufficiently occupied with the things which are, without tormenting or troubling myself about those which may indeed be, but of which I have no evidence."[8] As a consequence of these circumstances, Jefferson, as he put it, never

---

[5] Thomas Jefferson Randolph to Henry S. Randall, *ibid.*, III, 672; see also p. 555. See also Thomas Jefferson Coolidge, "Jefferson in His Family," *Writings of Thomas Jefferson*, XV, iv.

[6] Thomas Jefferson, *Notes on Virginia, ibid.*, II, 221.

[7] Jefferson to Samuel Miller, January 23, 1808, *ibid.*, XI, 429. Jefferson's convictions respecting the means of achieving knowledge in religious affairs were partly responsible for his crusade for religious freedom and toleration, the story of which is not properly the subject of this paper. Both the *Notes on Virginia, ibid.*, II, and the *Statute of Virginia for Religious Freedom, ibid.*, contain elaborations of these views.

[8] Jefferson to John Adams, August 15, 1820, *ibid.*, XV, 275, 276.

permitted himself to "meditate a specified creed."[9] What one learns, therefore, must be culled from his papers and correspondence; there is no single set of documents that give a systematic outline of his own religious ideas at any given period of his life.

Jefferson was not orthodox in his religious beliefs although he gave attention to the practices of his own particular church. Moreover, he thought that "the relations which exist between man and his Maker, and the duties resulting from those relations, are the most interesting and important to every human being, and the most incumbent on his study and investigation."[10] The evidence is abundant that Jefferson acted upon this conviction; we find that his religious beliefs were his own and that he came to them only after the most rigorous investigation and examination. Jefferson has given what was, in all probability, his own approach to the study of religion in a letter to his nephew, Peter Carr, about to commence his higher education. You must "divest yourself of all bias in favor of novelty and singularity of opinion" and "shake off all the fears and servile prejudices, under which weak minds are servilely crouched. Fix reason firmly in her seat, and call to her tribunal every fact, every opinion. Question with boldness even the existence of a God; because, if there be one, he must more approve of the homage of reason, than that of blindfolded fear." Read the Bible "as you would read Livy or Tacitus. The facts which are within the ordinary course of nature, you will believe on the authority of the writer. . . . But those facts in the Bible which contradict the laws of nature, must be examined with more care. . . ." Examine the pretensions of the author to inspiration from God and see if the evidence of his pretension is "so strong, as that its falsehood would be more improbable than a change in the laws of nature, in the case he relates." In reading the New Testament, keep in mind the opposing views of first those who say Jesus "was begotten by God, born of a virgin, suspended and reversed the laws of nature at will, and ascended bodily into heaven"; and second those who say Jesus "was a man of illegitimate birth, of a

[9] Jefferson to Thomas Whittemore, June 5, 1822, *ibid.*, XV, 373.
[10] Report of the Rector of the University of Virginia, October 7, 1822, *ibid.*, XIX, 414.

benevolent heart, enthusiastic mind, who set out without pretensions to divinity, ended in believing them, and was punished capitally for sedition. . . ." Jefferson continued by warning his friend not to be "frightened from this inquiry by any fear of its consequences. If it ends in a belief that there is no God, you will find incitements to virtue in the comfort and pleasantness you feel in its exercise, and the love of others which it will procure you. If you find reason to believe there is a God, a consciousness that you are acting under his eye, and that he approves you, will be a vast additional incitement; if that there be a future state, the hope of a happy existence in that increases the appetite to deserve it; if that Jesus was also a God, you will be comforted by a belief of his aid and love. In fine," he concluded, "you must lay aside all prejudice on both sides, and neither believe nor reject anything, because any other persons, or description of persons, have rejected or believed it. Your own reason is the only oracle given you by heaven, and you are answerable, not for the rightness, but uprightness of the decision."[11]

What did Jefferson think of Christianity after having applied these tests to its investigation? He thought he had "a view of the subject which ought to displease neither the rational Christian nor Deists, and would reconcile many to a character they have too hastily rejected."[12] Christianity, "when divested of the rags" in which a scheming priesthood "have enveloped it, and brought to the original purity and simplicity of its benevolent institutor, is a religion of all others most friendly to liberty, science, and the freest expansion of the human mind."[13] Indeed, it is "the most sublime and benevolent, but most perverted system that ever shone on man. . . ."[14]

Jefferson, believing thus that Christianity had been perverted from its true origins, set about examining the New Testament and other accounts of the life and teachings of Jesus and of the early Church. Following considerable study involving, among other

[11] Jefferson to Carr, August 10, 1787, *ibid.,* VI, 258–261.
[12] Jefferson to Dr. Benjamin Rush, September 23, 1800, *ibid.,* X, 174.
[13] Jefferson to Moses Robinson, March 23, 1801, *ibid.,* X, 237.
[14] Jefferson to Dr. Joseph Priestley, March 21, 1801, *ibid.,* X, 228.

things, an extract which he made from the Evangelists of those portions which met the tests of his reason, Jefferson prepared a syllabus in which he estimated the merits of the doctrines of Jesus as compared with some of the ancient philosophers. Jesus, he wrote, appeared among the Jews at a time when they, although believing in one God only, had degrading and injurious ideas about Him, and followed an imperfect ethical code "often irreconcilable with the sound dictates of reason and morality," and "repulsive and anti-social, as respecting other nations." Jesus' parentage "was obscure; his condition poor; his education null; his natural endowments great; his life correct and innocent: he was meek, benevolent, patient, firm, disinterested, and of the sublimest eloquence." His doctrines appeared under several remarkable disadvantages among which were: He wrote nothing Himself; the learned of His country, "entrenched in its power and riches," were in opposition; "unlettered and ignorant men," writing from memory long after the events had transpired, provide the only sources of information concerning Him; He fell an early victim to a "combination of the altar and the throne," at thirty-three, His reason not having attained its maximum of energy. Fragments only of His teachings have survived and these come to us "mutilated, misstated, and often unintelligible." These bits suffered disfiguration by the corruptions of schismatics interested in sophisticating His simple doctrines by "engrafting on them the mysticisms of a Grecian sophist [Plato], frittering them into subtleties, and obscuring them with jargon, until they have caused good men to reject the whole in disgust. . . . He corrected the Deism of the Jews, confirming them in their belief of one only God, and giving them juster notions of his attributes and government. His moral doctrines . . . were more pure and perfect than those of the most correct of the [ancient Greek and Roman] philosophers . . . and they went far beyond both [the Jews and the philosophers] in inculcating universal philanthropy . . . to all mankind. . . . He pushed his scrutinies into the heart of man; erected his tribunal in the region of his thoughts, and purified the waters at the fountain head. He taught, emphatically, the doctrines of a future state . . . and wielded it with efficacy, as an important incentive, supplementary to the other motives to moral conduct."[15]

Jefferson noted years later that the syllabus did not place him with Jesus in all His doctrines, for the syllabus was *"His* doctrines, not *all* of *mine.* I read them as I do those of other ancient and modern moralists, with a mixture of approbation and dissent." Points of difference included: "I am a Materialist; he takes the side of Spiritualism; he preaches the efficacy of repentance towards forgiveness of sin; I require a counterpoise of good works to redeem it, etc., etc."[16] These differences did not, however, keep Jefferson from referring to himself as a "Christian, in the only sense in which he [Jesus] wished any one to be; sincerely attached to his doctrines, in preference to all others; ascribing to himself every *human* excellence; and believing he never claimed any other."[17]

Jefferson thought the essential doctrines of Jesus to be "simple, and tend all to the happiness of man.

"1. That there is one only God, and He all perfect.

"2. That there is a future state of rewards and punishments.

"3. That to love God with all thy heart and thy neighbor as thyself, is the sum of religion."[18] Christianity, as Jefferson defined

---

[15] Syllabus of an Estimate of the Merit of the Doctrines of Jesus, Compared with those of others, enclosed in a letter to Dr. Benjamin Rush, April 21, 1803; both in *ibid.,* X, 379–385.

[16] Jefferson to William Short, April 13, 1820, *ibid.,* XV, 244, 245. Jefferson seemed to have some doubts concerning Jesus and His espousal of spiritualism, for in another discussion he wrote that the early Church Fathers were materialists and suggested that Jesus "told us only that God is good and perfect, but has not defined Him. I am, therefore, of His theology, believing that we have neither words nor ideas adequate to that definition." Jefferson to Ezra Styles, June 25, 1819, *ibid.,* XV, 203.

[17] Jefferson to Dr. Benjamin Rush, April 21, 1803, *ibid.,* X, 380. Jefferson revealed to Charles Thompson the knowledge of his "wee-little book" entitled "The Philosophy of Jesus" made from selections from the Evangelists. This booklet Jefferson offered as proof that he was "a *real Christian,* that is to say, a disciple of the doctrines of Jesus. . . ." January 9, 1816, *ibid.,* XIV, 385. See note 30 below regarding Jefferson's pamphlet.

[18] Jefferson to Dr. Benjamin Waterhouse, June 26, 1822, *ibid.,* XV, 383, 384. Compare these phrases with those used by Jefferson in his First Inaugural Address in which he spoke of America as being "enlightened by a benign religion, professed, indeed, and practiced in various forms, yet all of

it, very obviously was something quite different from orthodox Christianity, whether viewed by Catholics or most Protestants. Jefferson claimed, as did many of the reformers of the Enlightenment, that the pure, simple teachings of Jesus had in the course of centuries been so perverted and misconstrued that it was no wonder that honest men rejected the whole of it as a fabrication and looked upon Jesus as an impostor. Jefferson thought the priesthood, which term he used quite generally and often loosely, had "compounded from the heathen mysteries a system beyond the comprehension of man, of which the great Reformer . . . were He to return on earth, would not recognize one feature."[19] The "mild and simple principles of the Christian philosophy would produce too much calm, too much regularity of good, to extract from its disciples a support from a numerous priesthood, were they not to sophisticate it, ramify it, split it into hairs, and twist its texts till they cover the divine morality of its author with mysteries, and require a priesthood to explain them."[20]

Jefferson, in nearly every letter he wrote on religious subjects, struck hard at the priesthood with strong language. Through all his criticism runs the charge familiar to readers of the philosophes that those who professed to be the special servants of Jesus had converted His teachings into "an engine for enslaving mankind, and aggrandizing their oppressors in Church and State: that the purest system of morals ever before preached to man has been adulterated and sophisticated by artificial constructions, into a mere contrivance to filch wealth and power to themselves. . . ." These "in fact, constitute the real Anti-Christ."[21] Jefferson had

them inculcating honesty, truth, temperance, gratitude, and the love of man; acknowledging and adoring an overruling Providence, which by all its dispensations proves that it delights in the happiness of man here and his greater happiness hereafter. . . ." James D. Richardson, *Messages and Papers of the Presidents* (10 vols., Washington, 1911), I, 311.

[19] Jefferson to Charles Thompson, January 9, 1816, *Writings of Thomas Jefferson*, XIV, 386.

[20] Jefferson to Elbridge Gerry, March 29, 1801, *ibid.*, X, 254.

[21] Jefferson to Samuel Kercheval, January 19, 1810, *ibid.*, XII, 345, 346. See also Jefferson to John Adams, August 22, 1813, *ibid.*, XIII, 350; Jefferson to William Canby, September 18, 1813, *ibid.*, XIII, 377, 378;

reason to speak harshly of those whose bitterness he faced beginning with the opponents to the Virginia Statute for Religious Freedom. He felt the full force of the stinging denunciations of priests who "wished him to be thought atheist, deist, or devil, who could advocate freedom from their religious dictations."[22] He admitted abusing the priests "who have," he charged, "so much abused the pure and holy doctrines of their Master, and who have laid me under no obligations of reticence as to the tricks of their trade."[23]

The doctrine of the Trinity constituted one of the principal dogmas used by the priesthood to confuse mankind and keep it within the power of the clergy. "These metaphysical heads" usurp "the judgment seat of God" and denounce as His enemies "all who cannot perceive the Geometrical logic of Euclid in the demonstrations of St. Athanasius, that three are one, and one is three; and yet that the one is not three nor the three one."[24] Jefferson concluded that it was "too late in the day for men of sincerity to pretend they believe in the Platonic mysticisms" contained in the dogma of the Trinity. Such things constitute "the craft, the power and the profit of the priests. Sweep away their gossamer fabric of factitious religion, and they would catch no more flies."[25]

There were other rogueries, absurdities, and untruths perpetrated upon the teachings of Jesus by a large band of "dupes and impostors" led by Paul, the "great Coryphæus, and first corruptor of the doctrines of Jesus."[26] Platonists, Plotinists, Stagyrites, Gamalielites, Eclectics, Gnostics, and Scholastics with "their essences and emanations, their Logos and Demiurgos, Æons and Dæmons, male and female, with a long train of etc., etc., etc., or, shall I say at once, of nonsense," all added their own misconcep-

Jefferson to John Adams, October 13, 1813, *ibid.,* XIII, 389, 390; same to same, July 5, 1814, *ibid.,* XIV, 148, 149; Jefferson to Mrs. M. Harrison Smith, August 6, 1816, *ibid.,* XV, 59–61; Jefferson to William Short, October 31, 1819, *ibid.,* XV, 219, 220.

[22] Jefferson to Mrs. M. Harrison Smith, August 6, 1816, *ibid.,* XV, 60.

[23] Jefferson to Charles Clay, January 29, 1815, *ibid.,* XIV, 233.

[24] Jefferson to William Canby, September 18, 1813, *ibid.,* XIII, 378.

[25] Jefferson to John Adams, August 22, 1813, *ibid.,* XIII, 350.

[26] Jefferson to William Short, April 13, 1820, *ibid.,* XV, 245.

tions and glosses still further to confuse mankind and thus hold him in control.[27] Finding the doctrines of Jesus "levelled to every understanding, and too plain to need explanation," the Christian priesthood "saw in the mysticism of Plato materials with which" to "build up an artificial system, which might, from its indistinctness, admit everlasting controversy, give employment for their order, and introduce it to profit, power and preëminence."[28]

The union of Church and State represented to Jefferson the crowning achievement of the clergy in its quest for power. He had traced the incorporation of Christianity into English common law, beginning with an opinion issued in 1458 and ending with another in 1767. This was a plain usurpation and revealed to what lengths the priesthood would go. "What a conspiracy this, between Church and State!" Jefferson commented; "Sing Tantarara, rogues all, rogues all, Sing Tantarara, rogues all!"[29]

Largely for his own satisfaction, but partly to aid in rescuing Christianity from the many encrustations with which it was burdened, Jefferson adopted a procedure later to become quite common under the name of the higher criticism of the Bible, that of examining the life and teachings of Jesus as a problem in history. Jefferson compiled a little booklet which he titled "The Life and Morals of Jesus of Nazareth" by extracting excerpts from the four Evangelists, "selecting those only whose style and spirit proved them genuine, and His own," and including only facts of His life "within the physical laws of nature, and offending none by a denial or even a mention of what is not." The task of selection was not

[27] Jefferson to John Adams, October 13, 1813, *ibid.,* XIII, 389.

[28] Same to same, July 5, 1814, *ibid.,* XIV, 149. Jefferson went on to say that he had been reading Plato and had concluded that: "In truth, he [Plato] is one of the race of genuine sophists, who has escaped the oblivion of his brethren, first, by the elegance of his diction, but chiefly, by the adoption and incorporation of his whimsies into the body of artificial Christianity. His foggy mind is forever presenting the semblances of objects which, half seen through a mist, can be defined neither in form nor dimensions. Yet this, which should have consigned him to early oblivion, really procured him immortality of fame and reverence. . . . It is fortunate for us, that Platonic republicanism has not obtained the same favor as Platonic Christianity; or we should now have been all living, men, women and children, pell mell together, like beasts of the field or forest" (pp. 148–150).

[29] Jefferson to John Cartwright, June 5, 1824, *ibid.,* XVI, 48–51.

difficult, for the teachings of Jesus, Jefferson asserted, are as "distinguishable from the matter in which they are embedded as diamonds in dunghills. A more precious morsel in ethics was never seen."[30] These pure and unsophisticated doctrines "were professed and acted on by the *unlettered* Apostles, the Apostolic Fathers, and the Christians of the first century." Publication of them might serve as an "euthanasia for Platonic Christianity, and its restoration to the primitive simplicity of its founder."[31] Had Jesus' teachings "pure as they came from Himself, been never sophisticated for unworthy purposes, the whole civilized world would at this day have formed but a single sect." Creeds, formulas, and dogmas "have been the bane and ruin of the Christian church, its own fatal invention, which, through so many ages, made of Christendom a slaughterhouse, and at this day divides it into castes of inextinguishable hatred to one another."[32]

Jefferson, true to the progressive ideals of his age, looked to a reformation of Christianity especially in the United States where freedom of religious opinion and a divorce of Church and State prevailed. "This reformation will advance with the other improvements of the human mind," although it will, he noted regretfully, be "too late for me to witness it."[33] Evidences of this change he saw about him. Several letters written during the last six years of his life bespeak his faith in the triumph of what he called "rational Christianity." The Unitarian movement, which gained momentum after 1820, seemed to him to offer the greatest promise for a restoration of primitive Christianity in America. That it would "ere long, be the religion of the majority from North to South, I have no doubt," he wrote to Dr. Thomas Cooper; and to Dr. Benjamin Waterhouse he confided that he hoped there was "not a *young man* now living in the United States who will not die an

[30] Jefferson to F. A. Van der Kemp, April 25, 1816, *ibid.*, XV, 1–3. Several editions of the booklet have been published among them being one sponsored by William Jennings Bryan under Jefferson's title (St. Louis, Chicago, and New York, 1902). A photostatic copy can be found in *Writings of Thomas Jefferson*, XX.

[31] Jefferson to John Adams, October 13, 1813, *Writings of Thomas Jefferson*, XIII, 390, 391.

[32] Jefferson to Thomas Whittemore, June 5, 1822, *ibid.*, XV, 373, 374.

[33] Jefferson to Jared Sparks, November 4, 1820, *ibid.*, XV, 288.

Unitarian."[34] Such an advance, however, would not come easily, for much opposition would develop, especially among the Presbyterians. "The blasphemy and absurdity of the five points of Calvin, and the impossibility of defending them, render their advocates impatient of reasoning, irritable, and prone to denunciation." Consequently, their "ambition and tyranny would tolerate no rival if they had the power."[35]

While commending the efforts of those "younger athletes" who were willing "to encounter and lop off the false branches which have been engrafted [into Christianity] by the mythologists of the middle and modern ages,"[36] he warned the Unitarians against falling into "the fatal error of fabricating formulas of creed and confessions of faith, the engines which so soon destroyed the religion of Jesus. . . ." He feared that they might "give up morals for mysteries, and Jesus for Plato. How much wiser are the Quakers, who, agreeing in the fundamental doctrines of the Gospel, schismatize about no mysteries, and, keeping within the pale of common sense, suffer no speculative differences of opinion . . . to impair the love of their brethren. Be this the wisdom of the Unitarians, this the holy mantle which shall cover within its charitable circumference all who believe in one God, and who love their neighbor!"[37]

With respect to the fundamentals of religion, it can be noted that, in his view, there were but a few such basic tenets, and these were to be found in nearly all religions. He did not, as observed earlier, believe in revelation as a source of knowledge; conse-

[34] Jefferson to Cooper, November 2, 1822, *ibid.*, XV, 405; Jefferson to Waterhouse, June 26, 1822, *ibid.*, 385.

[35] Jefferson to Dr. Thomas Cooper, November 2, 1822, *ibid.*, XV, 403, 404. Jefferson summarized Calvinism in the following fashion: "1. That there are three Gods. 2. That good works, or the love of our neighbor, are nothing. 3. That faith is everything, and the more incomprehensible the proposition, the more merit in its faith. 4. That reason in religion is of unlawful use. 5. That God, from the beginning, elected certain individuals to be saved, and certain others to be damned; and that no crimes of the former can damn them; no virtues of the latter save." Jefferson to Dr. Benjamin Waterhouse, June 26, 1822, *ibid.*, XV, 384.

[36] Same to same, July 19, 1822, *ibid.*, XV, 391.

[37] Same to same, June 26, 1822, *ibid.*, XV, 385.

quently religious principles had to meet the tests of observation, experiment, and reason. He did not believe, therefore, in miracles, the divinity of Jesus, nor the doctrine of the atonement. He was convinced, as he said, by the writings of men more learned than he, that "Jesus did not mean to impose Himself on mankind as the Son of God" although "He might conscientiously believe Himself inspired from above. . . . Elevated by the enthusiasm of a warm and pure heart, conscious of the high strains of an eloquence which had not been taught Him, he might readily mistake the coruscations of His own fine genius for inspiration of an higher order."[38]

Jefferson, while not a Trinitarian, affirmed continuously a belief in God. He was not a Calvinist, nor could he ever become one, for Calvin "was indeed an atheist, which I can never be. . . . If ever man worshiped a false God, he did. The Being described in his five points, is not the God whom you and I acknowledge and adore, the Creator and benevolent Governor of the world; but a dæmon of malignant spirit."[39] Nor did he agree with Judaism which "supposes the God of infinite justice to punish the sins of the fathers upon their children, unto the third and fourth generation. . . ."[40] That there was a God, Jefferson had no doubts; but he thought Christians made a mistake in alleging revelation as necessary to prove the existence of God. He rejected the arguments of the atheists who asserted that it was simpler to believe "in the eternal pre-existence of the world, as it is now going on, and may forever go on by the principle of reproduction . . . than to believe in the eternal pre-existence of an ulterior cause, or Creator of the world, a Being whom we see not and know not, of whose form, substance and mode, or place of existence, or of action, no sense informs us, no power of the mind enables us to delineate or comprehend." Jefferson maintained the justifications familiar to

[38] Jefferson to William Short, August 4, 1820, *ibid.*, XV, 261. "And the day will come, when the mystical generation of Jesus, by the Supreme Being as His Father, in the womb of a virgin, will be classed with the fable of the generation of Minerva in the brain of Jupiter." Jefferson to John Adams, April 11, 1823, *ibid.*, XV, 430.
[39] Same to same, April 11, 1823, *ibid.*, XV, 425.
[40] Jefferson to Ezra Styles, June 25, 1819, *ibid.*, XV, 203.

deism, of design and universal belief. "I hold, (without appeal to revelation)," he wrote, "that when we take a view of the universe, in its parts, general or particular, it is impossible for the human mind not to perceive and feel a conviction of design, consummate skill, and indefinite power in every atom of its composition. The movements of the heavenly bodies, so exactly held in their course by the balance of centrifugal and centripetal forces; the structure of our earth itself, with its distribution of lands, waters and atmosphere; animal and vegetable bodies, examined in all their minutest particles; insects, mere atoms of life, yet as perfectly organized as man or mammoth; the mineral substances, their generation and uses; it is impossible, I say, for the human mind not to believe, that there is in all this, design, cause and effect, up to an ultimate cause, a Fabricator of all things from matter and motion, their Preserver and Regulator while permitted to exist in their present forms, and their regeneration into new and other forms. We see, too, evident proofs of the necessity of a superintending power, to maintain the universe in its course and order. . . . So irresistible are these evidences of an intelligent and powerful Agent, that, of the infinite numbers of men who have existed through all time, they have believed, in the proportion of a million at least to unit, in the hypothesis of an eternal pre-existence of a Creator, rather than in that of a self-existent universe. Surely this unanimous sentiment renders this more probable, than that of the few in the other hypothesis."[41]

Jefferson was unable to give a satisfactory answer to the problem of the nature of God. He did not feel alone in that position, however, for he discovered that Jesus "told us only that God is good and perfect, but has not defined Him. I am, therefore of His theology, believing that we have neither words nor ideas adequate to that definition."[42] He admitted having indulged himself little in these speculations, for when confronted with a proposition "beyond finite comprehension" he abandoned it as he did "a weight which human strength cannot lift . . . I think ignorance, in these

[41] Jefferson to John Adams, April 11, 1823, *ibid.*, XV, 426–428.
[42] Jefferson to Ezra Styles, June 25, 1819, *ibid.*, XV, 203.

cases, is truly the softest pillow on which I can lay my head."[43] If it were necessary, however, for him to reach an answer to the problem, he was inclined to extend materialism into the realm of religion. Several letters, especially to John Adams from 1820 to 1824, contain discussions of this issue, revealing a considerable amount of study and thought. Beginning with his "habitual anodyne, 'I feel, therefore I exist,' " Jefferson felt bodies which were not himself. There were other existences then; he called them matter. He felt them changing place; that gave him motion. An absence of matter he called void, or nothing, or immaterial space. "On the basis of sensation, of matter and motion," he concluded, "we may erect the fabric of all the certainties we can have or need. I can conceive *thought* to be an action of a particular organization of matter, formed for that purpose by its Creator, as well as that *attraction* is an action of matter, or *magnetism* of lodestone." From this point, he argued that to "talk of *immaterial* existences, is to talk of *nothings.* To say that the human soul, angels, God, are immaterial, is to say, they are *nothings,* or that there is no God, no angels, no soul." True, Jesus said that " 'God is a Spirit' but He has not defined what a spirit is, nor said that it is not *matter."* The early Church Fathers deemed it matter. The author of the Gospel according to John has been mistranslated and misunderstood. Truly translated, the first verses would read: " 'In the beginning God existed, and reason (or mind) was with God, and that mind was God. This was in the beginning with God. All things were created by it. . . .' " This text, Jefferson claimed, plainly declared the doctrine of Jesus "that the world was created by the Supreme, Intelligent Being. . . ." This has been perverted by modern Christians to build up the second person of "their tritheism, by a mistranslation of the word λογος [Logos]."[44] Jefferson concluded, therefore, that there was nothing inconsistent with belief in God and materialism, for God to be real was material: "It requires one effort only to admit the single incomprehensibility of matter endowed with thought, and two [efforts] to believe, first that of an

[43] Jefferson to John Adams, March 14, 1820, *ibid.,* XV, 241.
[44] Same to same, August 15, 1820, *ibid.,* XV, 273–275; same to same, April 11, 1823, *ibid.,* 429.

existence called spirit, of which we have neither evidence nor idea, and then secondly how that spirit, which has neither extension nor solidity, can put material organs into motion."[45]

When it came to the question of an afterlife, Jefferson, although evidencing a belief in a future state, wrote practically nothing on the subject. One learns of his belief not in direct statements, but indirectly in sentences such as the following written to his friend, John Adams, at the occasion of the death of Mrs. Abigail Adams: ". . . it is of some comfort to us both, that the term is not very distant, at which we are to deposit in the same cerement, our sorrows and suffering bodies, and to ascend in essence to an ecstatic meeting with the friends we have loved and lost, and whom we shall still love and never lose again."[46] Physical knowledge, however, of the country of spirits has been withheld from us by the laws of nature; and God, "for reasons unknown to us," has "chosen to leave us in the dark as we were" on this question. Jefferson admitted that in his younger years he had been fond of speculations which "seemed to promise some insight into that hidden country, but observing at length that they left [him] in the same ignorance in which they had found [him]," he had "for very many years ceased to read or to think concerning them. . . ." He thought it better, "by nourishing the good passions and controlling the bad, to merit an inheritance in a state of being on which I can know so little, and to trust for the future to Him who has been so good for the past."[47] In other words, immortality not just in the memory of posterity, but as a fact of existence was offered as one of the rewards of virtuous conduct.

Jefferson placed chief emphasis upon morality in all of his thinking about religion, for in the end, he thought that the ultimate test of religion was in the life of individual men and women; "if that has been *honest and dutiful* to society, the religion which has regulated it cannot be a bad one."[48] Indeed, he concluded, following a half century of reading and thought on religious

45 Jefferson to John Adams, March 14, 1820, *ibid.,* XV, 241.
46 Same to same, November 13, 1818, *ibid.,* XV, 174.
47 Jefferson to Isaac Story, December 5, 1801, *ibid.,* X, 299.
48 Jefferson to John Adams, January 11, 1817, *ibid.,* XV, 100.

subjects, that the "interests of society require the observation of those moral precepts only in which all religions agree (for all forbid us to murder, steal, plunder, or bear false witness,). . . ."[49] Moreover, he who steadily observes those moral principles in which all religions concur "will never be questioned at the gates of heaven, as to the dogmas in which they all differ."[50]

Jefferson concluded, after examining truth, the love of God, beauty, self-interest, and egoism in the broader sense as foundations for morality—revelation, of course, he ruled out of consideration—that "nature hath implanted in our breasts a love of others, a sense of duty to them, a moral instinct, in short, which prompts us irresistibly to feel and to succor their distresses. . . . The Creator would indeed have been a bungling artist, had he intended man for a social animal, without planting in him social dispositions." When the want or imperfection of the moral sense is found in some men, we endeavor to supply the defect by education, using love, or ostracism, or demonstrations that long-run honesty promotes interest, or offering the hope of rewards or penalties provided by the law, and ultimately "the prospects of a future state of retribution for the evil as well as the good done while here" as incentives. As to tests of conduct, "nature has constituted *utility* to man," as the standard measure of virtue.[51] This he thought not out of harmony with correct religious principles, for he believed that God "delights in the happiness of man here and his greater happiness hereafter."[52]

To conclude this survey of the religious views of Thomas Jefferson two questions might well be asked. First, did these views work for Jefferson? Second, what influence did they have upon the religious and intellectual development of the times? An adequate answer to both of these questions is wanting at present and awaits further study. We have the testimony of Jefferson, some of his intimate acquaintances, and certain members of his family, as well

---

49 Jefferson to James Fishback, September 27, 1809, *ibid.,* XII, 315.
50 Jefferson to William Canby, September 18, 1813, *ibid.,* XIII, 377.
51 Jefferson to Thomas Law, June 13, 1814, *ibid.,* XIV, 139–140.
52 Jefferson's First Inaugural Address, March 4, 1801, in Richardson, *Messages and Papers of the Presidents,* I, 311.

as the facts of his life. Certainly, if attention to the welfare of society is a test of the efficacy of religious opinions, the record is clear, for Jefferson devoted a long life to advancing with disinterestedness the cause of his countrymen. Members of his family have testified that he was a model husband, father, and grandfather. Finally, as he approached the end of his life, he evidenced no regrets at the imminence of death. During his last illness, he knew of his approaching end and remained calm and composed. When he thought he had heard the name of his minister mentioned the day before his death, he said he had no objection to seeing him as a "kind and good neighbor." He had nothing to recant.[53] Jefferson's friend and physician, Dr. Robley Dunglinson, observed after Jefferson's death that he had "never heard an observation that savored, in the slightest degree, of impiety."[54]

With respect to his influence upon the religious development of his times, it must be observed that Jefferson played a role incommensurate with his achievements in other endeavors, notably politics. Part of the explanation for this fact, as suggested earlier, is to be found in Jefferson's belief that religion was a matter between God and the individual, and part of the explanation is to be found in the politico-religious opposition to Jefferson which commenced early in his career and was maintained with virulence to the day of his death—and beyond. His chief significance in the realm of religious thought, aside from his crusade for religious freedom and tolerance, is the fact that he mirrored some of the religious tendencies of his own time, thus giving an insight into some of the thought currents of an unusually pregnant period of American religious development.

---

[53] Thomas Jefferson Randolph to Henry S. Randall, in the latter's *Life of Thomas Jefferson,* III, 543.

[54] Memorandum prepared for Henry S. Randall, *ibid.,* III, 549.

Selected Bibliography

Adams, Henry. *History of the United States During the Administrations of Jefferson and Madison,* 9 vols. (New York, 1891–1893).

Berman, Eleanor D. *Thomas Jefferson Among the Arts* (New York, 1947).

Boorstin, Daniel. *The Lost World of Thomas Jefferson* (New York, 1948).

Boyd, Julian P., and others, editors. *The Papers of Thomas Jefferson,* 17 vols. [to date] (Princeton, New Jersey, 1950–1965).

Bullock, Helen D. *My Head and My Heart* (New York, 1945).

Caldwell, Lynton K. *The Administrative Theories of Jefferson and Hamilton* (Chicago, 1944).

Chinard, Gilbert. *Thomas Jefferson, The Apostle of Americanism.* Revised Edition (Boston, 1939).

Dumbauld, Edward. *Thomas Jefferson, American Tourist* (Norman, Oklahoma, 1946).

Honeywell, Roy J. *The Educational Work of Thomas Jefferson* (Cambridge, Massachusetts, 1931).

Kimball, Fiske. *Thomas Jefferson, Architect* (Boston, 1916).

Kimball, Marie. *Jefferson: The Road to Glory, 1743 to 1776* (New York, 1943).

Kimball, Marie. *Jefferson: War and Peace, 1776 to 1784* (New York, 1947).

Kimball, Marie. *Jefferson: The Scene of Europe, 1784 to 1789* (New York, 1950).

Koch, Adrienne. *The Philosophy of Thomas Jefferson* (New York, 1943).

261

Koch, Adrienne. *Jefferson and Madison: The Great Collaboration* (New York, 1950).

Lehmann, Karl. *Thomas Jefferson, American Humanist* (Chicago, 1947).

Levy, Leonard. *Jefferson and Civil Liberties: The Darker Side* (Cambridge, Massachusetts, 1963).

Malone, Dumas. *Jefferson the Virginian* (Boston, 1948).

Malone, Dumas. *Jefferson and the Rights of Man* (Boston, 1951).

Malone, Dumas. *Jefferson and the Ordeal of Liberty* (Boston, 1962).

Martin, Edwin T. *Thomas Jefferson: Scientist* (New York, 1952).

Mayo, Bernard. *Jefferson Himself* (Boston, 1942).

Nock, Albert J. *Jefferson* (New York, 1926).

Peterson, Merrill D. *The Jefferson Image in the American Mind* (New York, 1960).

Randolph, Sarah N. *The Domestic Life of Thomas Jefferson.* American Classics Edition (New York, 1958).

Schachner, Nathan. *Thomas Jefferson: A Biography,* 2 vols. (New York, 1951).

Wiltse, Charles M. *The Jeffersonian Tradition in American Democracy* (Chapel Hill, North Carolina, 1935).

MERRILL D. PETERSON received his doctorate in American Civilization from Harvard University in 1950 after serving in the United States Navy during World War II. He has taught at Princeton and Brandeis universities and is now Jefferson Foundation Professor and Chairman of the Department of History at the University of Virginia. His first book, *The Jefferson Image in the American Mind,* was awarded a Bancroft Prize in 1961, and he has been a Guggenheim fellow. His other publications include *Democracy, Liberty, and Property* and *Major Crises in American History,* of which, with Leonard Levy, he is General Editor.

✪

AÏDA DIPACE DONALD, General Editor of the American Profiles series, holds degrees from Barnard and Columbia, where she taught American history, and a doctorate from the University of Rochester. Mrs. Donald has been awarded A.A.U.W. and Fulbright fellowships and has edited *John F. Kennedy and the New Frontier.* She is also co-editor of the *Diary of Charles Francis Adams.*

AMERICAN CENTURY SERIES

WHEN ORDERING, please use the Standard Book Number consisting of the publisher's prefix, 8090–, plus the five digits following each title. (Note that the numbers given in this list are for paperback editions only. Many of the books are also available in cloth.)